THE ELECTRONIC WORD

The University

of Chicago

Press

Chicago

and London

Richard A. Lanham

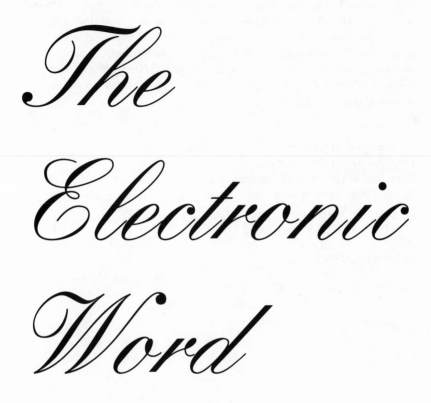

The

Electronic

Word

Democracy,

Technology,

and the Arts

Richard Lanham is professor of English at the University of California, Los Angeles, where he has taught since 1965, and directed the Writing Programs from 1979 to 1986. He is the author of numerous articles and nine books, including *Sidney's Old "Arcadia"* (Yale 1965); *A Handlist of Rhetorical Terms* (California 1968; 2d ed. 1992); *"Tristram Shandy": The Games of Pleasure* (California 1973); *Style: An Anti-Textbook* (Yale 1974); *The Motives of Eloquence: Literary Rhetoric in the Renaissance* (Yale 1976); *Analyzing Prose* (Scribner's 1983); and *Literacy and the Survival of Humanism* (Yale 1983).

The University of Chicago Press, Chicago 60637
The University of Chicago Press, Ltd., London
©1993 by The University of Chicago
All rights reserved. Published 1993
Printed in the United States of America
02 01 00 99 98 97 96 95 94 93   1 2 3 4 5

ISBN: 0-226-46883-6

Library of Congress Cataloging-in-Publication Data

Lanham, Richard A.
    The electronic word : democracy, technology, and the arts /
    Richard A. Lanham
        p. cm.
    Includes index.
    ISBN 0-226-46883-6.— ISBN 0-226-46884-4 (floppy disk)
    1. Computers and civilization. I. Title.
QA76.9.C66L363 1993
303.48'34—dc20   93-13884
                                                            CIP

Carolae coniugi rarissimae

Contents

Preface

The change in expressive technology about which these essays offer some preliminary reflections was announced in the January 1975 issue of *Popular Electronics* magazine. The cover carried a picture of the now-famous Altair 8800, a computer kit with 256 bytes of memory that sold for $397. The designer, Ed Roberts, had hoped to sell as many as four hundred of the machines. He took that many orders in one afternoon, in the course of a three-week period when his company's "status with its bank went from a negative value to plus $250,000."[1] The response to the machine was as significant as the machine itself. A new expressive medium had emerged—the personal computer—but the demand for the medium had *preceded* the medium itself. Technology was not creating a demand but fulfilling one that already existed.

The machine puzzles us less than the demand for it. In the decade since it became a commonplace device (as a typical lay user, I bought my first one—an Osborne!—in 1981), it has worked a revolution not only in computers but in the mythology surrounding them. It is now a personal companion rather than an impersonal giant serviced by a white-coated priesthood; it now comes in a small box instead of a large room; it is designed to perform daily tasks rather than gonzo calculations; it aims to enhance human intelligence, not substitute for it; it brings with it a bottom-up, networking managerial system rather than a top-down hierarchical one; above all, it allows us to manipulate words and images and sounds as well as numbers.

The revolution thus visited upon us has, given its magnitude, attracted very little attention. We have been preoccupied, ever since Marshall McLuhan made "media" a household word, with the much sexier world of broadcast television.[2] It was TV that was creating the global village full of couch potatoes with minds to match. It was TV that dramatized politics. It was TV that created a special channel to reenact rhapsodic sexual foreplay on a round-the-clock basis. Thus bemused, we failed to notice that the personal computer had presented itself as an alternative to the printed book, and the electronic screen as an alternative to the printed page. Furthermore, in the last three or four years, that alternative page has been enhanced so that it can present and manipulate images and sounds almost as easily as words. And it can do all this in 16.7 million colors. The long reign of black-and-white textual truth has ended. The nature and status of textual discourse have been altered. This movement from book to screen promises a metamorphosis comparable in magnitude, if not in hype, to broadcast TV.

A few people, in very recent books, have remarked upon the change. The classicist Jay David Bolter, for example, has surveyed the whole range of Western alphabetic expressivity and tried to locate electronically based discourse within it:

> The printed book ... seems destined to move to the margin of our literate culture. The issue is not whether print technology will completely disappear; books may long continue to be printed for certain kinds of texts and for luxury consumption. But the idea and the ideal of the book will change: print will no longer define the organization and presentation of knowledge, as it has for the past five centuries. This shift from print to the computer does not mean the end of literacy. What will be lost is not literacy itself, but the literacy of print, for electronic technology offers us a new kind of book and new ways to write and read.[3]

For the technologists—the hardware designers and the software programmers—this shift promises the millennium. They are all dedicated sci-fi fans, and the new world promised by that genre, utopian and dystopian, seems very like that promised by electronic text. They are occupied, even preoccupied, with the unprecedented nature of this new textual medium, and the redefiniton of "text" that it brings with it. Optimistic humanists are much harder to find. It is the pastist, not the futurist, for whom the end of the book promises the end of the world.

I survey some of these anxieties in chapters 8 and 9. They threaten to obscure the most interesting question posed by the coming of the electronic word: What can account for the extraordinary fit between this new expressive technology and the deep cultural hunger for it so handily allegorized by those hundreds of prepaid orders for the Altair 8800?

About this question, the pastists should by rights have something to say. For the changes brought by electronic text, including the very redefinition of what a "text" is, touch upon practically every central question on the current humanist agenda. The volatility of electronic text, its mixture of alphabetic and iconic information, and its essential typographical plasticity, seem, much more than film, the perfect fulfillment of the Italian Futurists' desire to abolish the book in favor of a more dynamic medium. Electronic text thus leads us to the many twentieth-century attempts to release language from the traditional rules print has dictated.

A volatile and interactive electronic text leads directly, as well, to our current debate about authoritative and canonical Great Books. To volatilize text is to abolish the fixed "edition" of the great work and so the authority of the great work itself. Such volatility questions the whole conception of textual authority built up since the Renaissance scholars resurrected Alexandrian textual editing. The "Great Books" view of Western culture that depends on these great fixed texts thus becomes imperiled. Not only does electronic text dissociate cultural greatness from the codex book form but, as we shall see, it threatens a reappraisal of that greatness. The electronic word incarnates the distinction between literate and oral cultures, now so hotly debated in a number of fields, that lies at the heart of our current literacy crisis. This debate is being pursued almost exclusively in terms of print, yet the expressive medium for which children, for which we all, should be trained is electronic. The higher-order conceptual skills that we all need today for a digital information society find their expression digitally as well. The current literacy debate is about mechanical drawing techniques in an age of CAD-CAM.

One of the computer screen's routine marvels is manipulation of scale, and such manipulation stands at the center of postmodern art. As we shall see in chapter 2, wherever you touch twentieth-century visual art and architecture, it seems both to foreshadow electronic expression and to provide an aesthetic ready-made for it. As I point out in chapter 1, the composition, notation, and performance of music have been transformed by digital expression. Because word, image, and sound are expressed in a common digital code, the arts take on a new and radical convertibility that threatens both their present compartmentalization and its academic departmental embodiment. So, too, poststructuralist literary theory, which has precipitated the current streetfight between Left and Right, turns out to be just such another proleptic aesthetic; poststructuralism and the common digital code seem part of the same event. As I suggest here, the whole Aristotelian basis of literary criticism is undermined by electronic expression, and so *pre*structuralist literary theory is similarly transformed.

The main intellectual debate of our time, I argue in chapter 3, is best understood as a resurrection of the ancient quarrel between the philosophers and the rhetoricians. This fundamental polarity depends heavily, it turns out, on the mode of presentation. Print—if I may telescope an argument presented more fully later—is a "philosophic" medium, the electronic screen a deeply "rhetorical" one. Once again, the quarrel, the item on the intellectual agenda, preceded the means of expression it so badly needs in order to sort itself out. Technology is *following* the main "operating system" disagreement in our time, not driving it.

Unlike print, electronic text defies proverbial wisdom. You can have your cake, give it away, then eat it, and still have it. Because it is so easily replicable, it takes us, yet again, to the heart of two of our deepest contemporary conundrums. We are trying, as we always have in America, but now with special urgency, to democratize the higher education needed for a technological culture. Electronic text suggests many new ways to do this. But it also threatens at every point the legal structure that has enabled our textbook-based Western education, along with the rest of our written culture. Copyright law is based on print. It was invented when print was invented, in order to protect it. It has been stretched to protect images and sounds but the stretching has always shown, and now electronic text breaks the intellectual fabric down completely. The humanist world has scarcely begun to confront this dilemma, and the law, which must confront it, is still trying to plot new epicycles on a Ptolemaic cosmos.

Electronic text creates not only a new writing space but a new educational space as well. Not only the humanities curriculum, but school and university structures, administrative and physical, are affected at every point, as of course is the whole cultural repository and information system we call a library. In the university world, it is disciplinarity and its departmental shadow that will be most transformed.

Profound changes in expressive medium always ask a fundamental question: What does this medium do to us and for us? We ask this in a deep way only when the new medium reveals what profound effects the old one has had on us. That question is now being asked by electronic text about *books*. And, since books underlie our whole humanistic cultural apparatus, about that apparatus as well. Those who feel that the end of the book is the end of the world assume, and less often argue, that books *equal* culture. To call that assumption into question, as electronic text does, takes us to the central crisis of the humanities today, our cultural accountability. Can we really argue that the arts and letters make us better? If not, how do we justify the public expenditures now made on them? How, for the matter of that, do we justify the time we spend teaching and cultivating them? I call this question the "Q" question and confront it in chapter 7.

Electronic text is reframing many more questions than I have itemized here: questions about the implications for verbal discourse of current work in behavioral neuroscience, for example, or the uncanny fit between digital expression and the human profile being established by behavioral biology. I argue in these essays that the change from book to screen, the emergence of electronic text, puts the major questions of our current intellectual agenda into a new relationship and sheds new light upon them. I've gathered these essays, several of which have been published earlier and in scattered places, into a book to elicit just this interrelationship. I think they strengthen and clarify and expand each other. They share a common focus, the change from book to screen and the intellectual context needed to understand that change. I've tried to underline this common focus by the revisions, major and minor, which I've made in the essays to knit them into a book.

Unlike most humanists discussing technology, I argue an optimistic thesis. I think electronic expression has come not to destroy the Western arts and letters, but to fulfill them. And I think too that the instructional practices built upon the electronic word will not repudiate the deepest and most fundamental currents of Western education in discourse but redeem them. It takes some temerity to look on the bright side of electronic technology these days. In chapters 8 and 9, I survey some recent accounts that do just this, as well as some that take issue with such digital optimism.

I've supplied headnotes to the essays because the often perplexed—perhaps I might say hypertextual—genesis of the argument constitutes part of the story and I don't want to hide it. I was trying to sketch a relationship, a *convergence* as I call it, of some very broad cultural forces, and I found it difficult to keep the drawing to scale. Perhaps the headnotes will help. I've revised each previously published essay so that the book can be read as a continuous argument, but I've also tried to leave sufficient repetition so that each chapter can be read individually.

◻   ◻   ◻

Writing these essays was much eased by support from the UCLA Committee on Research and by a John Simon Guggenheim Fellowship. I have also greatly profited from the advice and criticism of Michael Cohen, Lisa Spangenberg, Myron Tuman, and Jay Bolter. And for extremely helpful readings of the manuscript I must thank Linda Billingsley, Robert Winter, Donald McCloskey, and an anonymous reader for the University of Chicago Press.

My greatest debt for this work, as for all that I have done, is reflected in the dedication.

NOTES

1. Steven Levy, *Hackers: Heroes of the Computer Revolution* (Garden City, N.Y.: Anchor Press/Doubleday, 1984), 185. Levy's chronicle is the best history both of the personal computer and of the spirit that animated its creators.

2. McLuhan has recently been the subject of a very thoughtful biography by Philip Marchand: *Marshall McLuhan: The Medium and the Messenger* (New York: Ticknor and Fields, 1989).

3. Jay David Bolter, *Writing Space: The Computer, Hypertext, and the History of Writing* (Hillsdale, N.J.: Erlbaum, 1991), 2.

Acknowledgments

Chapter 1, "The Electronic Word: Literary Study and the Digital Revolution," was first published in *New Literary History* 20, no. 2 (Winter 1989): 265–90.

Chapter 2, "Digital Rhetoric and the Digital Arts," originally appeared as "Digital Rhetoric: Theory, Practice, and Property" by Richard A. Lanham in *Liter-acy Online: The Promise (and Peril) of Reading and Writing with Computers,* Myron C. Tuman, editor. Published in 1992 by the University of Pittsburgh Press. This longer and substantially different version is reprinted by permission of the publisher.

Chapter 3, "Twenty Years After: Digital Decorum and Bi-stable Allusions," first appeared in *Texte: Revue de Critique et de Théorie Littéraire* 8/9, "La Rhétorique du Texte" (1989): 63–98.

Chapter 4, "The Extraordinary Convergence: Democracy, Technology, Theory, and the University Curriculum," was originally published in *South Atlantic Quarterly* 89, no. 1 (Winter 1990): 27–50. Published by Duke University Press. Reprinted with permission of the Publisher.

An edited excerpt of chapter 5, "Electronic Textbooks and University Structures," was published in *Scholars and Research Libraries in the 21st Century,* American Council of Learned Societies Occasional Paper no. 14 (1990): 31–43.

An earlier version of chapter 6, "Strange Lands, Strange Languages, and Useful Miracles," appeared under a slightly different title in *Liberal Education* 76, no. 4 (September/October 1990): 7–13; copyright Association of American Colleges.

Chapter 7, "The 'Q' Question," was first published in *South Atlantic Quarterly* 87, no. 4 (Fall 1988): 653–700. Published by Duke University Press. Reprinted with permission of the Publisher.

THE ELECTRONIC WORD

1

*In this essay, first published in 1989, I tried to suggest the broad spectrum of changes brought by electronic text. Although I focused on literature, readers of the essay immediately began applying it to the other arts as well. One architecture critic has taken the process a step further, performing an experimental revision of the essay into the architectural idiom. Where I wrote "literature," he would substitute "architecture," "building," and so on; in place of my literary instances, he supplied examples from architecture and urban planning. I found the revision both illuminating and startling. Here was my text **in the process of being absorbed into another pattern of thought**. The revision depicted a reader applying what I had written to another conceptual world. One knows—hopes—that this happens, but it is rare to* see *it happening.*

We plan to distribute the revision to a group of architects and critics who will further gloss, annotate, and change it. We'll then take stock of the results. I hope that the essay will thus take a step toward doing what it is talking about—integrating the arts into a single critical inquiry. I hope the results may also shed some light on issues of copyright and originality as they affect academic publication in the volatile, additive medium of electronic text.

The Electronic Word: Literary Study and the Digital Revolution

*P*erhaps the real question for literary study now is not whether our students will be reading Great Traditional Books or Relevant Modern ones in the future, but whether they will be reading books at all. Our first round of technological perturbation, which pitted the codex book and Culture As We Know It against commercial television, didn't turn out so badly as we feared. The print media continued to thrive during TV's great expansion period.[1] And literature continued to be taught in American schools and colleges much as before; students read books and wrote papers and exams about them, which the professors then read, marked up (time and zeal permitting), and returned to the students. Compared to other areas of textual communication in the society around us, literary study has felt almost no pressure from changing technology. This grace period has now been ended by the personal computer and its electronic display of what, until a new word is invented, we must call "text."

The literary world, having gingerly learned to manipulate pixeled print ("pixels" are "picture elements," the dots that electronically paint the letters onto the computer screen) through word processing, has found personal computers handy engines to produce printed texts about printed texts. But our thinking has not gone much further than that. Meanwhile, the electronic word has been producing profound changes in the outside world. Some of the billions of dollars American business and government spend to train their employees are being spent in redefining the "textbook"—and, almost in passing, the codex book itself—into an interactive multimedia delivery system.[2] Sooner or later, such electronic "texts" will redefine the writing, reading, and professing of literature as well.

This changed status of the word affects the entire range of arts and letters. Digitized communication is forcing a radical realignment of the alphabetic and graphic components of ordinary textual communication. In music, notation, creation, and performance have been transformed. Digitization is desubstantiating the visual arts. This common digital denominator of the arts and letters forces upon us a rhetoric of the arts like none seen before. And the free marketplace in which the arts and letters live and breathe is being transformed as well, for perhaps the most immediate, certainly the most immediately felt, effect of the electronic word has come in the area of intellectual property. After the technology of the printing press enabled the rapid production of multiple copies of a work, copyright law emerged to establish a market for printed text. In a world of electronic word and image, literally every fundamental principle of that law, and hence of that marketplace, must be renegotiated.[3] But the most fundamental questions posed for literary study by the electronic word emerge where we would last think to seek them, in our fundamental poetics—and we might begin our survey there.

The late Eric Havelock, in his pioneering work on the Greek alphabet,[4] stressed that an alphabet that could support a high literate culture had to be simple enough to be learned easily in childhood. Thoroughly internalized at that time, it would become a transparent window into conceptual thought. The shape of the letters, the written surface, was not to be read aesthetically; that would only interfere with purely literate transparency. "Reading" would not, except in its learning stages, be a self-conscious, rule-governed, re-creative act but an intuitive skill, a literate compact exercised on the way to thought.

It took a long while for this ideal to be realized in a page of modern print, a page which should, in the famous words of one book designer, stand to its thought as a fine crystal goblet stands to the wine it contains.[5] The physical effort required to write on and read from wax tablet or parchment had first to be attenuated. The scribe's perennial temptation to elaborate the letters, to convert boredom into beauty, had to be overcome. Spaces had to be left between words (a convention invented, according to one authority, as a remedial technique to teach Latin to slow-witted seventh-century Celtic monks).[6] And, after Gutenberg, "transparent" print faces had to be modeled. But once all this was done, unintermediated thought, or at least what seemed like unintermediated thought, was both possible and democratizable. And this unselfconscious transparency has become a stylistic, one might almost say a cultural, ideal for Western civilization. The best style is the style not noticed; the best manners, the most unobtrusive; convincing behavior, spontaneous and unselfconscious.

Pixeled print calls this basic stylistic decorum, and the social ideal built upon it, into question. Electronic typography is both creator-controlled and reader-controlled. The screen upon which these words appear as I write has five sizes of a dozen Roman type styles and two Greek styles at its immediate command and literally hundreds more in second-level storage. I can enlarge the print if my eyes get tired, reduce it to check format and page layout, flow it around illustrations if I want. I can redesign the very shapes of the letters, zoom in on them until their transparency becomes an abstract pattern of separate pixels. I can alter the alphabetic/graphic ratio of conventional literacy in dozens of ways. I can reverse the basic black/white, figure/ground relationship. I can create and maintain a purely transparent verbal surface, but I need not. And as literary scholars above all should know, where the verbal creative spirit has room to play, play it will. When inspiration lags, I'll be tempted to see what a new type style might do for me. I can reformat a text to make it easier to read, or, using a dozen transformations, make it harder, or just different, to read. I can literally color my colors of rhetoric. I can heal the long hiatus of silent reading and make the text read itself aloud. At present this reading sounds a little funky, but it will become an expressive parameter as agile and wide as the others. I can embolden my own special key words and places. I can reformat prose into poetry. I can illuminate my manuscript in ways that would make a medieval scribe weep with envy. And when I have finished, I can print it out on a Linotron 300 electronic typesetter by pushing a keystroke or two. And so can you, as an electronic reader, do all these things, whatever I have chosen to do.

Desktop publishing, as this kind of razzle-dazzle is called, has turned a lot of commercial practices and relationships upside down along with our traditional notions of literary and cultural decorum. The textual surface is now a malleable and self-conscious one. All kinds of production decisions have now become authorial ones. The textual surface has become permanently bi-stable. We are always looking first AT it and then THROUGH it, and this oscillation creates a different implied ideal of decorum, both stylistic and behavioral. Look THROUGH a text and you are in the familiar world of the Newtonian interlude, where facts were facts, the world was really "out there," folks had sincere central selves, and the best writing style dropped from the writer as "simply and directly as a stone falls to the ground," precisely as Thoreau counseled. Look AT a text, however, and we have deconstructed the Newtonian world into Pirandello's and yearn to "act naturally."

We have always had ways of triggering this oscillation, but the old ways—printing prose consecutively and verse not, layering figures of sound and arrangement on the stylistic surface until it squeaked—were clumsy, slow, unchangeable once chosen, and above all author-controlled. And we used them sparingly because the final aim was stable transparency. Make these changes electronically and the oscillations alter radically in frequency and wavelength. The chain reaction goes critical. The difference is profound. You change Edens. And your new Eden becomes, not choosing one or the other attitudinal world, as the current deconstructionist streetfight trivializes it, but determining what kind of oscillation between them you want to create and what stylistic patterns will create it. You return circuitously, by electronic ambages, to that Renaissance sprezzatura, that rehearsed spontaneity which Newtonian science so unceremoniously set aside.

The interactive reader of the electronic word incarnates the responsive reader of whom we make so much. Electronic readers can do all the things that are claimed for them—or choose not to do them. They can genuflect before the text or spit on its altar, add to a text or subtract from it, rearrange it, revise it, suffuse it with commentary. The boundary between creator and critic (another current vexation) simply vanishes. As does the analogous boundary between prose and verse. And, as Richard Ziegfeld has pointed out so perceptively,[7] literary works are being created to exploit this radical interactivity. In interactive fiction, the reader determines the story's outcome by controlling its branching of events. Such decisions amount to literary criticism of a sort, in the same way that deploring Nahum Tate's happy ending of *King Lear* is an act of critical judgment. Suitably embedded in the fiction, a reader's comments about the plot's decision points become part of the fiction itself. The work snowballs into electronic orality, changes and grows as it moves from one screen and keyboard to another.

We might note here that interactive fictionalized modeling is already used in the everyday working world on a massive scale. All kinds of situations are being modeled—a literary critic might say dramatized—interactively. The great battles of the world, both past and future, are being fought electronically, both at home in Uncle Toby's garden and in the Pentagon. Buildings are being designed, constructed, and inserted into a specific townscape through which the prospective client is then walked. Political campaigns are rehearsed, peace treaties negotiated, interests balanced by gaming theory of all sorts. Evolution, human and animal, actual and potential, is being charted by a field of computer-based biology called "artificial life."[8] Into all these interactive environments the literary imagination, the fictional impulse, enters vitally. The personal computer has proved already to be a device of intrinsic dramaticality.

This dramaticality will now inform a reader's re-creation of electronic literary text. In the face of such volatility, it is reassuring to recall all the real literature that got written and fixed forever before pixels dissolved the literary monasteries.⁹ After all, establishing the fixed text has been the human-istic raison d'être since the Renaissance. To nail it down forever and then finally explain it, that has been what literary scholars do. All our tunes of glory vary this central theme, even our current endeavors to show once and for all why nobody can once and for all explain anything. The pixeled word, in fact, seems to sharpen both horns of our current Con- and Deconstruc-tive dilemma. An ever-varying chameleon text forever eludes definitive expla-nation, as the Decons would have it, but it also invites rearrangements that would allow the Cons to have their way with it. Like a Cretan bull leaper, the electronic reader must grab the dilemma firmly in both hands and flip.

Are even the classic printed texts safe from such gymnastics? Imagine growing up as an electronic reader, used to the broad interactive enfran-chisements just sketched. How would you feel about *Paradise Lost* as pre-sented to you in a codex book? Probably you'd prefer to access it from the CD-ROM disk which, in a few years, will contain all the texts you were asked to read—or ever could read—in your undergraduate career. Wouldn't you begin to play games with it? A weapon in your hands after 2,500 years of pompous pedantry about the Great Books, and you not to use it? Hey, man, how about some music with this stuff? Let's voice this rascal and see what happens. Add some graphics and graffiti! Print it out in San Francisco (the kooky face I used above) for **Lucifer**, and Gothic for God. Electronic media will change past literary texts as well as future ones. The electronic word, for both literature and literary history, works both ways.

We will wince at this playfully blasphemous rearrangement even more when it becomes commonplace in popular entertainment. Rock musicians are beginning to design pieces with alternative endings and performative sequences, much as "serious" experimental composers have done for a long time in "aleatory" compositions. Films, too, can be viewer-arrangeable using digital techniques. As Stewart Brand remarked at a Directors' Guild semi-nar on changing technology several years ago, in digital media there is no "final cut." Digitized films can now be released with alternative outtakes or alternative endings from which each viewer will assemble a private ideal ver-sion at home. No "final cut" means no conventional endings, or beginnings or middles either. Interactive literary texts will share this fundamental irres-olution. Obviously our poetics will require some basic non-Aristotelian adjustments.

And "books," the delivery system for texts, are changing as much as the texts themselves. Here, too, technology is forcing vital theoretical issues. As long as the codex book remains at the center of the humanities curriculum, we can with tranquil mind fuss about what we are really doing, what the core curriculum really should be, and so on, because we all really know what we really do. We read books and write about them and teach students about them. Yes, Homer may oxymoronically be "oral literature," and Chaucer may have recited his poems and Shakespeare written plays, but we deal with the book forms. It is the codex book which carries that vital symbolic charge, symbolizes our escape into our "real" world, constitutes our badge of office, furnishes our genuine home. What is valuable about what we do is what happens when we read books.

But if you are not going to read books any more, or are going to read them in different ways, you must decide what it is that happens when you do read them. You must know this if you are to recreate that ineffable something in another medium. You must decide what business you are really in. You can conclude, of course, that that ineffable something cannot be transplanted, that the business you are really in is Reading Books. Many areas of endeavor in America pressured by technological change have already had to decide what business they were really in, and those making the narrow choice have usually not fared well. The railroads had to decide whether they were in the transportation business or the railroad business; they chose the latter and gradual extinction. Newspapers had to decide whether they were in the information business or only the newspaper business; most who chose the newspaper business are no longer in it. A fascinating instance of this choice is now taking place in the piano industry. Steinway used to own the market, and it has decided to stay in the piano business. Yamaha decided it was in the keyboard business—acoustic and electronic—and has, with Roland, Korg, and other manufacturers, redefined the instrument. Time has yet to tell who will win, financially or musically. For all its fastidious self-distancing from the world of affairs, literary study faces the same kind of decision. If we are not in the codex book business, what business are we really in?

Even if we decide that books will be our only business, our assumption that the book is the natural and only vehicle for a written text has been irreparably shaken. We have been made to see more clearly the assumptions that come with a book: it is authoritative and unchangeable, transparent and unselfconscious, read in silence and, if possible, in private. And we see the particular literary and cultural decorum, and hence self and society, that it implies much more clearly too. This self-consciousness about the codex book will prompt basic rearrangements in literary history, and these rearrangements may not be restricted to the age of print. We have for a long time misread and mistranslated the Greek and Latin classics according to the philosophical coordinates of print rather than their native rhetorical orality. The electronic word is hastening this long-overdue revaluation. Literary history, that is, like literature and literary criticism, is being changed both forward and backward.

We have become, I might parenthetically remark, more self-conscious about prose itself. So used are we to thinking black-and-white, continuous printed prose the norm of conceptual utterance, that it has taken a series of theoretical attacks and technological metamorphoses to make us see it for what it is: an act of extraordinary stylization, of remarkable, expressive self-denial. The lesson has been taught by theorists from Marinetti to Burke and Derrida, and by personal computers which restore to the reader ranges of expressivity—graphics, fonts, typography, layout, color—that the prose stylist has abjured. Obviously these pressures will not *destroy* prose, but they may change its underlying decorum. And perhaps engender, at long last, a theory of prose style as radical artifice rather than native transparency.

Electronic text reveals, too, that books as specifically educational tools—textbooks—do have their limitations. People who study and create literature in universities seldom read the elementary and secondary textbooks their students have used to prepare for university study, but they would be horrified if they did. These volumes—physically ugly, worn out if distributed in the public schools, bound in vile peanut-butter-sandwich-proof pyroxylin covers, written in a prose style intentionally dumbed down by readability formulas that filter out all the pleasures of prose, written to offend no one—these volumes do a terrific job of teaching students to hate reading. The el-hi market, as this area of publishing is called, assiduously shuts out anything fresh or new; if electronic technology simply blew it to smithereens, none of us would have undue cause to repine. Or consider our old college friend the big Freshman Comp handbook. How many classes actually use more than a small part of it? It probably contributes more to physical fitness, as a mandatory dumbbell, than it does to the study of prose style. Enormous amounts of money, in these instances and in dozens of others, are spent on monstrously wasteful delivery systems. Even library books, if you think about it, have their limitations. What a blessing if each student had a private copy of each assigned text and could mark it up, individualize it just as scholars do with their own books!

No one knows what electronic "textbooks" will look like; we can hope that great inventions yet impend. Certainly the current textbook publishers, firmly in the book not the information business, are guilty of no fresh thinking. The current state of the art is being created in the gigantic world of business and government training programs. There, interactive video-and-text programs based on laser-optical techniques are proliferating, and radically renegotiating the customary alphabetic/iconic ratio. The single book sold in a single sale is being replaced by a delivery system that remains in place and is continually updated. The explosive growth in database storage capacity made possible by laser-optical techniques has only begun to be used effectively. An interactive compact laserdisc can hold 1,000 video stills, 2,000 diagrams, six hours of high-quality sound, and 10,000 pages of text—and have enough space left over to make it all work together.[10] Such a disk stands to a fixed text as interactive fiction stands to a paperback novel. It promises not the spindled mutilation that the sixties feared but an incredible personalization of learning, a radical democratization of "textbooks" that allows every student to walk an individual path. Stylistic levels can be reader-selectable rather than permanently dumbed down. All kinds of reading assistance—spoken accompaniments, language glossing embedded hypertextually, dynamically interactive bilingual texts—can enfranchise non-native-speaking minorities within the world of letters. Electronic "textbooks" are democratizing education in all the arts in the same way that the invention of printing reinforced the spread of Protestantism.

One possible pattern for textbooks is suggested by Lexis and Westlaw, the two electronic information networks that serve the legal profession. These continually updated on-line databases provide a legal library to anyone with a computer terminal, anywhere in the country. Imagine a major "textbook" continually in touch with all the teachers who use it, continually updated and rewritten by them as well as by the "authors." Imagine a department faculty collaborating to produce a full on-line system of primary and secondary texts, with supporting pedagogical apparatus, to be collectively updated and enhanced: it might encourage a real, and nowadays rare, collegiality. Lexis and Westlaw are expensive, but so are those never-read Freshman Comp texts.

We need not prophesy: the electronic revolution of the textbook is taking place right now. The whole of Greek literature is now on disk. Latin is following suit. Surely the modern languages must do likewise. What use will we make of this gold mine? Students nowadays seem to read only textbooks and only the chapters assigned. Often, required texts are so expensive that they leave no money for any other kind. None of that need be true any longer. We will have to think about canonical expansion from a technological as well as a theoretical perspective. If nowadays students read only what they are assigned, soon they can be assigned almost anything they should read—and will have their own copy of it. In university literature courses, we will soon have to teach students who have been brought up on interactive electronic "texts," and we will have to prepare them for a world of work that relies on the electronic word. I don't think we can sit out this technological revolution; why not use it?

Nowhere does technological pressure fall more intensely than on the relation between the arts. Digitization gives them a new common ground, a quasi-mathematical equivalency that recalls the great Platonic dream for the unity of all knowledge. Digitization both desubstantiates a work of art and subjects it to perpetual immanent metamorphosis from one sense-dimension to another. I keep returning to "Ovidian" as the adjective to describe its force, since such formal metamorphosis constituted Ovid's great epic subject. Perhaps the most striking instance of desubstantiation is real-light holography, whereby an insubstantial but totally "real" and persuasive sculptural image can be displayed. Such techniques will first be employed in cost-intensive industrial and military applications, but it is only a matter of time before sculpture gardens will be constructed in the same way. Such desubstantiation volatilizes our sense of artistic quiddity, of the existence of art objects. They live ultimately in the digital code, the sensuous manifestation only a temporary "printout." This changed essential location pushes images some distance toward the ontological status of words. (It also introduces the issues of possession and pricing, of art as investment-grade specie against which the minimalists, conceptualists, earth artists, and others have waged so notably unsuccessful a war in the last decades.) Digital equivalency means that we can no longer pursue literary study by itself; the other arts will form part of literary study in an essential way. Let me sketch how this is happening.

Ovidian digitization in the arts has gone furthest, perhaps, in the composition, notation, and performance of music. All three dimensions have been radically altered. Programs available widely and cheaply for use on computers like the one these words are being written on (through? by? with? from?) allow novices to compose pleasant-sounding music by enlisting the computer as co-composer. Far from regretting the role of chance in such a composition, or thinking that the computer diminishes human originality and skill, the authors of such programs often regard the physical skills needed for performance, and the theoretical knowledge needed for notation, as elitist prejudices. As one of them, Laurie Spiegel (author of Music Mouse), has said, "sheer physical coordination has nothing to do with musicality. … The ability to deal with and manipulate symbolic notation is irrelevant to musical ability. … All in all, we filter out 90 percent of the musicians and we're left with virtuosos who play piano like it's a sport—without soul."[11]

We ought not underestimate the metamorphic power of this technology just because such computer programs are inexpensive and widely available and have cute names like Music Mouse. The entire structure of Wagnerian sublimity which, at least until Cage, we all ascribed to music stands at risk in this new orchestration. Our sense of "musicality" as artistic rarity, as that combination of divine talent and endless effort which shows the real way to Carnegie Hall, has been called into question. What "musical talent" is thought to be may itself change. New combinations of physical and neurochemical activity may become valorized as "musical genes" under such a new system. In Laurie Spiegel's Music Mouse, you move the Macintosh mouse around on its pad and the linear motions are translated by the computer into musical sounds. Time and space, drawing and music, are made one by digitization. And if the music sounds good, as often it does, what does "good" mean here? "Who" has created the goodness? Such creation takes us deep into the aleatory world of chance so densely explored by experimental music since Cage. To yoke expressivity through one sense to expressivity through another by coaxed chance is Ovidian metamorphosis come true.

Using FM synthesizers and digital sampling techniques to convert sound into sight for purposes of musical notation and editing is now commonplace. Sounds are converted into a whole range of visual equivalents and then manipulated through a variety of transforms before being reconverted into sounds. The "art" of music is thus visualized. There seems no reason why the direction of this translation could not be reversed—although it has not, to my knowledge, been done—and programs be made available to "play" already existing visual patterns musically. One could choose the instrument or instruments on which the visual designs would be "played," the style and tempo of play, and one of a dozen or so choices of intonation system, from "well-tempered" to the "just" intonations of Harry Partch. All these permutations are available to performers without formal musical training. (The computer training required is something else.) We can now, in something like a strict analogy, speak of "music processing" in the same way we speak of "word processing." And the music processed can be arranged into orchestral patterns and performed, a one-person electronic orchestra, by the computer and its programmer. Creator, notator, editor/critic, and performer all fuse into the same creative source.

We can also speak of "image processing."[12] The technology for this is now familiar to us from the space probes and their presentation of digitally processed images on commercial television. Once an image has been digitized, it can be metamorphosed endlessly. Brightness and contrast can be reset. Gray levels can be plotted on a histogram and then manipulated. Pseudocolor can assign colors to levels of gray. Three-dimensional models can be synthesized through volumetric reconstruction. Filtering can elicit patterns the eye cannot normally see. The possibility of such metamorphoses renders the visual image as intrinsically volatile, as desubstantiated, as the musical one. And convertible into it. And these transforming techniques, as with literature, can transform the "fixed" canon of past art as well as setting the future in permanent motion. The Ovidian metamorphosis looks backward as well as forward.

In the digital light of these technologies, the disciplinary boundaries that currently govern academic study of the arts dissolve before our eyes, as do the administrative structures that enshrine them. It is not only the distinction between the creator and the critic that dissolves, but the walls between painting and music and sculpture, music, architecture, and literature. Might not they all, like a Wagnerian *Gesamtkunstwerk*, find a common literary reality as drama, as Cage so long ago predicted? The very volatility of it all, the relentless dramaticality of such continual modeling, might bring it about.

The other arts, that is, face the same metaphysical adjustment literature faces. If sculpture is not chiseling and casting and welding, what is it? If painting is not painting on canvas and selling it to buy more paint to put on more canvas, what is it? And because all the arts face the same technological pressures, they are going to find, create, new relationships through that technology, through their new digital equivalences. Such equivalences pose the most fundamental, and most obvious, challenges to the structure and purpose of the university arts curriculum, and to the place of literary study in it. The shocked responses to chance techniques of creation in experimental music[13] will no doubt be duplicated in responses to programs that create aleatory poetry.

But the shock created by aleatory technology marks only the beginning of the change in attitudes required by the digital metamorphosis of the arts and letters. For the same technological pressures on how past literature will be "read" and metamorphosed in the reading will bear upon the art and music of the past. What is a mustache on the *Mona Lisa*, compared to a Fourier transform practiced upon it? What does colorizing *Casablanca* amount to, compared to pseudocolor techniques applied to Titian? What will the first digital sketches of the Beethoven G-Major Concerto look like, or one of the Opus-17 Haydn String Quartets? How would they sound in Partch's "just intonation"? Such questions, if not precisely literary questions, will have literary analogues equally disconcerting. The university world has for half a century been desperately seeking a "core curriculum" for the arts and letters. And more recently we have yearned with equal hunger to expand the canon, to breathe air not yet passed through the Arnoldian purifier. The digitization of the arts promises a solution to both desperations.

What will emerge finally is a new rhetoric of the arts, an unblushing and unfiltered attempt to plot all the ranges of formal expressivity now possible, however realized and created by whom- (or what-) ever. This rhetoric will make no invidious distinctions between high and low culture, commercial and pure usage, talented or chance creation, visual or auditory stimulus, iconic or alphabetic information. And rather than outlaw self-consciousness, it will plot the degree of it in an artistic occasion. As a start, we might think of a new locational matrix for the arts, one based on the bi-stable decorum I have been discussing rather than on a stable, unselfconscious transparency.[14] It might look like this:

	Unselfconscious	Selfconscious
Object	Transparent	Opaque
Viewer	Through	At
Reality	Biogrammar	Drama
Motive	Hierarchy	Play

The classical notion of decorum, like modern equivalents—"clarity," "authenticity," and so on—measures an effect on the beholder. If a style works, if it creates the transparent illusion, it is decorous. "Decorum" is such a poor descriptive term precisely because it describes so many different kinds of verbal patterns yet allows only one virtue, unselfconscious transparency. We know that all literature, all the arts, are infinitely more various. A matrix like this one allows us to plot them on a common ground. We can define an artistic occasion in terms of object, perceiver, reality perceived, or animating motive. A text or painting can present itself as "realistic," a transparent window to a preexisting world beyond, and so fall at the left end of the "Object" spectrum; or it can present itself frankly as an invention, as pure fantasy, and so choose the right extreme. We can choose to read or view in the same way: either we assume that the object is "real" and stand to the left, or that it is "art" and stand to the right. The object will invite a certain placement but we can decline the invitation, "read" a fantasy as if it were a realistic description of a world as yet unknown, if we like. The social reality presented by the object can be pure human biogrammar, an act as natural and unthinking as a mother's love for her child, or as self-conscious as an actress playing the same scene, or it can be some "ordinary reality" halfway between. We can plot the motival structure that animates the object we see, or our viewing of it, or the creation of the object, on a spectrum that runs from the most intense competition for hierarchical ranking to the most spontaneous, gratuitous behavior, which we perform just for the hell of it, because the performative muscles want to fire: careerism at the left, saintly simplicity at the right.

Ordinary life, or perhaps I should say "Ordinary Life," mostly falls in the middle of these four spectra. *Homo sapiens* is one kind of species—practical and sensible—if, as we usually do, we think the center the norm and the two extremes extreme. We are a quite different animal—obsessed by competitive games on the one hand and unmotivated play on the other— if the two "extremes" constitute our basic norms, the two buttons that make us dance. The Greek philosophers championed the first view, the Sophists the second, and we have been debating the issue ever since. A matrix like this allows us to mix these two views as richly as does life itself. We can plot the range and, with a dynamic electronic version of the matrix, the frequency of the oscillation as well. We can, that is, do what experimental humanism has spent much of the twentieth century striving to do—substitute experiment and observation for authoritative critical guesswork.

The history of criticism in arts and letters has been largely a history of arbitrary and invidious discriminations, single fixations across these spectra of expressivity which then seek to prohibit all other such fixations. Art is an eternal object that exists beyond any beholder. Or it is a type of perception that can be applied to anything from the *Mona Lisa* to Duchamp's famous urinal. Great Art is individual expression, or that of a sublime collective unconscious such as created the medieval cathedrals. It stems from the play impulse. Or from ludic contention. It is good only when you don't notice it or, in Wildean inversion, only when you do. It is "real" only when it refers to the world of myth, or to self-conscious social drama, or to the mixed reality of "ordinary life" in between. Meaning is always in the reader, always in the text, or always in between.

Such exclusive fixes across the matrix have always been hopelessly inadequate to the full range of artistic expression, but the digitization of the arts shows us how silly they really are. Even the simplest work of art describes a complex wave-form across the matrix, a wave-form that varies as we read. We pass in and out of self-consciousness, take our stand first "out there" and then "in here," look and hear first "at" and then "through." Electronic media make us aware of how complex a measurement of bi-stable decorum can be. Indeed, always has been. But the parameters of this matrix are now *userdefinable*. We will be able to manipulate them more clearly than heretofore. By such manipulations and scaling changes, we will be able to glimpse patterns of order in a reality that seemed chaotic and upon which, consequently, we felt obliged to impose an arbitrary order, an individual "theory" of literature. The norms of electronic art will be so volatile that the volatility of a nonexclusive matrix will be the only norm; it will prove a great exposer of pontificating ukase.

Electronic media are essentially dynamic rather than static. This dynamism implies a new future for criticism, one where experimental measurement will figure as largely as critical fiat, and a new history of it as well. For the bi-stable decorum that supplies the premise of electronic text has been the fundamental premise of rhetorical education from the Greeks onward. We can use this electronic decorum to rewrite the history and criticism of Western literature wherever it has been influenced by rhetoric—and that is practically everywhere. Rhetoric becomes, through the digital equivalences such a matrix can plot, a general theory for all the arts and, as well, the central structure for a central curriculum in the arts and letters. Parallel Ovidian revolutions in the other arts change the status of the word by implication; this status is now being changed explicitly as well. Students of literature rarely interest themselves in business communication, but digital techniques have been metamorphic there too. Visual modeling is now employed for all kinds of communication that formerly took place in words, through written prose and discursive conversation. It is being used increasingly, for example, to supplement courtroom argument, especially before a jury considering complex abstract or historical relationships in civil cases. All kinds of conceptual relationships can now be electronically modeled in dynamic and compelling ways.

I see no reason why the matrix I present here in two-dimensional black-and-white could not be recreated in three-dimensional computer-graphics color. We could then use it to plot a particular pattern of attention—a complex literary response—dynamically, if not in real time (that would involve brain-scanning, I suppose) then in a convincing re-creation. We might accumulate a library of literary engrams, if that is the right word for them.

I have no wish to enter into the current debate about lateral hemisphericality in the brain, or the oral/literate debates that depend therefrom, but perhaps I can say under metaphorical license that the left-handed and right-brained are at last inheriting their ancestral lands. If we remember how much our education system depends on grades—"grades" both as merit badges and as age and ability groups—and how much grades depend on verbal testing and verbal cleverness (as vocal but not always verbal minorities remind us), we can glimpse the attitudinal and administrative readjustments that will be required. If a "musical" child can be musical without the long and expensive muscular training required, who knows what "verbal" talents may emerge, or what verbal training may be required, when words and images and sounds, when pixeled print and digital voice, mix in such profoundly metamorphic new ways. Perhaps we will learn the lesson Ovid's metamorphoses sought to teach, see how the literary imagination actually works. One thing is certain: the arts and letters will be one activity as never before.

Technological change, then, is forcing disciplined literary study to look outward to the changing literacy in the world around us. If the codex book is being revolutionized, surely we must ponder this process. We cannot preserve Western culture in pickle. It must be recreated in the technologies of the present, especially if these technologies prove more condign to the oral and rhetorical part of it. And surely we are impelled to this outward view by even the most fashionable and inward of our current activities, literary theory in all its manifestations. Theory is in fact rhetorical practice, as we are becoming increasingly aware, part of a returning rhetorical paideia that began with the didacticism of Futurism and Dada and has been colonizing the humanities and social sciences ever since. Our agonizing "deconstructive" readjustments have come from the figure/ground alternation of our two great tectonic plates, rhetoric and poetics. The movement from inward to outward gaze, from purity to application, comes from our most inward thoughts as well as from outward technological pressures.

The great *explanandum* of changing technologies in the arts and letters rests right here, in fact, in the extraordinary convergence between technological and theoretical pressures. Perhaps we shall find that the personal computer itself constitutes the ultimate postmodern work of art. It introduces and focuses all the rhetorical themes advanced by the arts from Futurism onward. Digital desubstantiation poses in the most acute way the issue of instrumental substance, to which Cage alluded when he closed the keyboard cover of a piano and rapped on it a time or two with his knuckles, and which Nam June Paik dramatized more vividly by taking an ax to the whole instrument. The interactive audience that outrageous Futurist evenings forced upon Victorian conventions of passive silence finds its perfect fulfillment in the personal computer's radical enfranchisement of the perceiver. Cage's games of chance and Oldenburg's experiments in visual scaling become everyday routines in personal-computer graphics. Preoccupation with game and play, which figures so strongly in experimental humanism from Futurism to the present day, has surrounded the computer from the beginning. Pioneer "hacking" was born in the play spirit and that spirit still animates the computer world—especially the personal-computer world.[15] Above all, digital technology poses, as we have seen, the abiding problem of postmodern musing—the status and purpose of art. By fundamentally altering its radix of presentation and reception, technology forces us to rethink fundamental equations we have preferred to answer with windy, self-serving spiritual protestations.

◻   ◻   ◻

The invention of printing brought a struggle between freedom to publish and profit therefrom, and state efforts to control publication. From this struggle emerged the concept of copyright, the protection of a writing as the author's intellectual "property."[16] Western literature for the last two centuries has been created in a marketplace stabilized by copyright laws. And it has, in America, in constitutional times, been rigorously protected by the First Amendment's guarantee of free speech. In the American literary world, if we have not taken this orderly marketplace and its First Amendment freedoms for granted, we have certainly grown to expect them. But this marketplace and its rules are based on print. Copyright law is a creation of print. And, as Ithiel de Sola Pool has argued in *Technologies of Freedom*, the strong bulwark of the First Amendment has been applied mostly to print as well. The electronic word does not fit into the existing copyright marketplace, nor can we be sure, as Pool makes clear, that the First Amendment will protect it as well as it has protected print. The electronic image finds itself similarly imperiled.

These marketplace changes affect literary studies in various ways. Let's start with the least exalted: our profits on textbooks, editions of literary texts, and literary texts themselves. The electronic word embodies a denial of nature: *copia* can be kept and yet given away. Making a digital copy for you does not impoverish me; the only substantial exchange of such a desubstantiated "property" is the physical disk that contains the data, and to send the text over a modem from your hard disk to mine involves no expenditure of substance at all. As software "publishers" have found out, the resulting duplication can bankrupt the producer and beggar the author. The policing required to prevent illicit duplication offends an open society and, a fortiori, that of scholarly interchange. Yet as our texts are all digitized the literary community will face the same problems. If "textbooks" are distributed via local area networks, telephone lines, or more capacious broadband conduits of some sort, how will we protect the intellectual property of those who have created these works? And if the works are excerpted and revised continually by those using them, as we know they will be, who will "own" the revised "property" then redistributed for yet further revision? Who will "own" an interactive novel after it has been repeatedly interacted with? The blurring of the creator/critic distinction here finds a direct legal and financial manifestation. Our ethics of quotation, and the stylistic formulas that embody it, is called into question by electronic media. The electronic word is, obviously, much easier to quote because it is much easier to duplicate and move around. We can embed much larger quotations in our text through hypertextual techniques (indicating by the shape of the cursor, for example, that a further text of a certain sort is embedded behind the surface text) than we could when they would grossly distort our own prose surface. Will these larger quotations exceed what is now reckoned as "fair use" under existing copyright laws? To litigate a copyright case you must have a "final cut," a fixed version, upon which to base your arguments. What if there isn't any?

The dilemma goes to a yet deeper distinction. Intellectual property in words may never have been rooted in a substance, an essence, but we could fool ourselves most of the time that it was. Words there on the page. Look at them. Compare them. That book there with the splendid red binding, that's mine. I wrote it. The Great American Novel. The definitive edition of The Great American Novel. The greatest critical discussion of The Great American Novel. The electronic word has no essence, no quiddity, no substance of this sort. It exists *in potentia* as what it can become, in the genetic structures it can build. It is volatile both in how it is projected onto an electronic screen and in how it works in the world. In both places, its essence is dynamic rather than static. How do we invest an intellectual property in an intellectual *potentiality*? Not in what something is but what something may become, the uses to which it may be put? The great catchphrase in copyright law (the lawyers call it a "principle") is "substantial similarity." As a legal principle, the phrase has always had its problems,[17] but what if the property litigated has been desubstantiated? Who owns a piece of music that has been created by tracing a drawing on a digitizer pad? Or the music created by a program responding to mouse and keyboard manipulations? Do I own the musical rights to my drawings?[18] The graphics rights to my music? And what if some lunatic literary scholar succeeds in his efforts to do dynamic three-dimensional models for rhetorical figures? When he uses them in the hypertext version of his *Handlist of Rhetorical Terms*, can he protect them as original expressions? Suppose I decide to make an interactive version of a conventional novel? Or illustrate it in an interactive way through hypertext? Do I need the author's permission or is this "fair use"? Suppose I use digital conversion to add voice and music to a fiction according to some fixed parameters?

Electronic information seems to resist ownership. To make sure that it does flow freely in the world of literary study, we will have to create a new marketplace based on a new conception of intellectual property and copy-right protection, and make sure that the constitutional guarantees of free speech made good in the print world prevail here too. Such a readjustment will not come easily. And if we modulate from the cash marketplace to the academic marketplace, surely the electronic word will pose puzzles there too. Academic life's real currency, the intellectual currency that determines the dollar amounts, is publication. How will the electronic word affect the elab-orate system of merit badges that, during the last hundred years, we have worked out on the basis of print? It is only when we compare print to its pixeled analogue that we realize how talismanic the physical book and jour-nal have become. Will we feel as good about a text that exists only in elec-tronic form, or as cheap printouts? Will an "offprint" communicated through electronic mail carry the same grooming charge to one's scholarly acquain-tance, stroke their amour propre as satisfactorily, as a real offprint with a real cover? In those departments where a "textbook" carries merit-badge status, will an electronic delivery system, with its inevitable several co-"authors" and subsequent re-creation by others, count as much as a real, coated-stock-heavy book? And what of the new forms of critical commentary that may emerge?

Let's assume that an enterprising young scholar undertakes to construct a hypertext edition of a famous novel with a vexed textual history. It will include all textual possibilities plus suggestions as to their relationships. These will be presented in certain carefully determined, related ways; the reader can dial up, as it were, different coherent combinations of alternate readings. And with them all the available, or at least all the good, com-mentary on the text, embedded behind a set of "buttons" that are reader-selectable. This commentary will be indexed to individual passages in the text and cross-indexed by a user-selectable group of categories. Various recorded readings will be available, too, as well as animated three-dimen-sional diagrams illustrating basic stylistic patterns. Surrounding the whole will be a pedagogical framework with user-selectable levels. If you want guid-ance on how this text-delivery system might be used in secondary schools, you make the appropriate selections and a suggested pedagogy is offered. For various university applications, specific guidance is likewise offered. And the whole is conceived on an open structure: each user can make comments and these will become part of the system.

Who "wrote" such a "text"? Who gets the royalties? Clearly it is origi-nal in its conception and realization. Is it then a copyrightable "expression," to use the law's terminology, or only an unprotectable "idea"? Are all its tex-tual uses "fair"? If it is a "textbook," in my department at least it cannot be awarded a merit badge, but isn't it "criticism" as well? And "literary history"? Therefore badgeworthy? And aren't some major theoretical issues raised by such a "text"? Hypertexts are, in more than a manner of speaking, three-dimensional. Fuguelike, they can carry on an argument at several levels simultaneously. And if we cannot read them simultaneously, we can switch back and forth with great rapidity. We talk a lot about "subtexts" and such, but what if several are actually there in residence? Again, electronic text literalizes a theoretical conundrum. Doesn't this further disempower, unpack, the force of linear, printed prose, following the argument developed above? And if the embedded texts consist of our own commentary on the text, our own or others', or somebody else's, or long quotations from the authorities whom we are presently treating, mustn't we avail ourselves of the nomenclature of musical arrangement to find terms adequate to this fugal, but at the same time totally literary, occasion?

Property issues of a nonlegal but very real professional sort will supervene when, as seems likely, we come to do our scholarly disputation electronically. Scholarly-journal publication, for example, would make much more sense done electronically. The audiences are usually specialized and small, library budgets for journals perennially tight, and storage a gigantic problem; publication schedules involve both long delays and lots of hurry-up mailing at proof stages; students often want to use journals but all the same journals at the same time, which makes them unavailable to most. Even the physical labor of reading old volumes—lugging them from the library, propping them open on your desk with both hands while the acidified paper crumbles to the touch—gets in the way.

All this fuss could be avoided if scholarly journals were "published" as on-line databanks upon which individual scholars could draw at will. The extraordinary delays in humanistic publishing could be avoided. The costs of such publication, if we consider the scholarly apparatus from producer to library storage and distribution, could be markedly reduced. And new informational opportunities would arise. We could update our own articles as we wanted to, and those revisions would be immediately available to the scholarly community. We could choose to include, as part of our work, subsequent comments upon it—either champagne or, for stout hearts, hemlock, or both.[19] Most of us now keyboard our writing electronically to begin with. After it goes through various permutations and rekeyboardings, we read it in print and then take notes on it—by electronic keyboarding. Keeping the process electronic from beginning to end would save much time and effort. And it would make the apparatus of "published" scholarship available to anyone anywhere in the world who had a computer terminal. Our sense of scholarly "location" would change. Academic urbanity would no longer be an affair of big research campuses. Such a system would be an extraordinarily democratizing one.

It would lead inevitably to real-time communication as well, an electronic bulletin board of sorts. What kind of merit badge, if any, could be awarded for participation in such a scholarly "conversation" is hard to say; we don't presently stigmatize similar conversations when they take place in conferences and in person, but we don't list them as publications either.

The censorial process by which our efforts are judged "worthy of publication" might change as the meaning of "publication" changed. The present rejection rate of publications in the social sciences and humanities is 80–90 percent and in the sciences 25 percent. Certainly we are tougher and more discriminating than our lab-coated brethren, but perhaps not that much more so. Rowland Lorimer, in a recent article in *Scholarly Publishing*, suggested a "tiered-acceptance" system which would expand the acceptance rate.[20] Or perhaps the whole judgmental system could be made more interactive as between referee and supplicant scholar. Maybe print publication is intrinsically a censorious technology and information would flow more efficiently in electronic form.

Whatever happens, however we rearrange our marketplace of ideas— as sooner or later we certainly shall—our sense of what "publication" means is bound to change. We will be able to make our commentary part of the text, and weave an elaborate series of interlocked commentaries together. We will, that is, be moving from a series of orations to a continuing conversation, and, as we have always known, these two rhetorics differ fundamentally. It seems reasonable to assume that as the definition and nature of "publication" changes, our system of academic rewards and punishments will change as well. If we keep an eye on these changes, they may change for the better. Above all, we may be able to introduce our students to the scholarly conversation sooner than we do now, and in more realistic and effective ways.

Issues of intellectual property, whether in the copyright marketplace or the (sometimes) less contentious marketplace of academic accomplishment and credentials, will then certainly arise as we move in slow and staggered steps from the printed to the pixeled word. Solving them will not be made any easier by a fundamental theoretical issue underlying them, the concept of artistic rarity. The ease, speed, and magical metamorphosis of digitized arts and letters put the "rarity = value" equation at risk. This equation cleaves to all our hearts, to our sense of self, status, and accomplishment. Yet electronic media do seem to imply that our individual voices will blend more quickly and thoroughly into the general conversation than heretofore. Not only our amour propre will suffer, but the Arnoldian aesthetic of the very best and most beautiful upon which we have built so much. The electronic word democratizes the world of arts and letters in far more ways than I can sketch here, but the political direction of the technological force is strong and unmistakable; value structures, markets ideological as well as financial and theoretical, will be reassessed.

Humanists are such natural Luddites and have become so used to regarding technology—and especially the computer—as the enemy that it takes some temerity to call the personal computer a possible friend. Yet this remarkable convergence of social, technological, and theoretical pressures suggests that it may be just that. Literary study, as by now we all know, takes place very largely in a university environment, and that environment is far more open and democratic than it used to be, and draws upon a student body far more multilingual and multicultural than any of us contemplated even twenty years ago. This diverse student body often lacks the pattern of cultural practices and expectations upon which literary study has depended in the last hundred years, and so we are being asked to explain our customs and delights as never before. And since our activities, like those of higher education generally, are often supported from public purses, we are being asked to document those unproven Arnoldian claims to cultural centrality and civic virtue by which we have set such traditional store.

The electronic word, as we have seen, asks this question—What business are we really in?—in equally forceful technological terms. It also suggests at least some tentative answers. If our business is general literacy, as some of us think, then electronic instructional systems offer the only hope for the radically leveraged mass instruction the problems of general literacy pose. If we are in any respect to pretend that "majoring in English," or any other literature, and all that it implies, teaches our students how to manipulate words in the world of work, then we must accommodate literary study to the electronic word in which that world will increasingly deal. Otherwise, we shall find ourselves, as engineering schools did half a dozen years ago, teaching manual mechanical drawing in a world of CADD (computer-assisted design and drafting). Electronic technology is full of promising avenues for language instruction; it will be lunacy if we do not construct a sophisticated comparative-literature pedagogy upon it. The bankruptcy of our long-fragile ideas of a humanities curriculum has been exposed by both changing demography and changing technology. And again electronic technology, through its central agency of digital conversion, suggests how we might begin constructing precisely the rhetoric of the arts that we so much need. The computer modeling that has become central to social and scientific think-ing of all sorts is a dramatic, that is to say a literary, technique through and through. Such techniques, used throughout the creative thought of a soci-ety, imply precisely the self-conscious dramatic conception of public reali-ty we now see advanced across the spectrum of the social and humane sci-ences.

The rhetorical paideia formed the basic pattern of Western education for most of our 2,500 years. Electronic technology looks like forming a cen-tral part of our return to this basic pattern. The rehearsal reality that classi-cal rhetoric created in the practice oration, we now model, in icon as well as word, on an electronic screen. Pixeled print destabilizes the arts and let-ters in an essentially rhetorical way, returns them to that characteristic oscil-lation between looking AT symbols and looking THROUGH them which the rhetorical paideia instilled as a native address to the world. Our present squabble in the public prints about teaching Western culture is usually ani-mated on both sides by a radical misapprehension about what "Western cul-ture" has always been. We are asked to believe that it has been a print-sta-ble collection of Great Ideas enshrined in Great Books, and we now quarrel about which books are, for our present needs, really Great. But Western edu-cation has in its essence been rhetorical, has been based, that is, not on a set of great ideas, but on a manner of apprehension; it has taught as central not knowledge but how knowledge is held. That characteristic grasp has been bi-stable, alternatively unselfconscious and purposive, and self-conscious and contemplative. It is this Thucydidean alternation of speech and narra-tive patterns and psychologies that has undergirded classical literature almost from its beginnings.[21]

We may view the strand of experimental humanism that started with Marinetti's Futurist Manifesto and the Dadaists, then returned as a specifi-cally rhetorical argument with Kenneth Burke and Richard McKeon, explod-ed again in all the sixties' isms, and then returned again in the seventies as "literary theory," as finally a didactic movement, a long and variously ani-mated argument about what humanistic study should do and be. Experi-mental humanism aimed to convert the Arnoldian foregone conclusions into an open-ended experimentality; to galvanize the silent and impassive audience into interaction; to invoke the medium as self-conscious condi-tion of the message; to expose scaling changes as movements to a different register of meaning; to precipitate game and play out of pompous purpose and plead directly to them; to readmit chance to the role it has always played in the human drama; to make war on taste in order to find out what species of censor it truly was; and through all these radically to democratize the arts.

To return us, that is, from a closed poetics to an open rhetoric. The electronic word, as pixeled upon a personal-computer screen, reinforces all these purposes, literalizes them in a truly uncanny way.

We may expect a deal of commentary greeting the electronic modification of print literacy as the death of the Western self.[22] Surely the opposite is taking place. The characteristically unstable Western self, by turns central and social, sincere and hypocritical, philosophical and rhetorical, is just what electronic literacy has been busy revitalizing. Allowing the simplicities neither of Arnoldian sincerity nor of deconstructive despair, it will force these extremes into that bi-stable oscillation which has created our richly felt Western life since Plato and Isocrates first started it rocking two-and-a-half millennia ago.

I hope I have been persuasive enough to coax you now into modeling literary study against a technological screen. So far as I can see it, our instinctive posture has been defensive, based on the book and the curricular and professional structures that issue from it. We conceive the humanities as a pickle factory preserving human values too tender and inert for the outside world. The world goes its way but supports us, museumlike, to show what, had it been composed of people like us, it might have become. The cozy conspiracy is sustained by both sides. The harsh world wants to imagine a finer world and we pretend to dwell in it. But our students and the society from which they come will not permit this illusion to continue unchanged; nor will a technology that has volatilized print; nor will our own thinking, our "theory," about what we are and do. All these are asking us to think systemically about literary study, to model it from kindergarten through graduate school. They are asking us to reconceive literary study, to think of it as permeating society in the way literary rhetoric has always done in the West, but with new technologies and through new administrative arrangements. We are being asked to explain how the humanities humanize. Surely it is by teaching and studying, and thus sustaining, that bi-stable oscillation which forms the heart of the Western self. That is the business we are in, and it rests on the bedrock assumption of Western culture itself, the assumption that if we understand this dangerous and inventive heart of human life, we will cherish it and, so cherishing, will work to preserve it. The electronic word stands on our side in this endeavor and for that we should return thanks.

Apoplexy seems to come more naturally than apocalypse to literary scholars when we think about technology. Apoplectic rage and scorn has been the common response to commercial television; apocalyptic soaring on the wings of new technology has been altogether less common. I have tried, though, to guard against both in this essay. Electronic text is a different but not less important affair than commercial TV, and it needs the separate argument I have given it here. I have tried as well to avoid the windy prophetic suspirations that come so easily when pondering future technologies, by concentrating on the present, on technologies that are all commercially available right now at reasonable prices and which can be observed in action. And yet I am willing to be, if not apocalyptic, still optimistic and excited about literary study in an electronic age. We have scarcely begun to think constructively about the electronic word. Although it brings compulsions with it, I hope we will think of it less as a technological *vis a tergo* driving us where we don't want to go than as an opportunity to go where we have never been, and to do things no one has done before. At the very least, we have been given an extraordinary opportunity to rethink literary study and its uses from the ground up.

The basic implications of electronic technology may be inevitable but what we make of them certainly is not. We are free to think about, and plan for, literary creation and literary study in ways more agile, capacious, and hopeful than any generation has possessed since literature began to figure in human life. And we must do so, we must learn to think systemically. Technology is sending the same message being broadcast by society's demands upon us and by our own thinking: We must take into our disciplinary domain the world of general literacy upon which literature depends, a world whose existence up to now we have simply assumed. If the prejudices of print and craft-guild muff our play, we shall have only ourselves to blame. Literary scholars have traditionally resisted and resented technological change. If we decide once again to view technology with a hostile eye, this time we may find ourselves making the pianos while someone else makes the music. But if we put aside our traditional resentments and fears, then we must decide what our "music" is and how to make it in the new ways.

NOTES

1. See Ithiel de Sola Pool, *Technologies of Freedom* (Cambridge: Harvard University Press, 1983), 21: "From 1960 to 1977 the circulation of daily papers in the United States grew by 5 percent, the circulation of magazines by 25 percent, and the distribution of books annually by 75 percent."

2. See George Melloan, "Public Education's Failures Plague Employers," *Wall Street Journal*, 21 June 1988, sec. A39: "The American Society for Training and Development (ASTD) recently estimated a $210 billion total annual cost,

not far below the $238 billion the U.S. spends on formal elementary, secondary and college education."

3. "And," as one copyright lawyer pondering a major media case told me, "since it took Congress sixteen years to revise the Copyright Act the last time, this may take a good while."

4. See esp. chaps. 3–6 in Eric A. Havelock, *The Literate Revolution in Greece and Its Cultural Consequences* (Princeton: Princeton University Press, 1982).

5. Beatrice Warde, *The Crystal Goblet: Sixteen Essays on Typography*, ed. Henry Jacob (London: Sylvan, 1955), 11–17.

6. Ivan Illich and Barry Sanders, *ABC: The Alphabetization of the Popular Mind* (San Francisco: North Point, 1988), 46.

7. Richard Ziegfeld, "Interactive Fiction: A New Literary Genre?" *New Literary History* 20, no. 2 (Winter 1989): 341–72.

8. Steven Levy has described this emergent field in *Artificial Life: The Quest for a New Creation* (New York: Pantheon, 1992).

9. George Steiner remarked on the historical connection between books and monasteries: "I would not be surprised if that which lies ahead for classical modes of reading resembles the monasticism from which those modes sprung. I sometimes dream of houses of reading—a Hebrew phrase—in which those passionate to learn how to read well would find the necessary guidance, silence, and complicity of disciplined companionship" ("The End of Bookishness?" *Times Literary Supplement*, 8–14 July 1988, 754). We may expect a warm welcome for this monastic alternative to technological change.

10. Stewart Brand, *The Media Lab: Inventing the Future at MIT* (New York: Viking, 1987), 23.

11. Quoted by Steven Levy, "Whose Music Is It, Anyway?" *Macworld* (Aug. 1988): 46.

12. For a handy summary discussion of image processing, see Brita Meng, "Reality Transformed," *Macworld* (Aug. 1988): 82–87.

13. Michael Nyman coined the term in his pioneering *Experimental Music: Cage and Beyond* (New York: Schirmer, 1974).

14. I discuss an earlier version of this matrix in "At and Through: The Opaque Style and Its Uses," *Literacy and the Survival of Humanism* (New Haven: Yale University Press, 1983), 58–86.

15. Steven Levy's *Hackers: Heroes of the Computer Revolution* (Garden City, N.Y.: Anchor Press/Doubleday, 1984) captures this play spirit perfectly.

16. In addition to Melville B. Nimmer's standard work, *Nimmer on Copyright*, 4 vols. (New York: Matthew Bender, 1963; continually revised), see Lyman Ray Patterson, *Copyright in Historical Perspective* (Nashville: Vanderbilt University Press, 1968); Alexander Lindey, *Plagiarism and Originality* (New York:

Greenwood, 1952), 62–104; and Benjamin Kaplan, *An Unhurried View of Copyright* (New York: Columbia University Press, 1966), 1–37.

17. Amy B. Cohen makes this point in a brilliant essay, "Masking Copyright Decisionmaking: The Meaninglessness of Substantial Similarity," *U.C. Davis Law Review* 20 (1987): 719–67.

18. Some of these issues have been opened by Patricia A. Krieg, "Copyright, Free Speech, and the Visual Arts," *Yale Law Journal* 93, no. 8 (July 1984): 1565–85.

19. See K. Eric Drexler, "Publishing Hypertexts Isn't Hypertext Publishing," in *Hypertext '87: A Digest*, ed. Mark Bernstein (Cambridge, Mass.: Eastgate Systems disk, 1987).

20. Rowland Lorimer, "Implications of the New Technologies of Information," *Scholarly Publishing* 16 (1985): 197–210.

21. I have developed this argument at length in *The Motives of Eloquence: Literary Rhetoric in the Renaissance* (New Haven: Yale University Press, 1976).

22. See, e.g., Illich and Sanders (n. 6 above).

2

The argument of this chapter was born backward and after a prolonged confinement. The original paper started out as a discussion of the humanities curriculum. Such discussions seem to gravitate naturally to a ponderous moralizing tedium. To avoid, or at least ameliorate, this native ponderousness, I thought I might show some slides. The principles of a new humanities curriculum had already, it seemed to me, been worked out in the twentieth-century visual arts; why not use visual equivalents for curricular structures? It seemed to work.

But then I started thinking about electronic text and how it might affect the humanities curriculum. And I started thinking, too, about how electronic text constituted an expressive medium far better suited to traditional oral rhetoric than to print. And then something arced in my mind between electronic text and the visual arts: they shared a common aesthetic!

I began to give talks about this common aesthetic. I wanted to illustrate the textual changes I was discussing in a way that people could see, but I couldn't afford the required multimedia display machinery. In fact, when I began talking about these matters, adequate display machinery for a large audience did not exist, except in very expensive installations ($80,000 light-belt projectors and the like). And I couldn't escape the logic that demanded an electronic form from the beginning for such a discussion. So, as a second-best, I showed the slides I had prepared to illustrate the curriculum to illustrate another relationship altogether. This worked too. When I lectured, people understood what I was talking about. The essay began to rewrite itself, through these public presentations, into its present form.

Cart and horse began to change places. I came to think that the most interest-ing thing about digital "text" was how directly it fulfilled the expressive agenda of the strand of artistic thinking and practice we nowadays call postmodern. So here I was committed to argue that electronic text expressed both the postmodern spirit and the classical rhetorical one better than print!

And so I argue that at least one strand of postmodern visual art, the one that starts with Italian Futurism and Dada, represents yet another instance of the gener-al revival of rhetorical thinking and education that I discuss in chapter 3. The cur-ricular issues which then dropped out of this essay reappear in chapters 5 and 6 below.

This process, long and labored as it seemed in the doing, showed me that these various issues, or branches of thinking, were all related, all part of one single phe-nomenon. I try in the essays which follow to describe that phenomenon from the dif-ferent points of view its essence requires.

Digital Rhetoric and the Digital Arts

We have always, from Pascal to the present, thought of computers, especially digital computers, as logic machines. Whether they helped us with our weaving, our business tabulations, our artillery trajectories, or our atomic bombs, we have always located them where we locate logic: at the familiar Platonic, mathematical center of human reason. It was a Monster of Pure Reason that threatened to fold, spindle, and mutilate the riotous Berkeley students of the sixties. It was the same monster that prompted Hubert Dreyfus to write his equally riotous satire of artificial intelligence,[1] a modern *Dunciad* after which neither satirist nor satirized has ever been the same. I would like, as a supplement and complement to this view from philosophy and theory, to suggest that in practice, the computer often turns out to be a rhetorical device as well as a logical one, that it derives its aesthetic from philosophy's great historical opposite in Western thought and education, the world of rhetoric. I argue, at the same time, that this fixation on logic has so bemused us that we have failed to notice the extraordinary way in which the computer has fulfilled the expressive agenda of twentieth-century art. It thus fulfills at the same time a very new visual agenda and a very old verbal one. I want to suggest some of these remarkable fulfillments here.

What happens when text moves from page to screen? First, the digital text becomes unfixed and interactive. The reader can change it, become writer. The center of Western culture since the Renaissance—really since the great Alexandrian editors of Homer—the fixed, authoritative, canonical text, simply explodes into the ether. We can see that happening in a typographical explosion called *SCRABrrRrraaNNG*, from a 1919 manifesto by Filippo Tommaso Marinetti (fig. 1).

Italian Futurism, which began with Marinetti's famous *Futurist Manifesto* in 1909, was a complex, and as things turned out an extremely prophetic, movement that combined theatrical evenings very like the Happenings

Figure 1. Filippo Tommaso Marinetti, "SCRABrrRrraaNNG,"
from *8 anime in una bomba—romanzo esplosivo*, 1919.
© Marinetti/VAGA, New York 1993.

of fifty years later with political outpourings of an apocalyptically Fascist
sort. It created a new, nonharmonic music which used both silence and noise
in ways that foreshadowed John Cage, and argued for the primacy of vision
over print in ways that point toward Marshall McLuhan. The final aim of
all this was, or at least sometimes was, the conflation of the arts into a single theatrical whole, something Marinetti called "Il Teatro di Varietà," a theater that seemed, at least for him, to find its most natural future home not
in live theater but in cinema—cinema being then the new technology. (He
would now locate it, I think, in the digitally driven "theme park" events

being designed by Lucasfilm, Disney, and MCA. The perfect example of "Il Teatro di Varietà" would be the Disneyland space-travel attraction called "Star Tours.")

I want to single out from this prophetic mélange of violent theater and political rant only one of its dominant interests: the attack on the printed codex book and its typographical conventions, an attack symbolized by Marinetti's *esplosione*. In a tract called *La cinematografia futurista* Marinetti and some of his pals single out the book as the chief villain of the old order:

> The book, the most traditional means of preserving and communicating thought, has been for a long time destined to disappear, just like cathedrals, walled battlements, museums, and the ideal of pacifism. ... The Futurist Cinema will ... collaborate in a general renewal, substituting for the magazine—always pedantic—, for the drama—always stale—, and killing the book—always tedious and oppressive.[2]

The book is seen as static, inelastically linear, sluggish; the new cinematographic form as dynamic, interactive, simultaneous, swift. This war on the book chose as its immediate target typographical convention, with results like *SCRABrrRrraaNNG*. Here we see the book and all it represents in the act of deconstructing itself—all unawares the little children played, even as early as 1919—*esplosione* at its center literally shattering typographical convention into distended fragments.

Subsequent collage techniques from Dada to the present day have diffused the force and direction of this attack, but Marinetti was taking aim at the founding convention of a literate society. I quoted in chapter 1 Eric Havelock's thesis that a culture, to be truly literate, must possess an alphabet simple enough to be learned thoroughly in early youth and unobtrusive enough in its calligraphy that a reader forgets about its physical aspects and reads right through it to the meaning beneath. The written surface must be transparent. Transparent and unselfconscious. We must not notice the size and shape of the letters. We may in some subconscious way register the cheirographic or typographic conventions but we must not *see* them. (Havelock, for example, points to early Greek vase-paintings where letters of the alphabet are used as decorative motifs, are noticed for their size and shape only, as registering the preliterate, still oral, use of the alphabet.)

It is to this stage that Marinetti—and electronic text—would return us. He seeks to make us aware of the enormous act of simplification that an ordinary printed text represents; he wants to make us self-conscious about a register of expressivity that as literate people we have abjured. It is common to call experiments of this sort "outrageous," but surely they aim at didacticism much rather. In a literate culture our conception of meaning itself—whether of logical argument or magical narrative—depends on this radical act of typographical simplification. No pictures; no color; strict order of left to right then down one line; no type changes; no interaction; no revision. In attacking this convention, Marinetti attacks the entire literate conception of humankind—the central self, a nondramatic society just out there waiting for us to observe it—and the purposive idea of language that rests upon it. He would urge us to notice that all this reality-apparatus is as conventional as the typography we are trained *not* to notice. There was a time when it did not exist: in the oral culture, in fact, out of which Greek rhetoric developed.

Marinetti's techniques have been employed often since then. Ted Nelson's *Computer Lib/Dream Machines* offers a handy example from the digital world (fig. 2).[3] Nelson's sometimes cutesy typographical games show more clearly than Marinetti the native didacticism of the genre. Here too, as often happens, the self-conscious typography advocates a theory of prose style—a campaign against "cybercrud" and for an unselfconscious prose style based on the "Clarity-Brevity-Sincerity" trinity—that the self-conscious typography contradicts at every point.

Concomitantly with the explosion of the authoritative text, electronic writing brings a complete renegotiation of the alphabet/icon ratio upon which print-based thought is built. We can detect this foregrounding of images over written words most clearly in the world of business and government communications, but it is happening everywhere. When the rich vocal and gestural language of oral rhetoric was constricted into writing and then print, the effort to preserve it was concentrated into something classical rhetoricians called *ecphrasis*, dynamic speaking-pictures in words. Through the infinite resources of digital image recall and manipulation, ecphrasis is once again coming into its own, and the pictures and sounds suppressed into verbal rhetorical figures are now reassuming their native places in the human sensorium. The complex icon/word interaction of oral rhetoric is returning, albeit *per ambages*.

The struggle between icon and alphabet is not, to be sure, anything new, as the history of illuminated manuscripts attests. This complex interaction of word and image never actually vanished; it only fell out of fashion. The tradition of mixing transparent alphabetic information with opaque pictures formed by the letters goes back at least to Simias, a Greek poet of the fourth century B.C.[4] It was revived first by Marinetti and then by the Dadaists, with a specifically aggressive purpose. And, to some degree, it lurks in any calligraphic tradition. Electronic display both invites manipulating the icon/alphabet mixture and makes it much easier to write.

As one instance of how such calligrams work, we might look at a

Figure 2. Ted Nelson, *Computer Lib/Dream Machines.*
Reprinted by permission of Microsoft Press. Copyright
© 1987 by Ted Nelson. All rights reserved.

prophetic pre-electronic example in Kenneth Burke's *Collected Poems, 1915–1967* (fig. 3).[5] Burke called these doodles "Flowerishes." The "text" of this particular typographical game is a series of comic apothegms: "In a world full of problems he sat doing puzzles," "One must learn to be just morbid enough," "They liked to sit around and chew the phatic communion," and so on. The core of Burke's philosophy of rhetoric has been his discussion of "orientation," the self-conscious perception of paradigms for apprehending reality that we customarily push to the side, to our peripheral vision. In this doodle, he uses the conventions of typography to pun on orientation. To "orient" ourselves to this self-conscious form of proverbial wisdom, we must, like an illiterate pretending to read, turn the book round and round in an effort to make sense of it. We are made aware of the book as a physical presence in our hands. The printed surface is rendered opaque rather than transparent by changes in typeface, font size, and sequentiality. Text must be read top to bottom as well as left to right, back to front, in a circle, every which

35

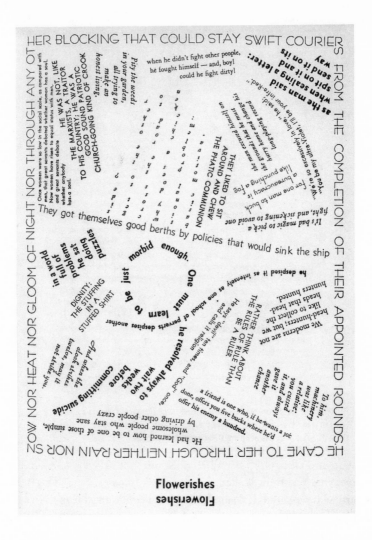

Figure 3. Kenneth Burke, *Collected Poems, 1915–1967*.
Copyright © 1968 Kenneth Burke.

way. Type is "poured," as it is in a desktop publishing system such as *Quark XPress*, rather than set. Spec-ing type in such a frame becomes an aspect of meaning rather than merely a transparent window to it. Does "a grandfather clock, run by gravity," mean something different because the words are presented in Gothic type? Typography becomes allegorical, a writer-controlled expressive parameter, just as it does on an electronic screen. Here, though, as so often, the electronic screen fulfills an already existing expressive agenda rather than prophesying a new one.

The most revered and central function of the literary canon is to transmit the canonical wisdom found quintessentially in the proverb. Burke deliberately calls that tradition into question, breaking the "literacy compact" by introducing visual patterns and typographical allegories to suggest that proverbial wisdom never comes into the world purely transparent and disembodied, totally serious, unconditioned by game and play, by the gross physicality of its display. No formal cause without a material one. Again, the electronic parallels are manifest. The electronic universe's playful attitude toward typographical convention drives the print-based imagination mad.

All kinds of interesting conversions take place when we move from book to screen. Proverbial wisdom, for example, becomes visual. Digital expression has resurrected the world of proverbial wisdom, but through vast databanks of icons rather than words. We buy what are, in effect, catalogues representing commonplace situations and appropriate responses to them: faces, hand gestures, signage of all sorts. Our computer font menus regularly include printer's dingbats— ❑ ❱ ❋ ▼ ❙ ◆ ❋ ✎ ✄ ❸ —but the range of readily available proverbial icons now runs to thousands. The traditional dependence on commonplaces in rhetorical education has been transmuted from word to image.

The same wind that carried away the authoritative text has also ventilated the reverent solemnity with which we view it. Again we encounter the digital aesthetic charted much earlier in the visual arts. The canonical image of this anticanonicity is Marcel Duchamp's urinal. My favorite emblem of compromised canonicity, though, is John Baldessari's *Quality Material* from 1967, which consists of five lines of black alphabetic text on a white ground:[6]

> QUALITY MATERIAL – – –
> CAREFUL INSPECTION – –
> GOOD WORKMANSHIP.
>
> ALL COMBINED IN AN EFFORT TO
> GIVE YOU A PERFECT PAINTING.

This textual painting does exactly what the computer screen does: it makes text into a painting, frames it in a new way, asks for a new act of attention—and smiles at the seriousness that text calls forth from us.

Baldessari, by a radical reversal of alphabetic and iconic information, denies an absolute beauty and fitness of things independent of humankind, a fitness we are first to discover and then breathlessly to adore. The painting would seem to suggest that such fitness is not out there in "reality," and it is not out there in sacred texts, either—timeless, unchangeable, self-explanatory, and canonical—excerpts of which, duly presented as "touch-stones," will impart the healing touch of sacred relics. Instead of a divine icon, we have a human text that substitutes the interpretation for the thing interpreted.

Doesn't electronic text often practice a similar comic reversal? The intrinsic motival structure of electronic text is as comic as print is serious. Let me illustrate this reversed polarity of seriousness by alluding to another familiar pre-electronic icon, Duchamp's most famous "Readymade," his mustachioed *Mona Lisa*. The title of this work, the letters L.H.O.O.Q., if pronounced in French, yield the words "Elle a chaud au cul," or in some-what fractured French, "This chick has hot pants." What, in the process, has happened to "Mona Baby"? First of all, she seems to have undergone a devastatingly effective and economical sex-change operation. By desecrat-ing Perfection, Duchamp has elicited a sexual ambiguity in the picture we had not seen before and could learn to see in no other way. Outrageous art as didactic criticism, once again. Second, Duchamp calls our attention to a powerful canonical constraint. The timeless perfection Mona Baby repre-sents condemns us to passivity. No interaction allowed. Canonical vision moves in only one direction, does justice to an external reality that exists independent of us, but never recreates that reality in the act of perceiving it. The traditional idea of an artistic canon brings with it, by the very "immortality" it strives for, both a passive beholder and a passive reality wait-ing out there to be perceived, the best that has been thought, said, or paint-ed perhaps, but unchangeable in its perfection, a goddess we can adore but never ask out to play. And so Duchamp asks her out to play. Criticism again. And, again, not so much an attack on the artistic canon as a meditation on the psychology of perception that canon implies. One perceptive critic has called this Readymade full of "quiet savagery." Not at all. Playful didacti-cism rather. Interactivity deflates solemnity—even as it does with electron-ic text. If we need a tutelary goddess for digital writing and reading, Mona Mustache is the perfect wo/man, or god/dess, for the job.

Electronic expression fulfills this deep urge in the modern visual arts; it asks the *Mona Lisa* out to play. It was not an accident that the hackers whom Steven Levy describes started out playing with model trains.[7] We can observe the interactive playful drive replacing Arnoldian solemnity in the work of the Swiss sculptor Jean Tinguely. Tinguely welded together junk contraptions that crash, bang, and thump, jiggle, make (for a small coin donation) an abstract drawing, and generally convert the museum into a combination toystore and playground. He took the world of civil engineering and converted it into game in much the same way that the personal computer has begun to convert history into a game, letting us play our way into everything from the Battle of Britain to the fate of the human biosphere.

In photographs of Tinguely's exhibitions the people who come to see them often figure prominently. I saw why this was so in the autumn of 1982, when I spent an entranced afternoon in a huge Tinguely exhibit mounted at the Tate Gallery in London. Instead of a reverential art-gallery hush, the whole place was a symphony of sounds, the whangs, bangs, and whistles of the sculptures blending with the exclamations of the participants—for that is what we were—and the delighted outcries of the children. Most of them had speedily found the great *Rotozaza*, a huge sculpture that takes balls and, after moving them through a series of Rube Goldberg maneuvers, flings them out into the crowd. The viewers then retrieve them and feed them back into the machine.

Part of the show was that part of the Tate which was *not* part of the show, the galleries that still preserved the reverential quiet of a conventional exhibition. But now you heard this silence as one of Cage's "silences," something that you consciously attended to, that you began to "hear." Might I suggest that these conventional galleries allegorize the printed text, as read in a digital age? They are still the same, and yet we listen to them in a different way, and hear silences we have not heard before. And in this new kind of gallery, this new kind of text, we hear voices and we move around.

With Tinguely's kind of junk sculpture comes, needless to say, a flood of Marxist moralizing. Behold the detritus of modern capitalism, the sordid remnants of a junk culture, and so on. The machines themselves, though, when they are working in their native environment—moving, clanking, and whistling, the spectators busy catching the balls, pushing the buttons, commissioning their abstract drawings for a sixpence—don't work this way at all. The machines exude high spirits and good humor. They do not damn a machine culture; like electronic text, they redeem it by returning it to play.

Let me, just for fun, report my own embodiment of this process, as I stood in the Tate exhibition before a machine called *Autoportrait Conjugal,* which dates from 1960. Two objects depend from the bottom of the machine. One is a weight, the other a stuffed bird. When the machine goes into action, a little ladder in the middle moves from side to side and the weight acts as a pendulum, imparting to the stuffed bird a pendulous twitch. I went to the exhibit with a very dear old friend, a remarkably tolerant and sophisticated woman with a wonderful sense of humor, who is also a keen bird-watcher. She had in fact arrived in London from a strenuous birding trip to the Pribilof Islands. She immediately noticed the dead bird and, after identifying it, began to excoriate Tinguely. She knows me extremely well, and when she saw me trying to flail my face into something resembling moral outrage, she remarked, "I'll bet you find this extremely funny, don't you?" Meaning by "this" both the stuffed bird swinging back and forth at the bottom of the bungee cord, and her outrage at it—which I anticipated—and my efforts to prevent her from seeing that I did indeed think that the dangling bird was, for reasons I could not explain, extremely funny. Finally I burst into laughter. And so did she. Tinguely had written a comedy and both of us had played our parts. *Autoportrait Conjugal* functioned as what the classical rhetoricians called a *chreia*, a little argumentative firecracker that got the argument of a speech going fast.

Electronic text contrives interactive events of precisely this sort, leavens with comedy the serious if not solemn business of clear, brief, and sincere human communication. Is it too fanciful to detect it supplying this comic leaven to the world of work? Aren't we finding that the world of computer-aided design and manufacture, for example, is deeply playful in the kinds of effort it calls forth? After all, screen space is free. You can make carefree mistakes and correct them, doodle with impudence.

Perhaps the most widely debated, though far from the most important, issue involving electronic text is whether writing on a computer creates verbal flatulence or not. Certainly it restores to centrality another element of classical rhetoric, the use of *topics*, of preformed arguments, phrases, discrete chunks of verbal boilerplate, which can be electronically cut, pasted, and repeated at will. Classical rhetoric argued that repetition, without intrinsically changing the object repeated, changes it absolutely, and modern philosophers like Andy Warhol have dwelt upon this theme, replicating everything from Brillo boxes and soup cans to rich and famous faces.

Think, since we have the *Mona Lisa* in mind, of Warhol's *Thirty Are Better Than One,* from 1963. In this painting, which gives us thirty Monas instead of one, her priceless canonical rarity vanishes even as we bring it to self-consciousness. The same aesthetic operates at the heart of electronic text, though we seldom notice it for what it is—an aesthetic of collage, the central technique of twentieth-century visual art. Collage is now a commonplace narrative technique too, as in David Hockney's recent work with photo collage and color photocopies; but my favorite example remains a golden oldie from the 1950s: Richard Hamilton's "Just What Is It That Makes Today's Homes So Different, So Appealing?" (fig. 4). Couldn't this—collaged up as it is with clip art and advertising icons—just as well be called "Just What Is It That Makes Today's Desktop So Different, So Appealing?" Perhaps this technique of the *topos* ought not surprise us; the iconographic computer desktop, after all, was modeled after the memory system in clas-

Figure 4. Richard Hamilton, *Just What Is It That Makes Today's Homes So Different, So Appealing?, 1956.* © Richard Hamilton/VAGA, New York 1993.

sical Greek rhetoric, or so at least says Nicholas Negroponte of MIT. One can even obtain a startup icon (a *turn-on* icon perhaps we should call her) who looks like the lady in Hamilton's painting and who varies the size of her bosom to indicate the amount of data on the disk. *Gentilezza per gentilezza.*

To replicate and juxtapose at will, as collage does, is to alter scale, and scaling change is one of the truly enzymatic powers of electronic text. When you click in the zoom box, you make a big decision: you are deciding on the central decorum of a human event, on the boundary-conditions within which that event is to be staged, and hence on the nature of the event itself. Nobody has toyed with scale as much as Claes Oldenburg, whose gigantic pool balls, electric switches, umbrellas, and baseball bats reached a culmination of sorts in the Swiss Army knife made into a supersize Venetian gondola.[8] When I saw it, it was majestically rowing its way down the courtyard at the Museum of Contemporary Art in Los Angeles. As the oars moved, the viewer's scale switched back and forth from knife to gondola, and the plain courtyard became alternately trouser pocket and Venetian canal.

To change scale is, as with repetition, to transform reality utterly, without changing it at all. To make art of scaling changes means making us self-conscious about perceptual distance and the conventions, neural and social, that cluster around it. That distance itself can so change an object—give it, to use Duchamp's phrase, a "new idea"—locks us into a conception of art as essentially interactive. This interactivity is the very opposite of canonical passivity.

Oldenburg's *Batcolumn*, erected in Chicago in April 1977, shows how a scale-game works. To render a baseball bat epic in scale, as Oldenburg has done, perpetrates one of those play/purpose reversals so common in Pop art and beyond, the same reversal we create when we zoom in on a letter until we dissolve its meaning into the abstract formal pleasure of the pixel patterns themselves—Havelock's decorative letters on Greek vases again. Oldenburg's bat ceases to be an instrument to hit a ball and becomes an object to be contemplated, to crane your neck up at, a skyscraper of a baseball bat. Yet the eye, less adaptive than the mind, still wants it to be a bat of normal size, and so yearns to make everything else increase in scale to fit it, conjuring up an enormous ball diamond with gigantic players scaled to fit the bat. If the skyscrapers surrounding it dwarf us, then the *Batcolumn* expands us again, restores a more equal relationship with our environment, a playful epic scale. The *Batcolumn* is a thing of beauty, a new shape, but also and more important, it represents one of Duchamp's "new ideas," the idea of scale. Twentieth-century art has often aimed to recreate epic scale in a new form; the big bat does so by scaling up an everyday object. Epic scale, then, but radically democratized.

We do the same thing when we zoom on the screen—we draw far closer to the text than ever we could with the naked eye, and in the magic world we thus enter, the text becomes gigantic, enormously weighty, a physical space, a writing sheet large enough to wrap up the world. Language does indeed become a field of meaning over which we wander. A zooming session leaves the student of rhetoric with a renewed and expanded sense of how much the basic decisions about reading and writing and speaking have to do with scaling arguments, fitting them to time and place. Enlarging and diminishing them is what the basic figure/ground decision that empowers human vision is all about. The scaling powers of electronic text create an extraordinary allegory, almost a continual visual punning, of the stage sets implied by written discourse. The future of rhetorical figuration, which McLuhan in an inspired phrase called "the postures of the mind," looks, after a long hiatus, promising once again.

Scale-change stands at the heart of Roy Lichtenstein's comic-book paint-ings, too, and they tell us a good deal about how scale-change operates on the images that electronic display can so easily mix with alphabetic text. Think for a moment of the well-known frame *Live Ammo* (1962). There, a form of commercial art usually presented in a format a couple of inches square suddenly finds a meticulous rendering almost six by eight feet. Again, an artifact of daily life is wrenched, through huge scale-change, into the domain of art. But another profound reversal operates. As these images appear in the funny papers, they function purely transparently, provide immediate access to the narrative they depict. They are the graphic equiv-alent of Havelock's "literate compact"; they trigger no self-consciousness, provide a pictographic "pure story," "romance" at its most mythically sim-plified, most unselfconscious. Lichtenstein reverses this convention. The surface is rendered maximally self-conscious. We look at the surface pattern, AT the design rather than THROUGH it. Lichtenstein points this out specif-ically in a small (sixteen by sixteen inches) black-and-white from 1962 called *Magnifying Glass*. In this small painting (shown most recently in the "High and Low" exhibition mounted by the Museum of Modern Art),[9] the microdot pattern, which in the comic-papers printing technique constitutes the transparent means for creating the narrative image, is deliberately framed in a magnifying glass, made into a self-conscious and opaque design motif, something we are forced to look AT and not THROUGH. So too with the characters in the narrative. "I use them for purely formal reasons," Licht-enstein has said, "and that's not what those heroes were invented for." This AT/THROUGH reversal appears in twentieth-century art in various guises, from the Italian Futurists onward. It is a favorite Lichtenstein motif. In his brushstroke paintings, for example, when he makes monumentality out of artistic means, the AT/THROUGH oscillation fairly jumps out at you.

Such an oscillation between looking AT the expressive surface and THROUGH it seems to me the most powerful aesthetic attribute of elec-tronic text. Print wants the gaze to remain THROUGH and unselfconscious all the time. Lichtenstein's *Magnifying Glass*, like the electronic screen, insists on the continual oscillation between unselfconscious expression and self-conscious design that formed the marrow of the classical rhetorician's art and pedagogy. *Magnifying Glass* is a painting about a different kind of seri-ousness, a different kind of perception, one that *forgets intermittently*—but must never *forget forever*—the means of perception, the carefully tuned illu-sions from which Western social reality has always been constructed. It is a painting, too, about what happens to text when it is painted onto an electronic screen, when we can change fonts, zoom in on the pixels until their "meaning" metamorphoses into purely formal pleasure. Again, this oscillation happens continually in electronic text without our recognizing it for what it is, or seeing how deeply runs its cardinal allegory.

Some of Lichtenstein's paintings seem as if created by and for electronic means. I am thinking now of the "Haystack" paintings or the series of Rouen Cathedral, where the microdot technique resembles a pixeled screen seen very close up and the series of paintings seems a series of screen-prints of a dynamically changing electronic representation. One of Lichtenstein's commentators, Lawrence Alloway, remarks that he was "interested in the paradox of a systematically executed Impressionism."[10] That systematic creation has now found electronic expression in a computer program called Monet that paints impressionistic pictures by means of digital algorithms.[11] Perhaps not every aspect of contemporary art will find such heady digital fulfillment, but it is certainly tempting to think of all the series paintings— not only of Lichtenstein, but of Warhol and others—as prophetic. They seem to reach out for the dynamic image as much as Marinetti sought the dynamic word.

It is not accidental, I think, that *animation* has come to be so dominated by digital techniques. Traditional gel-animation takes much longer than its computer-graphic successor, but more important than that, it creates action out of a medium static to begin with. Computer graphics emerge from a medium in itself dynamic. This difference leaps out in the stylistic evolution of comic-book graphics. Even print-based comics exude a computer-graphics feeling. They look like printouts from a program-in-progress. A journal like *RAW*, a folio-sized compendium of "serious" comics, looks like a Marinetti typographical explosion, but in color and ten seconds later. It illustrates the profound remixture of the alphabet/icon ratio that awaits printed text. When Lichtenstein picked out comics, he was being prophetic as a great artist should; it was the narrative/iconic relationship that he zoomed in on.

Serious comics teach one important lesson so obvious that we don't notice it: the impact of adding color to the alphabet/image mix. Both newspapers and magazines are developing the habitual use of color in new ways. But we are only beginning to understand how the black-and-white convention of print will be changed by a color display. The history of typography is another story but clearly every aspect of it has been revolutionized by digital technology. Hot type was *set*. Digital typesetting programs *pour* or *flow* it. We encounter this change in liquidity everywhere in contemporary printed texts, especially in the relation between words and pictures.

Clearly every stage of this revolution has been predicted by the post-modern visual arts. What has collage done from the beginning but imitate this pouring of text around image? What are Jasper Johns's letter paintings but invitations to look AT letters rather than THROUGH them, to think of letters as three-dimensional visual images in color? Oldenburg makes the page three-dimensional by taking letters and numbers and inflating them like overstuffed chairs, as in *Soft Calendar for the Month of August* (1962). Edward Ruscha painted a big red *Annie* over a yellow ground, as the top half of a square whose bottom half was plain blue, making a simple word vibrate against a color exercise à la Josef Albers. And in 1961 Lichtenstein painted a four-foot-square comic-book canvas showing a man looking into a completely dark, wholly black room through a round peephole. Through the peephole we glimpse a man, and a bright yellow background. The caption reads, "I can see the whole room *and there's nobody in it!*" Surely here is the electronic world of three-dimensional color looking back into the world of black-and-white print!

The sheer dynamic power of zooming in and zooming out on an image, this transformatory power of scale-change, seems frozen into a series of snapshots in the tremendous, and tremendously large, paintings of James Rosenquist. When I saw the Rosenquist exhibition in Denver, I felt as if I were a homunculus walking inside a gigantic, multifaceted computer display. The computer's power to transform the imagistic clutter of modern visual life by zooming in very close to it seemed to be what Rosenquist's paintings were about. Rosenquist started out as a billboard painter. His heroic efforts to bring commercial signage into the art gallery (I am not being ironic; *F-III* is a genuinely epic painting) find an exact counterpart on the electronic screen. Rosenquist flies us through the air up to one of his enormous billboards hanging over the city street and then rubs our noses in the billboard. We see it as line and shape and color and pattern, we look AT it rather than THROUGH it. The electronic screen allows us to practice this transformation on the images it displays. It flies us magically through the air, allows us to get closer to an image than normal human focus allows. It can and often does do what Rosenquist's paintings do—transform the public commercial landscape by scale-change, by flying us through and around it. Don't we witness the same process when a life scientist uses computer graphics and virtual-reality goggles to walk into a complex molecule the size of a room, wander around it and try, as it were, various possible junctures on for size?

We might reflect, too, on how easily another dominant theme of contemporary art—quotation—finds expression on an electronic screen. The storehouses of graphic images that all of us now have on our machines at home are, in effect, mass-produced and copyright-legal quotation devices. Our startup screens are often shifting art galleries of personal quotation—mine today started up with a Ferrari Testa Rossa—and iconic badges. When we have "quoted" the image we want, we can now process it in the same way we process words; we can, that is, "quote" it in the same way one painter quotes another. And the same democratization of "originality" takes place. Electronic display, in fact, spells out the pun in "original." It can easily call up the "original-as-root image" (the *least* original or most topical version) and make it, through now-commonplace manipulation routines, into an "original" in the Romantic "never-seen-before" sense of the word. The digital computer seems a machine created for Art-about-Art.

It also seems created to provide the perfect means for another contemporary artistic technique—the creativity of chance. The genuine ghost in this machine is the spirit not of Alan Turing but of John Cage. Even the simplest computer painting program builds in enormous resources for chance generation that seem taken right out of Cage's exhortation and practice. Take as an unpretentious example a program called Kid Pix.[12] It is as antilinear as Cage himself could have wished. When it is running in "Small Kids Mode," the user need not even know how to read. Scale-manipulation is a principal means of creation in the program—it has a built-in magnifying glass, à la Lichtenstein—but its many kinds of drawing implements depend on random variation. Patterns can be created, enhanced, juxtaposed, dynamically mixed, timed to fade in and out, poured in and out and away, all by random methods. Alphabetic information, in the Kid Pix environment, becomes iconic in the way it does on a Greek vase or in a medieval manuscript. And the program makes possible the three-dimensional layering that so many contemporary painters and collage-makers have striven for. It does so in reverse, going into the surface rather than out from it to build up layers. Kid Pix offers to kids a three-dimensional writing space—it comes with the territory.

We can study an architectural version of the basic electronic AT/THROUGH oscillation in one of the most controversial attempts at postmodern monumentality, the now-famous Centre Pompidou in Paris, the "Beaubourg" as it is called, designed by Richard Rogers and Renzo Piano. The façade reenacts a ritual in contemporary architecture, the reversal of use and ornament. The architects have turned the building inside out, put its plumbing on the outside instead of hiding it in utility shafts. They have made decoration out of ducts, play out of purpose, much as Duchamp did with *Fountain*. The building becomes an allegory of motive as well as a museum, a visual representation of the play/purpose reversal at the heart of postmodern architecture.

This oscillation between use and ornament, between purpose and play, pops out everywhere you look in the history of computers, and especially of private desktop ones. Play continually animates the operant purpose, indeed often becomes it. I have mentioned Steven Levy's history of the personal computer, *Hackers*, which recaptures this motivational mood perfectly. The play impulse symbolized purity of motive to the computer world (as so often to the academic world), and its loss has seemed the loss of innocence itself. I would urge the opposite case—play is as native to electronic text as it is to rhetoric. The purposive Suits and Bean-counters mistake the spirit of the place.

This motivational struggle is dramatized in the long-running struggle between the IBM world and the Apple world. The Apple world, born in personal computers not mainframes, has from the beginning been dominated by the play impulse. It colored motive, style, mood, personality type. Apple's graphics-based computers were built upon, assumed, a transformed alphabet/icon ratio. IBM—serious, indeed humorless—still cannot understand the revolution of electronic text or what it means to their business. Characteristic motivation, not technology, separates the two camps. The quarrel opposes an old way of looking at the world's business and a new way. About how the new way works, the postmodern arts have everything to tell us. The themes we are discussing—judgments about scale, a new icon/alphabet ratio in textual communication, nonlinear collage and juxtapositional reasoning, that is to say bottom-up rather than top-down planning, coaxing change so as to favor the prepared mind—all these constitute a new theory of management. The graphics-based digital computer—the computer as an instrument and work of art—implies this new theory at every point. Apple, because of the circumstances of its creation, knows this and IBM has yet to learn it. That's the real difference between them.

Classical rhetoric, and hence all of classical education, was built on a single dominant exercise: modeling. The key form was the oration, and it was rehearsed again and again in every possible form and context. *Declamatio*, as the modeling of speeches came to be called, stood at the hub of Western education, just as computer modeling is coming to do today. The world of electronic text has reinstated this centrality of modeled reality. The computer has adopted once again, as the fundamental educational principle, the dramatizing of experience; most important, it has dramatized the world of work. Today we model everything digitally, and usually visually, before we build it, manufacture it, or embrace it as policy or sales program. This ubiquitous modeling has reintroduced into the world of work literary and artistic coordinates which had been, as much as possible, banished from industrial enterprise in the mechanical age. It is not in the museum but in the marketplace, as a managerial agenda, that the extraordinary convergence of artistic impulse with its electronic expression has found its most striking instantiation.

Nothing in the world of postmodern art better illustrates this convergence than the work of the environmental artist Christo Javacheff. His *Running Fence, Sonoma and Marin Counties, California, 1972–76* embodies this rehearsal-reality and everything it implies. It is an epic *declamatio* of the modern integrated visual arts, a didactic rehearsal-reality event of the greatest scale, grandeur, beauty, and meaning. It allegorizes perfectly the influence that electronic expression is now having on the world of work.

In October 1972 Christo made the first drawings of a gigantic "fence" projected to run through farmland and end in the sea. He began to look for a site in northern California or Oregon. The fence was to run for twenty-four-and-a-half miles and to be built in segments eighteen feet high and sixty to eighty feet wide. By July of the following summer he had settled on an area around Petaluma, California, formed the Running Fence Corporation, and placed an order for 165,000 yards of woven nylon fabric. The period from July 1973 to April 1976 was taken up by eighteen public hearings to get the permits to build the fence, by several court sessions, a huge Environmental Impact Statement, and applications to fifteen government agencies, these activities all made possible through the kind offices of nine lawyers. Finally, after a tense final hearing, the project was free to proceed. On 7 September 1976, the part-time army of fabric-installation workers, 360 strong, began to deploy the fence. *Running Fence* turned out to be even more beautiful than Christo had imagined, sailing through the early morning fog, celebrating cows in their fields and the rolling hills in their glory, sailing like a silver ribbon toward the sea, punctuating the day from the dusk, scaling, scaling, forever scaling the landscape with its band of silver white, making from the air a ribbon of light across the earth, until at dusk it plunged into the sea.

Running Fence sounded all the notes in our current aesthetic chord. It was calculated to be of an age and not for all time, mortal rather than immortal, to represent what we cannot do forever, and should not do for long, to the land, to allegorize not our vainglory but our solemn sense of our own limitations. It was completed at noon on 10 September. On 21 September the dismantling began and by 23 October, eight days ahead of schedule, the entire fence had been removed and the pole anchors each driven three feet into the ground.

This powerful allegory of the world of work was not lost on the beholders. As one businessman wrote in the local paper, "the Running Fence will depict the evolution of man from the sea, his enormous efforts to survive and build on the land, and the ultimate destruction of that for which he has strived with such intensity for so very long. It is, indeed, a true artist and businessman that can conceive and execute so huge a philosophical symbol of the determination of man and the futile and transitory nature of his efforts. ... In all this I know whereof I speak. I am retired after forty years as an industrialist and rancher and all the businesses and enterprises that I developed are now gone. Little remains to show they were ever here. I have no regrets, it was great fun, but that is the way it is."[13]

Christo earned praise as a businessman by financing this project, as he does all his gargantuan projects, entirely himself. A huge book was published about the making of the fence.[14] Christo signed 3,000 copies of the book, which includes, besides all the gorgeous photographs of the project, a full history of it, copies of the relevant government documents, film stills, and—a relic of the project—a small square of its nylon cloth. I own copy number 133, and what a book it is! For it is no more a normal codex book than the Fence was a normal fence. Like the square of cloth it contains, it is not a book about a work of art which it describes, a work past or present which remains detached from it. The book is part of the work of art, formed part of its essence and design from the beginning. Christo has reached out in time as well as space, included in his work of art the object itself and all the processes, from the beginning, that brought it into, and out of, being. This insistence on art as process rather than product, interactive temporal event rather than untouchable timeless masterpiece, I take to stand at the center of contemporary thinking about art, and about more than art.

I take the *Running Fence* book as a model of how codex books will work in an electronic world. We will construe them not as absolute entities but as part of an expressive process both alphabetic and iconic, an entity whose physicality is manifest, whose rhetoric is perfectly self-conscious, that is to say whose place in a complex matrix of behavior forms a native part of its expression. Most students of the matter agree that books will not vanish. They will, however, like the *Running Fence* book, send out nerve-tendrils to the complex expressive world surrounding them. The book for *Running Fence* is one kind of "printout" among many, which, taken together, form a record of the artistic event.

I would also take the *Running Fence* itself as a model for how the digital computer might function in the everyday world of work. Christo testified before the Sonoma County Board of Supervisors that "the work is not only the physical object of the fence. The work of art is really right now, and here [that hearing itself]. Everybody is a part of the art, that is, through the project of the *Running Fence,* and it is a most exciting thing, and there is not one single element in this project that is make-believe."[15] Christo has chosen to work in behavior, in human motive, as well as in canvas and light; he has chosen to make art out of economic cooperation, out of the processes of collective work. In America nowadays, these are all bureaucratic processes, and Christo has transformed them into self-conscious art. By subtracting the practical purpose, the enduring object—fence, pipeline, building, whatever—from the process, he has allowed everyone involved (and that includes all of us) to focus on, to become self-conscious about, the process involved, the process of human cooperation. To look AT it rather than THROUGH it. I think we can use electronic text in the same way and for the same purpose. The self-consciousness of the device at least beckons us along this path far more cordially than ever print did.

I suggest, then, that we can use the digital computer, and more specifically electronic text, as a work of art very like Christo's *Running Fence.* It is always inviting us to play with ordinary experience rather than exploit it, to tickle a text or an image a little while using it, to defamiliarize it into art. And, as with scaling-change, as with both the objects and the actors in *Running Fence*—the hearing, the plan, the rendering, the Environmental Impact Statement; the construction worker, the councilman, the artist—human purpose will be both the same and utterly transformed. Is this radical democratization of art, this interweaving of play and purpose, so different from the range of hopes that computers inspired in the first generation of hackers who developed them?

❑   ❑   ❑

I have been using some examples from the visual arts to sketch out what is sometimes called the postmodern critique, an argument whose elements we have now before us: art defined as attention, beholder as well as object; thus an art that includes its beholder, and the beholder's beholder, an outward frame-expanding, an infinite *pro*gress rather than *re*gress; interactive text, that is, art and criticism mixed together, and so art and life as well; a continually shifting series of scale-changes, of what literary theory would call contextualisms; a resolute use of self-consciousness to turn transparent attention to opaque contemplation, especially, as we began by noting, in regard to the typographical conventions of fully literate reading; above all, a pervasive reversal of use and ornament, a turning of purpose to play and game, a continual effort not, as with the Arnoldian canon, to purify our motives, but to keep them in a roiling, rich mixture of play, game, and purpose. All of this yields a body of work active not passive, a canon not frozen in perfection but volatile with contending human motive.

Is this not the aesthetic of the personal computer? And is such an aesthetic not part of a world view larger still—as I have tried to suggest by choosing my illustrative images from the pre-electronic world? This larger world view occurs not only in the visual arts from which I have taken my examples, but in perception psychology from the transactionalists onward (the work upon which the Pop artists drew so heavily), in American role theory from George Herbert Mead to Erving Goffman, in evolutionary biology from the New Darwinian Synthesis onward, in Havelock's and Ong's formulation of the literate-oral polarity in Western discourse from classical Greece to the present day, in the East-West polarity which, using Balinese culture as ur-type, first Margaret Mead and Gregory Bateson and then Clifford Geertz have established, and in literary theory, which encapsulates much of this thinking. It occurs, indeed, practically everywhere we care to look in the contemporary intellectual landscape, as I argue in detail in chapter 3.

I have been suggesting that technology isn't *leading* us in these new directions. The arts, and the theoretical debate that tags along after them, have done the leading, and digitization has emerged as their condign embodiment. We needn't worry about digital determinism. We must explain, instead, the extraordinary convergence of twentieth-century thinking with the digital means that now give it expression. It is the *computer as fulfillment of social thought* that requires explanation.

How find a frame wide enough to provide such explication? To explain reading and writing on computers, we need to go back to the original Western thinking about reading and writing—the rhetorical paideia that provided the backbone of Western education for 2,000 years. Digital expression indeed fulfills the postmodern aesthetic, but also a much larger movement that comprehends and explains that aesthetic—a return to the traditional pattern of Western education through words. We are still bemused by the three hundred years of Newtonian simplification that made "rhetoric" a dirty word, but we are beginning to outgrow it. Digital expression, in such a context, becomes not a revolutionary technology but a conservative one. It attempts to reclaim, and rethink, the basic Western wisdom about words. Its perils prove to be the great but familiar perils that have always lurked in the divided, unstable, protean Western self.

NOTES

1. Hubert L. Dreyfus, *What Computers Can't Do: The Limits of Artificial Intelligence* (1972; rev. ed., New York: Harper and Row, 1979).

2. Luciano De Maria, ed., *Marinetti e il Futurismo* (Milan: Mondadori, 1973), 189–90; my translation.

3. Ted Nelson, *Computer Lib/Dream Machines* (Redmond, Wash.: Microsoft Press, 1974; rev. ed. 1987), 27.

4. See, in this regard, Albertine Gaur's discussion in *A History of Writing,* rev. ed. (New York: Abbeville, Cross River), 179–81.

5. Kenneth Burke, *Collected Poems, 1915–1967* (Berkeley and Los Angeles: University of California Press, 1968), 88–92; fig. 3 reproduces p. 88.

6. John Baldessari, *Quality Material,* reproduced in Jean Lipman and Richard Marshall, *Art about Art* (New York: Dutton, 1978), 51.

7. Steven Levy, *Hackers: Heroes of the Computer Revolution* (Garden City, N.Y.: Anchor Press/Doubleday, 1984), 6–11.

8. See Claes Oldenburg, Coosje van Bruggen, and Frank O. Gehry, *Il Corso del Coltello/The Course of the Knife* (New York: Rizzoli, 1987).

9. Roy Lichtenstein, *Magnifying Glass,* reproduced in Kirk Varnedoe and Adam Gopnik, *High & Low, Popular Culture & Modern Art* (New York: Museum of Modern Art, 1990), 229.

10. Lawrence Alloway, *Roy Lichtenstein* (New York: Abbeville, 1983), 53.

11. Monet (Delta Tau Software, 1992).

12. Kid Pix (Broderbund Software, 1991).

13. Werner Spies, *The Running Fence Project: Christo,* rev. ed. (New York: Abrams, 1980), unpaged.

14. *Christo: Running Fence, Sonoma and Marin Counties, California 1972–76* (New York: Abrams, 1978).

15. Spies (n. 13 above).

3

Several years ago, when I was running the UCLA Writing Programs, I visited a large state university in the Midwest to speak and to consult about their writing program. As part of the consulting, I met with the campuswide faculty committee charged with approving the proposed new courses in rhetoric. One member of the committee, a chemist, asked me if this "rhetoric business" had the staying power to become a proper university subject, something worth serious intellectual inquiry.

It was a short question, genuine and well meant, but it required a longer answer than that occasion permitted. How could I adequately explain that rhetoric had not always been a synonym for public flummery and outright lying? That the modern university subjects had spun out of a rhetorical center not much more than one hundred years ago? That for two millennia rhetoric had been the heart of Western education, had supplied its traditional unity, the lack of which we now so deplore? That it was rhetoric which, for most of Western history, had shaped the basic curriculum that taught people how to read, write, and think? It would have taken all morning to make the case, to explain how a subject so long the center of Western education had fallen into such disrepute that its very name meant nothing.

And even if I had persuaded the committee, it would have taken all afternoon to make the second case that needed making, that this "rhetoric business," banished during the Newtonian interlude in Western thinking, was now returning, in one way or another, in every discipline on campus that used words. That second case I try to make in this essay, published in 1989.

The hazards of such an undertaking manifest themselves speedily enough. Not only does one confront the Platonic prejudice against "rhetoric," endemic still in Western thinking. Not only do the issues loom enormously large. Not only does one trespass on many disciplines outside one's own. More than all this, I am haunted by the ghost of monstrous egotism: it turns out—goodness, how lucky—that the discipline which makes a general sense of things turns out to be my own. I can only reply that such indeed is how things seem to have worked out. The French historian H. I. Marrou has written the history of early Western education as the history of rhetoric, and that history has been carried forward into modern times by many others. We need not debate what the "rhetorical paideia" used to be. I try to sketch here—and indeed throughout the book—what it has now become.

The proximate cause of my undertaking such a task emerges at the beginning of the chapter. The final cause has been the graduate seminar in style and behavior that I've taught over the last twenty years. There I have tried to follow the "rhetorization" of contemporary thought in its various strands. It is this "rhetorization" that electronic text expresses so much more adroitly and empathetically than print.

Twenty Years After: Digital Decorum

and Bi-stable Allusions

An Emergent Paideia

Recently, I have been revising my *Handlist of Rhetorical Terms*, published over twenty years ago.[1] On its first appearance, it was noticed as a useful student guide in a marginal area. That was a condign reception for a compilation which seemed, even perhaps to its compiler, the chronicle of a forgotten mood. But, surprisingly, the book proved a steady seller; it has remained in print, and its pattern of use suggests something of what has happened to the study of formal rhetoric in those two decades. Students did use it, and much more than I thought they might. Mature scholars in English studies, and then people working in other European languages ancient and modern, found it useful for new kinds of rhetorical analysis. Finally, when letters started arriving from anthropologists and art historians, I began to suspect that use of this modest compendium was reflecting a much larger change in our intellectual landscape.

In retrospect, it is not hard to see why the book found an unexpected readership. The expansion of rhetoric's sphere of influence during this period is astonishing, so astonishing that I have come to conceive the intellectual history of this period as the return, after a long Newtonian interlude, of the rhetorical paideia as our dominant theory of knowledge and education. Some of this development might have been predicted, but one element in the mixture did not exist to dazzle prophecy—the digitized word displayed on a personal computer screen. Even now it is not easy to survey this extension of rhetoric's domain, to envision how rhetoric is again functioning *systemically* as a way of thinking, and no one has even tried to relate this renewed systemic rhetoric to the electronic form in which it is increasingly expressed. Suitably daunted by ultracrepidarian angst, I record here some tentative readings in rhetoric's expanded domain and venture a few preliminary observations on their relation to the electronic word.

The most obvious area of rhetoric's revival—literary theory—is so familiar as hardly to need elaboration. The "architectonic" view of rhetoric[2] that Kenneth Burke developed from the 1930s onward has underwritten the Derridean explosion—there is no other word for it—of literary theory since the Hopkins symposium in 1966 put it on the map. Although, incredibly, Derrida appears not to have known Burke's work, deconstruction's enfranchising hypothesis that rhetorical analysis can be used on nonliterary texts and on the conventions of social life itself is the pivotal insight of Burkean dramatism.[3] And if Burke's work does not fall in our period, certainly the realization of its importance does.

The reemergence of rhetoric in other fields of inquiry is less familiar than the well-documented battlegrounds of literary theory. Perhaps the most important development for people thinking about "architectonic rhetoric" has been the movement from a physics-based model to a biological one as a vehicle for thinking systemically about dynamic processes. Jeremy Campbell has called attention to the distinction between "closed" and "open" systems:

> Open systems do not behave in the same way as closed systems. ... Under certain circumstances, open systems reach a steady state in which they are far from equilibrium, or maximum entropy, and they maintain that state. They are highly "improbable," highly complex. What is more, such a steady state can be reached from different starting points, and in spite of disruptions along the way. The state is what is called "equifinal."[4]

Campbell is not talking about rhetoric, but it is interesting to conceive rhetoric in such terms, as a complex system with a different principle of stability than we normally premise. Ernst Mayr quotes Max Delbrück on what it is like to move from physics to biology:

> A mature physicist, acquainting himself for the first time with the problems of biology, is puzzled by the circumstance that there are no "absolute phenomena" in biology. Everything is time-bound and space-bound. The animal or plant or micro-organism he is working with is but a link in an evolutionary chain of changing forms, none of which has any permanent validity.[5]

Surely Delbrück's feelings on moving from physics to biology parallel the feelings of someone moving from Platonic philosophy to Isocratean rhetoric, and surely students of rhetoric can learn from the analogy. As an example, consider the implications for rhetorical study of recent work in evolutionary biology.[6]

The intellectual structures of formal rhetoric have formed part of Western culture for so long, and yet we have for so long suspected and despised rhetoric as simply hypocrisy and deception, that it is very difficult to recognize it for what is—an information *system*. Systems, at least for humanists, have never escaped from the Platonic orbit; they are closed patterns organized like human society in the *Republic*. Everyone has a single job; every element a fixed place; the aim is perfect stasis, with an emphasis on both "perfect" and "stasis." Our notion of systems is Platonic philosophy on the one hand and physics on the other. What Plato wanted above all to exile from his utopia, like Thomas More after him, was *style*, the unabridged range of ornament, of purposeless play. Rhetoric defines itself as a counter-system to the Platonic political order by admitting stylistic, ornamental behavior, by acknowledging that such behavior lies at the heart of human life, is what human politics is all about. If stylistic behavior is acknowledged as part of the complex human "reason," then rhetoric becomes the systematic attempt to account for this complex "reason," and find agreements within it. If, on the other hand, stylistic motive and behavior is split off and denigrated, in the manner of Plato, or More, or Peter Ramus, then rhetoric becomes the series of ad hoc fixes Plato despised it for being.[7] Behavioral biology provides a teleonomic explanation for the stylistic, playful component in human behavior, and suggests how that behavior works in animals other than *homo sapiens*. Two of the most profound students of rhetoric in our time, Kenneth Burke and Eric Havelock, both saw that the enfranchising framework for rhetoric had to be found in human evolution.[8] That foundationalist framework has now been provided, and rhetoricians might well avail themselves of it.

The evolutionary explanation sheds light on two ranges of motive to which rhetoric has anchored itself, game and play. Human purpose is energized by the competitive urge; that is why we convert all our serious activities into games. This competitive impulse finds its explanation in the hierarchical behavior of primates and lower animals. Conversely, recent descriptions of animal play and courtship display-behavior provide an evolutionary record as well as a teleonomic explanation of ornament, of the display impulse as against the competitive impulse, and so cast light first on the origin and use of rhetorical figuration, and second on the structure of human motive that rhetoric seeks to analyze and control. These two clusters of motive—game and play, usually intricated with one another—together constitute the loyal opposition to "being serious" in that binary pairing which has served Western thought so long and well.

My favorite instance of play behavior as rhetorical motivation is Alpha, a chimp described in Desmond Morris's *Biology of Art*, when she is feeling the first primate temptations of the periodic sentence. Confronted with a blank sheet of paper, she tended to restrict her scribbling to the surface of the paper, to mark the corners of a blank sheet before filling it in, to mark a centered figure, to balance an offset figure, and to complete an imperfect figure.[9] Resemblances like these strike humanists—such is our species conceit—as trivial or irrelevant, and yet the correspondences between rhetorical ornamentation and animal display-behavior are so extensive and so obvious that we must attend to them. Consider, for example, the cluster of techniques described by *amplificatio*. Eric Havelock essayed a biological rather than literary explanation: "Our species seems to have an inner biological motivation which seeks to vary its own forms of expression."[10] Marshall McLuhan, the scholar who, perhaps more than any other since the Second World War, opened rhetorical study to new ways of thinking, argued for rhetorical figures as "individual postures of mind" that allow thinking to occur in certain ways and not others.[11] They are also postures of the body, and we can now begin to realize how this is so.

It is about the origin of posturing itself that biological explanation has the most to teach us. Consider, for example, an explanation of the "antirhetorical prejudice"[12] that emerges at the end of a wide-ranging and seminal essay by the zoologist Richard D. Alexander, "The Search for a General Theory of Behavior."[13] Alexander is concerned to explain why hypocrisy evolved as the primary human attribute, the posturing axis of our social decorum, and why we so resist seeing that this is so. His discussion of why we resist the Darwinian hypothesis can map seamlessly onto the history of the antirhetorical prejudice:

> Selection has probably worked against the understanding of such selfish motivations becoming a part of human consciousness, or perhaps even being easily acceptable. We can recognize a triple paradox that the only organism capable of at least a feeble analysis of its own attributes must use the very attributes to be analyzed to carry out the analysis, when a central one of those attributes is a rather strong tendency to reject the results of all such analyses!
>
> Consider the argument that group-living intensifies reproductive competition between individuals and requires continual pressure from some outside selective force such as predators to persist. It implies that human society is a network of lies and deception, persisting only because systems of conventions about permissible kinds and extents of lying have arisen. (96)

He goes on to suggest an alternative explanation of the human social convention which sounds—he does not of course develop it in these terms—

like a biological definition of rhetorical and social decorum:

> I can conceive of only one possible argument against the notion that
> society is based on lies. It is an intriguing argument and involves the
> definition of "lie." Consider the ten commandments: "Thou shalt love
> thy neighbor as thyself." But this admirable goal is clearly contrary to
> a tendency to behave in a reproductively selfish manner. "Thou shalt
> give the impression that thou lovest thy neighbor as thyself" might be
> closer to the truth. ... One might even add: "Whether thou knowest
> it or not!" (96–97)

And so surface the evolutionary origins of our cardinal stylistic maxim: "The
greatest art is the art that conceals its own art."

> Sincerity is easier when one lacks full realization of motivations rep-
> rehensible to fellows. ... It is not difficult to appear sincere if one is
> sufficiently ignorant about his own motives to believe in fact that he
> is a just, moral, ethical person with mandates from Heaven for what-
> ever particular actions he may feel are necessary or profitable to carry
> out. For an individual who must carry out all of his actions within a
> social group of one sort or another, sincerity is an invaluable asset.
>
> The significance of these arguments for the problem of under-
> standing how man goes about interpreting his universe is almost
> unimaginable. He will not see in himself what he does not wish to see,
> or what he does not wish his neighbors and fellows to see; and he is
> reluctant to see in other organisms what he will not see in himself. All
> of biology, all of science, all of human endeavors have been guided to
> some large extent by this circumstance. (97)

The entire history of rhetoric has proceeded under the cloud of this self-
interested disinclination to know ourselves. As Eric Havelock wrote about
our resolute Platonic blindness toward the rhetorical ideal of life, "There
has been a block in the mind, an unconscious unwillingness to use the equipment."[14] Evolutionary biology tells us where that block comes from.

As part of the professional self-consciousness coming upon American
disciplinary inquiry now that most of our scholarly disciplines are a century old, the techniques of rhetorical analysis have begun to affect our thinking in another way. They are being used to describe both how formal academic research actually gets done and how rhetorical are its conventions of
presentation. Donald N. McCloskey has provided a model study of conventions of presentation and debate in *The Rhetoric of Economics*.[15] His argument is extended to all the social sciences by a number of distinguished essays
in *The Rhetoric of the Human Sciences*.[16] How unwelcome the acknowledg-

ment of a rhetorical ingredient in human experience can be, how satirically reductive the onset of such rhetorical self-consciousness can prove, the
violent responses to deconstruction have shown. The same pattern of denial
can be found much earlier, in the critical reception of James Watson's can-
did account of the discovery of the DNA structure in *The Double Helix*.[17]
Many people involved in the discovery, including Watson's partner Francis
Crick, denied the motives of competition and pure play that Watson
stressed.[18] Yet chronicles of how modern science is done are often rhetorical
analyses of careers as much as impersonal analysis of experiments. Susan Allport's *Explorers of the Black Box: The Search for the Cellular Basis of Memory,*[19] Gary Taubes's *Nobel Dreams: Power, Deceit and the Ultimate Experiment,*[20] and Robert Kanigel's *Apprentice to Genius: The Making of a Scientific
Dynasty*[21] are all studies in the art of persuasion as it occurs in the no-holds-
barred career wars of modern big science. Competition, a truly Homeric
urge to always be the best, *aien aristeuein,* animates the heroes of these chronicles, and their publications look, in intention and strategy, very like heroic speeches in the *Iliad.* Their authors do not perhaps appreciate this dimension in their work, but collectively they provide stunning examples of how
rhetorical patterns of thought and analysis are being used again to examine
human behavior.

Derek Freeman wrote a very different chapter in the rhetoric of inquiry
by debunking Margaret Mead's early Samoan anthropology, *Margaret Mead
and Samoa: The Making and Unmaking of an Anthropological Myth.*[22] Freeman's discussion of the scholarly environment and expectations that surrounded and distorted Mead's work will surely remain one of the landmarks
in the rhetorical self-consciousness growing in all the learned professions.
The issues he unmasked continue to be debated.[23]

The most thoughtful study of the rhetoric of physical science I have
encountered is Bruno Latour's *Science in Action.*[24] Latour's conception of
scientific truth is frankly and avowedly rhetorical: "Laboratories are now
powerful enough to define reality. To make sure that our travel through
technoscience is not stifled by complicated definitions of reality, we need a
simple and sturdy one able to withstand the journey. ... If, in a given situation, no dissenter is able to modify the shape of a new object, then that's
it, it *is* reality, at least for as long as the trials of strength are not modified"
(93). "The picture of technoscience revealed by such a method [looking at
the history of discovery as well as the discovery itself] is that of a weak
rhetoric becoming stronger and stronger as time passes, as laboratories get
equipped, articles published and new resources brought to bear on harder
and harder controversies"(103). One could scarcely ask for a clearer instance

of how, during the last twenty years, the methods, and more especially the epistemological assumptions, of the rhetorical world view have permeated how we think about scholarly inquiry.

The rhetorical component becomes more integral yet in a distinguished example of this genre, James Gleick's book on nonlinear systems, *Chaos: Making a New Science*.[25] Gleick does not dwell upon the rhetorical ruthlessness of the modern scientific career, as do Allport, Taubes, and Kanigel. Nor does he focus on the rhetoric of science as his main subject, as Latour does. What makes the book interesting for the rhetorician (besides a prose style that is a constant delight—you can catch him, sometimes, worrying over the placement of an indefinite article) is his analysis of scientific progress as a rhetorical study in the economy of attention. The dispersal of nonlinear thinking in the last twenty years or so was conditioned at every level by complex professional attention-structures, and Gleick analyzes this rhetorical ingredient acutely. Chaos theory, when it coalesced, took shape as an informing doctrine which, considered as an information system, operates very like the traditional rhetorical paideia, as a centripetal disciplinary focus, a body of thought that can function *as a general theory of knowledge*. Chaos theory stands to Newtonian science, one might raffishly analogize, as rhetoric stands to logic.[26]

Or at least we may say that rhetoric—considered as an information system that functions economically, that allocates emphasis and attention— resembles what is now called, in many fields, a nonlinear system. That is, it is dynamic rather than static, a constantly changing emergence rather than a fixed entity; global rather than specialized into disciplines and constituent parts; a system that seeks to describe the confusion of everyday experience rather than narrowing it into a delimited, predictable field of study. If we can, at least in a provisional and suggestive way, think of rhetoric "chaotically," we may be able to discern how the binary opposition in Western thought between the philosophers and the rhetoricians has been reincarnated in the age of electronic text.[27]

In many ways, the study of chaotic systems overturns what we have come to think of as human reason, for it presents counterintuitive conclusions, including the impossibility of prediction, at every point. Since chaos theory deals with scale-change, this thinking postulates a continually interactive audience as part of the experience studied, an audience whose intuition is continually being trained in a particular habit of perception. Its resemblances to rhetoric as a theory of behavior, one that considers human behavior as complex beyond prediction and yet subject to certain rules, and one which for that reason emphasizes the improvisational ability—trained intuition—must strike any student of rhetoric forcibly. "Intuition is not something that is given," one of its main inventors argues, it is something in which you have to train yourself.[28]

Chaos theory embraces fractal geometry, the study of irregular surfaces, as well as weather systems and wave mechanics. Benoit Mandelbrot, the discoverer of fractals, believes that he has formulated the science of *decoration*—a geometrical and mathematical theory of style, as it would eventually amount to.[29] We therefore come upon a *mathematical* explanation for ornamentation to complement the behavioral explanation being supplied by the biologists. Again, the "ornamental" and "purposive" poles have undergone a figure/ground shift. If Mandelbrot is right, the underlying geometry of the world is decorative, not utilitarian.

Both rhetorical self-consciousness and rhetorical nomenclature have begun to penetrate still other disciplines in the last two decades. For an example of how deeply rhetorical thinking has entered art criticism, we might consider the work of the dazzling and prolific historian of modern and postmodern architecture, Charles Jencks. Jencks's core argument, through a series of books culminating in *Post-Modernism: The New Classicism in Art and Architecture*,[30] has been that modernism rejected the rhetorical ingredient in architecture and that postmodernism has been resupplying it. Mies's steel and glass boxes are the equivalent of what I have called the C-B-S, or Clarity-Brevity-Sincerity school of prose style. They aim—to bounce a handy pun off Mies's glass walls—at transparency, at a design surface that represents pure aesthetic form, pure architectural "meaning," with no intervening stylistic surface of self-conscious ornament and direct signing. Postmodernism, by contrast, accepts a self-consciously ornamented surface and builds its effects from an oscillation between the surface and the "meaning," between the façade and the interior, between the building as sign and the building as shelter.

In the book where this argument is perhaps most immediately available for the nonspecialist, *The Language of Post-Modern Architecture*,[31] Jencks uses the duck/rabbit bi-stable illusion (which most of us who are not perception psychologists take, as perhaps does Jencks, from E. H. Gombrich's *Art and Illusion*) to illustrate this oscillation between surface and interior. Jencks's controlling paradigm in this very well-known study is frankly linguistic. "The modes of architectural communication," for example, are categorized as "metaphor, words, syntax, and semantics." But the real argument is rhetorical not linguistic or semiological. He wants to resituate architecture within the framework of its day-to-day use as what, to borrow a phrase from Kenneth Burke, we might call "equipment for living." He wants, like John

Cage with music, to take it out of the concert hall and reinstall it in real life: "Architecture is often experienced inattentively or with the greatest prejudice of mood and will—exactly opposite to the way one is supposed to experience a symphony or work of art."[32]

If one thinks of postmodernism in the visual arts as an argument for such a de-museumization, it becomes clear that it is arguing for moving the domain of art from poetics back into rhetoric. Jencks's repeated use of classical rhetorical terms like *chiasmus* then seems less an adaptation from a foreign field than a natural argument from within rhetoric itself; so does Robert Venturi's reading, in *Learning from Las Vegas*,[33] of that cityscape as a rhetorical surface rather than, as a modern planner would have it (at least after it had been torn down and "redeveloped"), as a poetic one. Jencks describes postmodern architecture—in a word to which I will return later—as *schizophrenic*, as alternating between two codes, one geometrical and Platonic and the other baroque and frankly emotional in its appeal, rhetorical in essence.[34] One might argue, as I do in the previous chapter, that all postmodern art is rhetorical in this schizophrenic way, toggling from Platonic to rhetorical premises and back again, and that it is neither extreme which constitutes its "postmodernity" but rather the schizophrenic rocking motion between them.

I use these scattered samplings to suggest a larger argument: that the last two decades have brought rhetoric, both as discipline and as world view, from the periphery to the center all across the disciplinary landscape. If we remember that this emergence of rhetorical thinking has been accompanied, at least in American colleges and universities, by a writing-across-the-curriculum pedagogy that stresses the rhetoric of the disciplinary languages involved, and if we remember all we have read about how the learned professions are going through similar identity crises, we can begin to estimate how radically rhetorical the atmosphere of professional self-consciousness has become. Such self-consciousness represents a broad-based willingness, if not proclivity, to look AT what we are doing, at its stylistic surface and rhetorical strategy, as well as THROUGH it, to the Eternal Truth which we all, at the end of the day, hope somehow we have served. The characteristic postmodern schizophrenia dwells here too.

In no area of professional activity has this acute self-consciousness been more apparent than in the law. In its principal manifestation of rhetorical thinking, the controversy surrounding "critical legal studies," students of rhetoric will, as with literary theory, hardly need special guidance, so familiar is the ground.[35] The "crits" have approached the law in the same way Latour has looked at scientific laboratories, arguing that legal argument *con-*

stitutes the reality of the law. (Alas, since this argument threatens to lead them where they do not want to go, toward what I have called the "hard defense" of rhetoric,[36] they then become Platonists and present a Divine Social Agenda that lies behind the obfuscatory and class-biased "rhetoric" of those who don't share that agenda.) But the key arguments of formal rhetoric have penetrated more deeply than this familiar foundationalist disagreement. As an example of how rhetorical thinking has penetrated into the body of everyday law, let us look briefly at an extended treatment of an area not in the critical limelight, Michael Sean Quinn's article on "Closing Arguments in Insurance Fraud Cases."[37]

Responding to current analyses of jury trials as dramatistic and rhetorical, Quinn defends them, and the arguments upon which they are built, as fundamentally a *logical* not a *rhetorical* affair. He creates two contenders for his legal arena, the *Rational Method* and the *Method of Manipulation*. The *Rational Method*:

> My thesis simply is that both words in the phrase "jury argument" should be taken literally and very seriously: what is presented to the *jury* is an *argument*. Arguments consist of premises and conclusions. According to the Rational Method, every conclusion should be (to some degree) demonstrated, that is, shown to be logically supported by premises which are themselves supported. ... Nor is the Rational Method for the faint-hearted. It calls for candid, frank, even blunt speaking. (747)

The *Method of Manipulation*:

> [T]rial lawyers win trials if they groom successfully, eat power breakfasts, obtain superior psychological wisdom, adapt their personalities accordingly, use power words, shun wimp-talk, use compelling body language, pick just the right jurors, ingratiate themselves with the jurors, push their buttons deftly, and so forth. (748)

If Quinn has already embraced the antirhetorical prejudice, his sense of his own craft is solidly rhetorical: "Litigation is the struggle to control the content, structure, and flow of information" (748). Rhetoric, the economics of attention, the allocation of a scarce resource, has always created the theoretical world within which litigation took place. Quinn goes on specifically to repudiate this domain: "It is currently fashionable to analogize the rhetorical theory of closing arguments closely upon the *dramatic arts* and *storytelling* (the Literary Analogy)."[38] In place of this Burkean dramatism he urges something he calls a *Broader Rational Theory*.

This theory works when there is a fair fight between knowledgeable, well-prepared, and otherwise evenly matched lawyers who stay pretty much within the rules, present their cases to a jury which is, at most, weakly biased, in a proceeding presided over by an intelligent and fair-minded judge who mostly follows the law, within the limits of practicality, who tries hard to rule correctly, and who uses his common sense. ...

According to the Broader Theory, the trial of a lawsuit can be, should be, and often is a largely rational process, although competitive and adversarial. (749–50)

But then he immediately begins to trap himself in the characteristic postmodern schizophrenia. Lawyers are storytellers; storytellers have to project a trustworthy persona, ergo, lawyers must appear "trustworthy, truthful, reliable, reasonable, and in possession of integrity" (751) if the jury is to believe the story they tell. So lawyers must learn to believe sincerely what they are paid to advocate: "Similarly for the trial lawyer, the best way to appear to be something is actually to be that thing" (751). This is not far from the good advice of the English comedy-team Flanders and Swann: "Always be sincere—whether you mean it or not," or from Richard Alexander's revised evolutionary ethic.

Quinn goes on to quarrel in detail with the idea of lawcourts as dramatic arenas constructing a dramatic reality, getting himself deeper and deeper into self-contradiction. He argues that the closing argument—counsel's only chance to tell consecutively and without interruption a story that throughout the trial can be told only in fragments—should bring that story together into a convincing whole. And opposing counsel should strive to *"(re)fragment, fictionalize, deconstruct,* and *ambiguate* the opposing story"* (756, Quinn's emphasis). That is, one should not reply to its rational arguments but *destroy it as a story.* Quinn thus waffles back and forth between adherence to drama and to logic, between rhetoric and philosophy. So on *reasons* in the closing argument:

A closing argument should provide a jury with *reasons* to decide the case favorably. In accordance with the precepts of the Rational Method, the reasons provided should make sense. They should be able to withstand at least modest critical scrutiny, for meretricious arguments are soon found out. (757)

In other words, if your arguments are meretricious, hide the duplicity somehow; make them *seem* reasonable if they cannot be so. After a number of these oscillations, he solves the problem he refuses to confront by denying its existence: "There is no tension between the concept of rational discourse and ardently attempting to use maximally persuasive language" (759). Maybe he can argue this way because he believes that "manipulative lawyering will not get as good results over time as the employment of the Rational Method"(762). Finally, he argues for a presentation of self that returns to the art of decorum basic to Western culture since the Sophists introduced it to Plato's Greece: "The truth of the matter is that authenticity, which always involves at least implicit self-disclosure, and craft should be integrated" (810). Trial lawyers should neither "gain access to their true inner selves" nor let their craft hang out either. The best art, that is, is the art that hides art. At the end of a *logical* defense of closing argument, he returns to what is (as we shall find later) the crucial rhetorical premise—without, of course, knowing that he has done so.

I don't mean to belittle Mr. Quinn or his remarkable article but to make an opposite point. Even a busy litigator, operating in an area of law not noted for its argumentative or theoretical elegance, returns—because rhetoric has again become so vital a method of operation in his intellectual world—to a schizophrenia that, as we have now seen, is both quintessentially postmodern and historically foundational for Western thinking. It may be that the schizophrenia is *systemic,* unavoidable.

A survey of rhetoric's reintegration into the field closest to law—management theory—is long overdue. The field resists summary, alas, not only because it is vast but because it does not think of itself as having any organizing premise other than "bottom-line" efficiency. Yet its rhetorical basis is emerging in a broad range of thinking about American industrial enterprise. Peter Drucker, for example, whom one might almost call the reigning philosopher of management theory, formulated this definition of management in a recent book:

> Management is about human beings. Its task is to make people capable of joint performance, to make their strengths effective and their weaknesses irrelevant. This is what organization is all about, and it is the reason that management is the critical, determining factor. These days, practically all of us are employed by managed institutions, large and small, business and non-business. We depend on management for our livelihoods. And our ability to contribute to society also depends as much on the management of the organizations in which we work as it does on our own skills, dedication, and effort.
>
> Because management deals with the integration of people in a common venture, it is deeply embedded in culture. What managers do in West Germany, in the United Kingdom, in the United States,

in Japan, or in Brazil is exactly the same. How they do it may be quite different. Thus one of the basic challenges managers in a developing country face is to find and identify those parts of their own tradition, history, and culture that can be used as management building blocks.[39]

A Greek Sophist, wandering from *polis* to *polis* in the eastern Mediterranean, could hardly have put his mission more clearly. Drucker embraces the Sophist's role even more closely a page or two later:

> Thirty years ago, the English scientist and novelist C. P. Snow talked of the "two cultures" of contemporary society. Management, however, fits neither Snow's "humanist" nor his "scientist." It deals with action and application; and its test [is] results. This makes it a technology. But management also deals with people, their values, their growth and development—and this makes it a humanity. So does its concern with, and impact on, social structure and the community. Indeed, as everyone has learned who, like this author, has been working with managers of all kinds of institutions for long years, management is deeply involved in spiritual concerns—the nature of man, good and evil.
>
> Management is thus what tradition used to call a liberal art—"liberal" because it deals with the fundamentals of knowledge, self-knowledge, wisdom, and leadership; "art" because it is practice and application. Managers draw on all the knowledges and insights of the humanities and the social sciences—on psychology and philosophy, on economics and history, on the physical sciences and ethics. But they have to focus this knowledge on effectiveness and results—on healing a sick patient, teaching a student, building a bridge, designing and selling a "user-friendly" software program.
>
> For these reasons, management will increasingly be the discipline and the practice through which the "humanities" will again acquire recognition, impact, and relevance. (231)

Isocrates could not have said it better, and would no doubt have agreed with Drucker that, in our time, the humanities have moved from the Humanities to the Graduate School of Management.

Drucker is arguing that management decisions must make sense in terms of people—both inside the company and outside it—as well as profits, and that the most skilled manager is one who can toggle from one domain to the other and back, hold the two in mind at once. It might surprise him to learn how closely his conception of management skill resembles the aristocratic governing techniques that Castiglione's *Book of the Courtier* recommends. It is as if he were trying to unite, in one perceptive conscience and consciousness, the two theories of management that have peopled the textbooks since the 1950s, Douglas McGregor's "Theory X" and "Theory Y." "Theory X" companies are managed in a traditional top-down, authoritative way. Employees are told only what they need to know, and know they must do as they are told. "Theory Y" companies work from a bottom-up, participatory theory of management in which workers should be generalists who know as much as they can possibly learn about a broad range of jobs, and do those jobs as need arises.

Students of rhetoric will recognize these patterns as the Platonic version of labor found in the *Republic* and the rhetorical version of general skillfulness and improvisational virtuosity. It is no secret to even the most closeted of humanists that the major movement in industrial enterprise the world over has been from "X" to "Y." This movement represents a complete reversal, from an adversarial to a cooperative theory of management. For students of rhetoric, it will be familiar as the movement from one pole of rhetorical thinking to its extreme opposite, from rhetoric as the theory of polarized debate to rhetoric as the theory of social harmony through ritualized two-sided argument. It is on a spectrum between these two extremes, precisely in the rhetorical arena, that the extraordinary (and, to those involved in them, often heartbreaking) changes in American—and indeed in the world's—industrial enterprise have taken place.[40]

Conflict resolution has been pondered in another area of contemporary thinking, one that takes us in a broad circle back to the evolutionary biology where we began: the study of game and play. This inquiry began from two opposite poles, cultural and mathematical, poles which have merged only in the world of electronic games. The cultural study of play and game (although it certainly has a pedigree going back to Schiller's *Letters on the Aesthetic Education of Man* and beyond) begins in our time with Johan Huizinga's *Homo Ludens*.[41] Huizinga's discussion of "the two cardinal moods of life—play and seriousness,"[42] prompted a series of studies from a cultural point of view, such as Roger Caillois's *Les Jeux et les Hommes: Le masque et le vertige*,[43] and David L. Miller's *Gods and Games: Toward a Theology of Play*.[44] The polarity Huizinga identified resurfaces in such disparate locations as Gregory Bateson's discussions of conflict resolution,[45] Clifford Geertz's essay on Balinese cockfighting,[46] and Alan Dundes and Alessandro Falassi's suggestive study of the Palio festival in Siena, *La Terra in Piazza*.[47] Dundes and Falassi describe a modern Italian city united, by common planning for and competition in a chivalric horse-racing festival, into something very like a Greek *polis*. Their description of the civic psyche that supports the Palio teams provides as good a description of what it must have been like to live within Greek rhetorical culture as we are likely ever to get. Bateson's essays in *Steps to an Ecology of Mind* analyze the peacemaking function of play and game as a counterweight to the overweening purposiveness of Western culture, and offer the best analysis to date of rhetoric as an *irenic* structure of thought. Geertz's dramatistic social anthropology (the connections with Kenneth Burke's thought are striking) reads cultures as texts and finds the decorum of a culture through intuitive interpretation rather than quantitative evaluation.[48]

In the Balinese culture Geertz describes, or the Sienese one analyzed alternately from both inside and outside by Falassi and Dundes (Falassi is Sienese, Dundes American), a figure/ground reversal has taken place in the traditional Western conception of "serious" behavior: the "play" sphere is "serious" and the "serious" world derivative and ornamental. The social, role-playing self is defining, and society is conceived as a self-consciously reenacted drama. The motival structure of games and play, in which display and triumph take precedence over the "practical" accomplishment of "real" work, replaces the bourgeois world of sensible purpose. In the art of such a culture, "ornament" and "content" reverse places and establish a stylistic decorum whose polarities are reversed 180 degrees from our customary ones. It is of this world that Carlyle spoke when he remarked "The first purpose of clothes was not warmth or decency but ornament," it is this world that Eric Hoffer described with his apothegm, "A vigorous society is a society made up of people who set their heart on toys," and that Isocrates was envisaging in the *Antidosis* when he talks about the gymnasium of the mind. I have discussed this reversal of cultural values at length in my *Motives of Eloquence*, as forming the center of rhetoric as a system of thought.[49] In such a light, it is easier to conceive the genesis of the modern social sciences—based as they are on a dramatistic rather than an ethical conception of human behavior—as deriving from classical rhetorical culture.[50] Obviously, if life in such a culture is fundamentally "literary," how we think about literature will be reversed as well, and indeed a number of studies have explored this reversal.[51]

Game theory per se, the area of applied mathematics that tries to chart the boundary-condition strategies of human conflict, has produced a vast body of thinking, most of it beyond my mathematical understanding.[52] But it conditions the modern study of rhetoric because it represents an attempt to analyze conflict by the most *unrhetorical* of means. Its premise of self-interest is as narrowly purposive as that of classical economics, but its effort to synthesize a *logical* solution to the problem of human cooperation produces some surprising conclusions. Robert Axelrod's *The Evolution of Cooperation*[53] builds a convincing model for how human cooperation may have arisen from the bedrock of rational self-interest. If we put these two orchestrations of human conflict, cultural and mathematical, into oscillation, we can begin to understand the intellectual world from which was born perhaps the most remarkable manifestation of the rhetorical world view in modern life—computer-based gaming and simulation.[54]

Viewing human culture as a binary opposition between two kinds of motive, serious and playful, reincarnates the classical quarrel between the philosophers and rhetoricians. The same quarrel made another entrance onto the rhetorical stage as an argument not from motive but from technology—the distinction between literate and oral cultures that began with Parry and Lord's discussion of oral formulas in the Homeric poems. Father Walter J. Ong, a principal voice in this debate, has summarized it in *Orality and Literacy: The Technologizing of the Word*, and there is no need to do that again.[55] Father Ong argues that the rhetorical world *was* the oral world; that they were isomorphic, and that the subsequent application of the rhetorical system of education to written utterance always carried with it the world of orality. That world is now familiar to us all: a world in which poetry was the cultural memory system; a world in which all human communion was what Malinowski called "phatic communion" and Bateson "ticking-over behavior," conversation that took place just to keep human reality in being; a world in which "even business is not business: it is fundamentally rhetoric";[56] a world in which there was no "central self," with its richly ironic interiorities; a world in which all thinking was narrative and situational, immersed in the particulars of time and place rather than floating free in general conceptual thought; a world in which words were indeed "winged," and the idea of "originality" had yet to emerge.

Robert Pattison has taken strong exception to the arguments of McLuhan, Havelock, and Ong. They are, he thinks, all wrong: "By itself, writing is an inert force. It provokes change only within the living organism of the human community, and the changes it does stimulate make sense only when studied in conjunction with the consciousness of language prevalent in the culture where it is employed." "Like the other technologies of language, from which it is distinct in many ways, reading has few inborn powers. It acquires its dynamic from the ideological framework in which it is deployed."[57] Yet Pattison's analysis of the problem is binary, too. "At the present the West faces a crisis not unlike that of the Middle Ages. We have produced two literacies, one of formal language as encoded in grammars and dictionaries, another of the living language found in daily intercourse and in popular art. ... One of these, advocating a formal, correct grammar, is at the moment the ideology of established authority. ...The other ideology, the ideology represented by the informal, oral literacy we see growing up around us, is as yet undeveloped" (84–85). The class struggle of our time can be seen as a struggle between literate and oral worlds, between—I am putting words in Pattison's mouth—between a controlling literacy and a disenfranchised orality.[58] We can thus view the basic binary relationship *conceptually*, as in the nature of human motive; *technologically*, as depending on the media of communication; or *socially*, as depending upon the class structure of a particular society.

◻   ◻   ◻

Generalizing across so many fields—and I have only sampled those areas of contemporary intellectual and artistic life that lend themselves to detailed rhetorical analysis—must of necessity be dangerous and seem foolhardy. But four basic themes do emerge.

First, during the last twenty years, rhetoric has moved from the periphery to the center of our intellectual focus. We seldom give this movement its right name because "rhetoric" has become such a dirty word that any sensible person shrinks from using it. And obviously, much of the work done in these areas is done by people ignorant both of one another's work and of rhetoric's predominance in Western education for two millennia.

Second, the emergent pattern of rhetorical thinking is, as it was during its past history, *centripetal*. It offers that vital center for the humanities which wanderers in the "core curriculum" wilderness have for so long sought. Clifford Geertz has wished for a "useful miracle" that would give today's specialized scholarly worlds a common language;[59] the rhetorical paideia has throughout its history tried to provide such a miracle. (I develop this argument further in chapter 6.) We might, as a way of focusing a confused babel of disparate inquiries, conceive the current disciplinary scene as an emergent reunification of the disciplines that fissionated out from their rhetorical center into the modern learned disciplines about a century ago. With the disciplinary universe as with the cosmic universe, a big bang has blown everything apart and now we debate whether it will continue to fissionate forever or start reuniting.

Third, all the fields I have so cursorily surveyed display at the center of their current debate some binary oscillation, an alternation of figure and ground. In chaos theory, the stability of the Lorenz attractor,[60] never repetitive but somehow orderly, toggles in and out of Newtonian thinking, from a conventional and natural to an unconventional and trained "intuition." In the law, it is a replay of the classic Greek debate about the nature of two-sided argument.[61] For management theory, it is defining the indispensable management skill that balances bottom-line applications with the larger strategies that long-range global competition is forcing upon everyone. The attempt to balance "Theory X" and "Theory Y" management theories addresses binary stability as a systemic ideal.[62] In architecture, Jencks's choice of the rabbit-duck figure, the perception psychologists' "bi-stable illusion," to figure forth the postmodern schizophrenia is dead accurate: a building like the Centre Pompidou, its façade alternately the undisguised guts of the building and finely ornamented surface, creates precisely the same bi-stability. The postmodern debate in architecture is about the nature of ornamentation, a topic dear to rhetoric schools since Gorgias got the figures off to a rolling start. The coming-of-age self-consciousness that the learned professions and disciplines all feel contains another genre of binary oscillation, as we have seen: the disinterested pursuit of truth on the one hand, the self-interested pursuit of victory in increasingly bureaucratic career-wars on the other. Those who think about game and play generalize this oscillation between truth and career into a general view of culture—and, in doing so, themselves toggle back and forth between the logical arguments of mathematical game theory per se and the rhetorical analyses of culture begun by Huizinga. The sociobiological debate between the culturalists and the genetic-determinists (to give both their extreme names) reduces itself, from a rhetorical perspective, to the debate about the nature and sources of "decorative" behavior, transposed up an octave from the traditional rhetorical orchestration. Kenneth Burke long ago separated readers into "hysterics" and "connoisseurs," those who look THROUGH a textual surface to the "content" that can confirm or deny their hysterical need for consolation, and those who look AT a stylistic surface and contemplate it in a Wildean manner. This frontstage/backstage oscillation moves naturally enough into the Derridean *sous rature* world where difference itself becomes the key issue.

Fourth, this binary oscillation begins to suggest that rhetorical culture may again be conceived *systemically*, as an information system, a system which—because it has been so familiar to us for so long—we have the greatest difficulty recognizing *as a system*, as a means of allocating the limited resources of human attention in accordance with social need.

The Electronic Word

All the changes the last two decades have brought are so disparate and confusing, and the territorial fears one feels in confronting them so great, that I hesitate to introduce another. Yet the biggest change of all for rhetorical inquiry has come not in the learned conversations or in the practicing professions but in the technology that expresses them. For surely the greatest change, falling for the most part outside the academic study of rhetoric but affecting and illuminating it at every point, has been the coming of the electronic word, the movement from letters printed on paper to digitized images projected onto the phosphorous screen of a computer.[63]

The basic changes from print to electronic screen we are now coming to comprehend in their full force. The fixed printed surface becomes volatile and interactive. The definitive and unchangeable text upon which Western humanism has been based since the Renaissance, and the Arnoldian "masterpiece" theory of culture built upon it, are called into question, put into play. Typography becomes allegorical, a new authorial parameter expressive in the very manner suggested by the Italian Futurists when our century began.[64] The graphical and typographical tricks to which the electronic surface lends itself make us self-conscious again about our own apparatus of vision. Francis Crick suggests that we think of "the visual system as a bag of tricks" rather than a passive registrant of a world simply out there.[65] Edward Wilson has made much the same point from an evolutionary perspective: "The brain depends upon elegance to compensate for its own small size and short lifetime. As the cerebral cortex grew from apish dimensions through hundreds of thousands of years of evolution, it was forced to rely on tricks to enlarge memory and speed computation. The mind therefore specializes on analogy and metaphor, on a sweeping together of chaotic sensory experience into workable categories labeled by words and stacked into hierarchies for quick recovery."[66] Print invites us to forget all these tricks, to look through a deliberately transparent and fixed black-and-white surface of verbal symbols to the conceptual universe beyond. Electronic text's bag of visual tricks makes us self-conscious about the bag of neural tricks that create our own vision, and puts this self-consciousness into oscillation with the visual conventions of transparent print. Shirley Strum, in her thoughtful study of baboon behavior and culture, has made an analogous point: "We often forget that we are animals ourselves—that we watch the outside world with specialized senses, with a brain that is geared to integrate this information in a specific way and with a set of emotions strongly invested in one view of how the world works or should work."[67] The perceptual field of the "reader" becomes considerably richer and more complex in electronic display.

This richness creates a strong feedback field around print. We have come to regard print as so inevitable that we have ceased to notice its extraordinary stylization. Print, after all, is a trickery too, not a historical inevitability. Print represents a decision of severe abstraction and subtraction. All nonlinear signals are filtered out; color is banned for serious texts; typographical constants are rigorously enforced; sound is proscribed; even the tactility of visual elaboration is outlawed.[68] Print is an act of perceptual self-denial, and electronic text makes us aware of that self-denial at every point and in all the ways which print is at pains to conceal. Not the least implication of electronic text for rhetoric is how the implicit self-denials of the print contract are being renegotiated.

The domain of prose style, for a start, is bound to change. Kenneth Burke reflected on the limited boundary conditions of prose long ago in *Counter-Statement*: "Much of the difficulty with imaginative prose today lies in the fact that our categorical expectations require a manner poorly adapted to the fuller potentialities of prose."[69] Our categorical expectations expand in an electronic environment. The ideal decorum for prose style has always been thought unselfconscious transparency; like the typography that enshrined it, it should be a crystal goblet to set off the wine of thought it contained. In an ideal world, prose would not be needed at all. We could look on ideas as in themselves they really are, unmediated by language. Yet, as every writer soon learns, transparent crystal words are hard to fabricate. Prose "right out of the old guts onto the goddamn paper," as Terry Southern put it, just won't do. Instead, the prose stylist finds himself taking rhetorical figuration and placing it in tension with the linear prose surface. A figure like chiasmus wants to fold its ABBA pattern up on itself, curl language into a symmetrical double layer, make the prose line run backward. Printed prose can't do that, and so the prose stylist finds his work in carefully tuning the tension between the diagrams that the figures want to describe and the linearity that printed prose permits. Likewise a pun wants to superimpose two senses on a word, and hence write two sentences based upon it that share the same space. You can draw a line through such a word, as Derrida might do, but that is to leave the domain of printed prose style, which is an aesthetic of controlled self-denial and suppressed visual and auditory suggestibility. We can underline or boldface the alliterating syllables in an alliterative text but, like the fingers pointing to rhetorical figures in eighteenth-century texts, such typographical contrivances make us uncomfortable —they, too, break the crystal-goblet rules. (That their original readers were not made uncomfortable suggests that their prose decorum was considerably more self-conscious than our own.) We do not usually think of prose style as conditioned, radically and intrinsically, by the conventions of writing and then, more narrowly, of print, but it is this conditioning that electronic print teaches us to detect.

We can, then, think of electronic prose as moving back toward the world of oral rhetoric, where gestural symmetries were permitted and sound was omnipresent. Any prose text, by the very nature of the denial/expression tensions that create and animate it, oscillates back and forth between literate self-denial and oral permissiveness, but electronic text does so much more self-consciously, simply by the volatile nature of the written surface. A volatile surface invites us to intensify rather than subdue this oscillation, make it more rather than less self-conscious.

Consider, for example, how we might think about a pivotal concept in rhetorical theory and practice, amplification. The standard advice about how to amplify through the various topics and categories is straightforward, but when we come to the crucial question of when enough is enough, of when *brevitas* should supervene, the rhetorical wisdom is bankrupt. We amplify enough to suit the context and no more. And yet, since the context is *created* by the amplification, such advice is useless. This version of the postmodern schizophrenia has been with rhetoric since the beginning, and writers have been limited to one solution. You decide, by that broad range of intuition which the rhetorical paideia trained you for but never could specify, what "length" an argument or description should be for the present use and let it go at that. Having to make such a choice does not inhere in the nature of the universe; it is forced upon us by writing and especially by print. When we speak to a live audience, we can expand or contract our matter as changing conditions demand. Electronic text restores to us some of that oral flexibility. Every major word-processing program features an outlining program and increasingly students are learning to write using such an outliner. We need only incorporate these stages of brevity/amplification into the final product and we have offered our readers a choice that converts amplificatio into an audience choice. And if we use a hypertextual program like *Guide* or *HyperCard*,[70] the choices become three-dimensionally complex.

Since the introduction of word-processing, the writing community has been heating its imagination with the question of whether or not "writing on a computer" makes one more long-winded. We can now appreciate how print-bound such a question is. We might much better put the matter this way: In the long history of Western prose style, Asiatic expansiveness has always contended with Stoic brevity. Expansiveness has won more often than not in the long run, but from seventeenth-century one-thing/one-word exhortations until recent postmodern experiments in fiction, the Stoics have had things their own way. Now electronic text is making us self-conscious again about this struggle *as a choice*, as a decision to create a reality as against fabricating a window to a preexistent reality already "out there." Its ease of choosing allows the reader to toggle back and forth between two conceptions of "the right length," and consequently between the two different conceptions of human reality, the one we make up "in here" and the one that exists "out there." If you dial up the short version of reality, you can use it for transparent navigational purposes; dial up the long version and then look AT it rather than THROUGH it, and it can stimulate you as literature always does to construct a new reality for it to describe. In this fashion, electronic text can oscillate between prose and poetry, or perhaps more accurately, between the prosaic and poetic uses of language.

The interactive audience of oral rhetoric obviously has returned in force. The ritualistically silent audience of the nineteenth century was an audience of "readers" observing a print convention. The rowdy and involved audience that the Futurists and Dadaists teased and abused into being is an audience from what Father Ong would call "secondary orality." The electronic audience is radically interactive. When Peter Ramus split rhetoric into sound argument on the one hand and Cecil B. De Mille *opsis* on the other, he banished memory and delivery to a limbo from which electronic text is only now beginning to rescue them. The question of how electronic memory operates, through its complex search and indexing procedures, to substitute for the stupendous feats of human memory that are commonplace in oral cultures, is one to which the answer has only begun to emerge. Clearly the human memory is weakened still further from the radical weakening inflicted by writing and then by print. Equally clearly, it is immensely enhanced by the awesome search and retrieval powers of digital memory, as the CD-ROM version of the *Oxford English Dictionary* (for example) demonstrates. One way or another, memory is again a major player as in the days of oral rhetoric.

And, through the iconic powers of electronic text, *gesture* has returned even more strongly than memory. As we saw in chapter 2, the digitized word is renegotiating the icon/alphabet ratio which we have since the invention of printing taken almost as holy writ. The oscillation between verbal and visual appeal which *ecphrasis* used to build into speech and writing now finds itself extraordinarily enhanced. Personal computers can create very sophisticated custom graphics, and growing libraries of images, visual topoi, await collage. This alternation of word and picture has swept through the world of business communication and we may expect scholarly communication to come limping behind.

Rhetoricians, like all humanists, harbor a built-in prejudice against what Rudolf Arnheim called "visual thinking," but it can't last much longer: "In order to evaluate the important role of language more adequately it seems to me necessary to recognize that it serves as a mere auxiliary to the primary vehicles of thought, which are so immensely better equipped to represent relevant objects and relations by articulate shape. The function of language is essentially conservative and stabilizing, and therefore it also tends, negatively, to make cognition static and immobile."[71] The digitization now common to letters and shapes creates a mixed text of icons and words in which "static and immobile" and dynamically mobile cognitive styles toggle back and forth into a new bi-stable expressivity. Texts have long had illustrations, to be sure, but that relationship was fixed, and it seldom favored the illustrations and always protected the conventional self-denials of prose expressivity. We have now to do with a relationship, both more balanced and radically dynamic, between two different kinds of signal. Susanne Langer stressed their difference long ago:

> Visual forms—lines, colors, proportions, etc.—are just as capable of *articulation*, i.e. of complex combination, as words. But the laws that govern this sort of articulation are altogether different from the laws of syntax that govern language. The most radical difference is that *visual forms are not discursive*. They do not present their constituents successively, but simultaneously, so the relations determining a visual structure are grasped in one act of vision. Their complexity, consequently, is not limited, as the complexity of discourse is limited, by what the mind can retain from the beginning of an apperceptive act to the end of it.[72]

As readers, we have to learn to alternate between these two kinds of syntax, verbal and visual. If we add to this binary expansion the sound and color rapidly becoming part of the mix, we can envision how rhetorical practice will literalize all its visual metaphors—beginning, one would think, with the "colors" of rhetoric. And if voice and musical sampling are added to the palette, we take yet another step back toward the full range of oral expressivity. We shall find, as the icon/alphabet ratio continues to be redefined, all kinds of other kinships with that earlier time when rhetoric was narrowing its expressive repertoire to cope with writing's narrowed and intentionally self-denying expressive range.

We've noticed earlier how rhetorical theory has been used to interpret the visual arts. But if Baxandall's study of *Giotto and the Orators*[73] shows that Charles Jencks is doing nothing radically new in describing postmodern architecture in terms of rhetorical figures, digitization does introduce something new. As I argue in chapter 1, for the first time the arts, through their common digitization, have become directly interchangeable. We can convert sound signals into visual ones and vice versa. We can operate on the digital signal in all kinds of ways to blur completely the distinction between sight and sound and produce a code expressible as either. This blurring will compel us to rethink the metaphorical structure of our rhetorical terminology, depending as it does so heavily on visual metaphors for verbal meanings. Such a development parallels the radical reconstruction of Western poetics forced upon us by the unstable electronic text and interactive reader/writer.[74] And if the scholarly disciplines may be, as we saw in our jetliner view of them, coming to share a common rhetorical center, we may find in the digitization of the arts a way to let them share the common descriptive vocabulary of rhetorical figuration as well. Many rhetorical figures, after all, work by moving information and power from one sense to the other, precisely as chiasmus moves it from sight to sound. Electronic text can do this more directly and effectively.

Father Ong has remarked on "the degree to which the oration as such tyrannized over ideas of what expression as such—literary or other—was" in the Middle Ages and the Renaissance.[75] Indeed, the influence of this paradigmatic form has lasted until the present day. The digital computer both strengthens and weakens the oration as a compositional form and educational technique. On the one hand, what the computer does best, besides counting, is *modeling*. It has made learning through *rehearsal-reality* possible across the complete range of human thinking and planning. *Declamatio* was education by endless rehearsal-reality, and the computer has simply adopted and expanded this basic expressive technique. On the other hand, electronic text is clearly finding its way to a new, and a new *kind* of, paradigm for writing—interactive on-line conversation. Such a form represents a movement into nonlinear hypertextual space where the classic oration cannot follow. We need not fear that this means the end of human thought, however; the oration gave way to the letter in the Middle Ages,[76] and that gave way to the essay in the Renaissance. It is hardly surprising that the basic instructional form for verbal composition should change again in a digitized verbal world.

It should not surprise us either that electronic text brings with it a characteristic mix of human motivation very different from that of print. The strategic self-denials of print, its linear, black-and-white transparency, bias expression toward the disembodied concepts of Platonic philosophy. The computer world was born under the opposite star of game and play, and its playful humor and game-centered characteristic structures have endured. Taken in the aggregate, its motival mix pushes the electronic word toward rhetoric as strongly as print urges us to get serious and do some real thinking. The strong resistance that humanists often exhibit to the changing icon/alphabet ratio, to the growing influence and power of computer and video graphics as "comic-book culture," reveals the struggle of these conflicting biases.

When this different motival mix is wired into the on-line classroom, it seems also—our experience with such classrooms is still very tentative—to alter the pedagogical environment in some marked ways.[77] In a classroom based on networked personal computers, the teacher no longer provides the authoritarian focus. Teacher is but one voice on-line, and other voices too timid to speak in class are often emboldened by the different and more protected role an on-line conversation provides. This technique is also being used for business meetings, where it has a similarly enzymatic effect on hierarchical structures. Such a conversation, inasmuch as I have observed it, toggles back and forth between the oral and the written word, to recreate in fact the bi-stability emergent in so many disparate fields of inquiry. The on-line environment creates a different species of decorum. Whether it is more sociable and less aggressive than present patterns remains unclear, but it may turn out that way.

Digital Decorum

Perhaps the hoariest of all chestnuts in the rhetorician's notebook is the caution that every stylistic virtue has its corresponding vice. "All the variations of oratorical style are capable of being used in season or out of season," cautioned Aristotle.[78] Quintilian echoed the sentiment: "Style may ... be corrupted in precisely the same number of ways that it may be adorned."[79] Likewise the *Ad Herennium* author: "But in striving to attain these styles, we must avoid falling into faulty styles closely akin to them."[80] This tradition spills over naturally from style into lifestyle, as Plutarch, writing on the education of children, notes in the *Moralia*:

> I advise then (for I return now to my original theme) that, as one should always be careful to avoid the theatrical and melodramatic style, so, on the other hand, one should exercise the same caution to avoid triviality and vulgarity in style; for a turgid diction is unfitted for a man in public life, and a barren style is too unimpressive; but as the body ought to be not merely healthy but also sturdy, so also speech should be not merely free from fault but vigorous too. For the cautious is merely commended, but the audacious is admired as well. It so happens that I entertain the same opinion also in regard to mental disposition. For a man should not be bold, on the one hand, or, on the other, pusillanimous and cowering, since the one resolves itself into impudence, and the other into servility. Always to pursue the middle course in everything is artistic and in good taste.[81]

The difference between good taste and bad, between an elegant ornament and its *propinqua vitia*, has always proved impossible to specify through rule, and touchstones are always pressed into use. But the criterion has always been clear: self-consciousness. Stylistic self-consciousness is the ultimate evil. Aristotle, in a passage following the one quoted, warns us that "it is better not to have everything always just corresponding to everything else—your hearers will see through you less easily thus." Fake it, he counsels, but hide the faking. Likewise, Longinus counsels that a figure is always better when it looks natural, does not seem to be a figure.[82] As a modern Plutarch put it, "Verbal cleverness commonly lowers the tone of meditation: one does not address God in that way."[83] Or anyone else, either. The operative rule of Western aesthetics from Aristotle onward has been that the best art is the art that hides its own art, appears natural. "Always be sincere," to vary Flanders and Swann, "especially if you don't mean it." It is self-consciousness that converts the three good styles of the *Ad Herennium* into their antitypical *vitia*. Self-consciousness is the ultimate villain for speaker as well as audience. "Indeed," Augustine remarks in *On Christian Doctrine*, "I think that there is hardly a single eloquent man who can both speak well and think of the rules of eloquence while he is speaking."[84] He goes on, naturally, to talk about the art of concealing art.

I've shown in chapter 1 how we might chart verbal expression, spoken and written, on a matrix of self-consciousness. Let me reproduce the matrix for ease of reference.

	Unselfconscious	Selfconscious
Object	Transparent	Opaque
Viewer	Through	At
Reality	Biogrammar	Drama
Motive	Hierarchy	Play

We can plot the spectrum of self-consciousness on four continua: the text, the perceiver, the nature of the "reality" perceived, and the motive animating the perception.[85] Decorum—that good taste which cannot be taught but yet somehow must be learned, since it lurks at the center of everything—can be charted, in any one occurrence, as a matrix plot across these four continua. The complete matrix creates something like a "chaotic" universe, a place where the diversity is infinite and unpredictable yet occurs within definable limits. From such a limited reality we can create all of human social and stylistic reality. We mean by "decorum" a felt sense of how the fixings fall across the continua during an integral event, literary or social. Decorum is not a fixed relationship between text, beholder, and event beheld, but the permitted range of dynamic variation. It is this permitted range that we must interiorize but *not bring to self-consciousness.*

And yet anyone studying language must do this, must break down the compelling urge to *see through* our means of seeing to the "reality" established by that seeing.[86] Fabrication of the "decorous," unselfconscious Western reality, stylistic or social, is done through a trick, a series of tricks, just like perception itself, and we want to know how the trick is done. The art historian E. H. Gombrich, when he wanted to learn how Constable's *Wivenhoe Park* created its illusion of reality, imposed a grid upon it and then looked at each individual square, deliberately denying the integrating powers of the "tricky" eye.[87] Rhetoricians have always done this for verbal design by creating as detailed a nomenclature as possible for verbal effects. The monstrous regiment of Latin and Greek rhetorical terms works as a "Wivenhoe grid," interfering with our integrative powers, making us look AT the verbal surface rather than THROUGH it to the "reality" our decorous trickery has created.

Rhetoric as a method of literary education aimed to train its students to toggle back and forth between AT and THROUGH vision, alternately to realize how the illusion is created and then to fool oneself with it again.[88] The literature such an education created—and this means most of Western literature until the nineteenth century—works the same way, by alternating speech and narrative, self-conscious and unselfconscious language, in the fashion that Thucydides established.[89] To study Western literature is to master the particular binary oscillation between kinds of consciousness that each text advances, to plot the fixings of each across the continua of self-consciousness. And to understand that particular mixture is what it means to "read" that text. To feel that characteristic oscillation is to understand the decorum of that work, and hence that part of Western culture, *from the inside.* Such dynamic knowledge puts us *inside the work looking out.* We can, if we like, shut the oscillation down and study, for example, only the rhetorical figuration, or only the philosophy. This, in fact, is how Western literature has been studied and taught for most of its history. We study "what Plato said," ignore the exquisitely wrought style that contradicts the "saying"—and miss entirely the ontological schizophrenia at the center of his being.

It is because our characteristic social reality is built on a trick, a radical hypocrisy, that Western culture has always feared the stylistic analysis upon which a rhetorical education depended. How deep down into the behavior chain the fear goes, Richard Alexander's analysis of the origins of hypocrisy has shown us. The best defense against this fear of exposure is the fixity of written language: the infinite variables of the self-consciousness matrix are, for the moment, controlled. It is this temporary stay, the first line of defense, that electronic text puts in jeopardy. Electronic text renders our decorum again self-conscious and interactive; it continually reminds us that the real basis of that decorum, of our social reality, is not fixed but bi-stable, the reality illustrated by the bi-stable illusions like the rabbit and/or duck. Digital decorum is frankly and openly bi-stable. It creates a reality in which figure and ground can continually change places.

This is a toggle to boggle the mind. It means that the two basic theories of language are placed in permanent oscillation. Language was in origin ornamental; language was in origin purposive. The anthropologist Marshall Sahlins asks whether need creates culture or culture creates need, and calls this question the founding contradiction of anthropology.[90] It is the founding contradiction of rhetoric as well—and of all Western culture. We solve it by a characteristic decorum that oscillates, at different frequencies and wavelengths, between the two. We have hidden that oscillation from ourselves, as a behavioral necessity, and electronic text now brings it to light. Such an oscillation is, I would argue, the fundamental renegotiation now demanded of our Western reality. It is this renegotiation we have seen occurring across the spectrum of Western inquiry, from professional self-consciousness to management theory. It is easy to generate despair, existential or deconstructive, from such a renegotiation—all you do is shut down the oscillation that shows the way out of the either/or choice. But such despair is needless and sentimental. The machinery to combat it has been with us from the beginning; it is in fact biogrammatical, as Alexander shows. Rhetoric and philosophy, to give the polar positions their familiar nicknames, don't mix but they can alternate, and that is quite good enough.

The centrality that the rhetorical paideia claimed, and which literary education has always claimed by analogy, came from the allegorizing of this generative oscillation. The bi-stable *illusion* of literary decorum was the source of infinite *allusions* built upon it. This allusive power is the premise upon which Quintilian relied, but which he never stated—and perhaps had never fully conceptualized—when he answered so positively his root question of whether the great orator was necessarily a great man.[91] The rhetorical paideia's aim was clear: to teach decorum, both linguistic and behavioral, and to teach the second by means of the first. To teach this would be to teach the appropriate and acceptable behavioral repertoire. One was also teaching, at the same time, the means of contravening that decorum, of being "revolutionary." That too had its style. But "direct" revolutionary behavior was not taught, any more than direct anything else. You could not do it, any more than you could teach "clarity." It had to go through words, and be compared to decorum. Real revolution meant abolishing rhetorical education. Such an abolition would sever the vital connection between verbal and behavioral education by fracturing the decorum that held them together. Alexander Pope saw this threat clearly; is that not what the *Dunciad* is all about? The social psychologist George Herbert Mead saw this clearly, too— you become socialized by learning to play all the positions on the team, get an introduction to the cultural drama by continued and varied rehearsal. Play moves into "reality" and back.[92]

Once you abolish rhetorical education, then you must ask, "How, then, do I teach decorum?" What else do I use for my behavioral allegory? Property? Stuff? And what about the teaching of language? Once it has become simply instrumental, the clear, brief, and sincere transmission of neutral fact from one neutral entity to another, it loses its numinosity and then its power, as our present literacy crisis attests. If you pursue only clarity, you guarantee obscurity. And people lose their vital interest in language, as any composition teacher can attest. The "literacy crisis" is not only a social crisis, a crisis of instructional leverage, of educational policy, although it is all of those. It comes from the repudiation of the rhetorical heart of Western education, and its linguistic and behavioral education in decorum.

This felt center, as our tentative survey has sought to suggest, may be returning. And it is precisely at this point that electronic text can have its strongest effect. I have been arguing that the binary switch that creates decorum, stylistic and social, constitutes the enabling logic of Western education. Electronic text can, for the first time, dynamically model this switch. Through allegorical typography, through manipulation of icon/alphabet relations, through nonlinear hypertextual juxtapositions, through the intricated real-time collages that digital memory makes possible, the electronic word can model the process of establishing our enabling decorum.

It can be argued that such a self-conscious decorum is unbearable for a general cultural audience, that only a stable and unchanging utopia can serve as a cultural ideal. So George Steiner has suggested: "Much of the truest of our culture was animate with ontological utopia....It is not certain, moreover, that one can devise a model of culture, a heuristic program for further advance, without a utopian core."[93] But it is the ontological utopias that have caused all the trouble! The bi-stable model for utopia holds a much greater hope for peace.

We have, in fact, an excellent illustration of how the bi-stable model works, in the Western system of jurisprudence, based as it has always been on two-sided argument. Michael Quinn's self-contradictions, in the article on closing arguments considered earlier, were honorably come by: they emerge from the fundamental self-contradiction that galvanizes the legal framework within which he thinks. The oscillation, in Anglo-Saxon jurisprudence, between the common law and statute law embodies the very AT/THROUGH oscillation we have been considering.[94] The ability to live with the self-contradiction it reveals—that social conventions have to be made by people, and change according to changing circumstance, and yet at the same time be considered as conceptually true and morally binding— is at the heart of any education for citizenship in Western culture. And it is a similar ability to live with an ethics both rule-based and situational at the same time that Western decorum, through its rhetorical educational system, has always tried to teach.

Technology will not *force* us to see our vital decorum more clearly. But technology will certainly *affect* this decorum, whether we like it or not— the motival structure does differ from that of print. But the logic of the argument I have been trying to construct moves away from technological determinism and toward an opposite conclusion, cultural convergence. What is remarkable about the newly self-conscious and renegotiated conception of Western decorum created by the electronic word is that, as our survey of "rhetoric" in nonrhetorical fields shows, *it happened everywhere else first*. Or at least *at the same time*. Postmodernism in the visual arts and in music supplied the aesthetic of electronic display half a century before we started processing our words electronically. The return of rhetorical patterns of thought, which we now call "theory," prompted a rethinking of our axial decorum in all of the fields I have so hastily surveyed and a great many more. Evolutionary biology pushed decorum's biogrammatical roots back beyond our primate history. What is extraordinary is not how digital technology has compelled us toward a fundamental cultural reevaluation, but rather how that technology can—if we use it right—express so eloquently an omnipresent reevaluation already in being.

The deconstructionists have made the binary oscillation of Western decorum a desperate affair. It is not a desperate affair; it is an error-checking operation. It represents, as Gregory Bateson made clear in *Steps to an Ecology of Mind*, a way in which style can control content, formal pleasure balance conceptual thought, self-consciousness satirically ventilate our hierarchical urges. The bi-stable utopia promises peace as Plato's static Republic never could. We have no cause to regret that we were born in interesting times. After all, rhetoric as we know it was born in the midst of a radical change in technology—the invention of writing. We are passing through a change equally great right now. Writing created one breed of seriousness; electronic text is now creating another. The new one is more suited to "the felt necessities of the time," and we will have failed as humanists and rhetoricians if we do not employ it for the purposes to which it so cordially invites us.

NOTES

1. Richard A. Lanham, *A Handlist of Rhetorical Terms: A Guide for Students of English Literature* (Berkeley and Los Angeles: University of California Press, 1969); the subtitle was dropped from the second edition, published in 1992.

2. The term is Richard McKeon's. For the best explanation of how McKeon used it, see Mark Backman's introduction to *Rhetoric: Essays in Invention and Discovery*, ed. Mark Backman (Woodbridge, Conn.: Ox Bow, 1987).

3. Burke developed the theory in *Counter-Statement* (1931), *Permanence and Change* (1935), *Attitudes Toward History* (1937), *The Philosophy of Literary Form* (1941), *A Grammar of Motives* (1945), and *A Rhetoric of Motives* (1950). All these works have been published in revised editions by the University of California Press; see n. 8 below.

4. Jeremy Campbell, *Grammatical Man: Information, Entropy, Language, and Life* (New York: Simon and Schuster, 1982), 101.

5. Max Delbrück, quoted by Ernst Mayr, *The Growth of Biological Thought: Diversity, Evolution, and Inheritance* (Cambridge: Harvard University Press, 1982), 69.

6. For a student of rhetoric, two good entry-points to this field are Robin Fox and Lionel Tiger's *The Imperial Animal* (New York: Holt, Rinehart and Winston, 1971) and David P. Barash's *Sociobiology and Behavior* (New York: Elzevier, 1977) and *The Whisperings Within* (New York: Harper and Row, 1979). The book that started the sociobiology fuss, Edward O. Wilson's *Sociobiology: The New Synthesis* (Cambridge: Harvard University Press, 1975), is suggestive, almost to the point of bewilderment, for anyone who wishes to pick up the Aristotelian burden of connecting rhetoric once again with what we know about the deep motival structure of *homo sapiens*. Perhaps even more pertinent for students of rhetoric and its conception of human motivation is Mary Midgley's fine study, *Beast and Man: The Roots of Human Nature* (Ithaca: Cornell University Press, 1978). Wilson has developed the broader arguments of his last chapter ("Man: From Sociobiology to Sociology," 547–75) in a subsequent book, *On Human Nature* (Cambridge: Harvard University Press, 1978); there he argues that evolutionary biology and the central cultural myth it expresses ought to function as an "antidiscipline" to the humanities, subtly and slowly introducing them to the teleonomic universe behavioral biology has created.

Applying this argument to rhetoric is an illuminating instance of Burke's "perspective by incongruity." A good place to begin such an undertaking is with the work of Konrad Lorenz, and a good introduction to that is to be found in Richard I. Evans, *Konrad Lorenz: The Man and His Ideas* (New York and London: Harcourt Brace Jovanovich, 1975). Irenäus Eibl-Eibesfeldt's *The Biology of Peace and War: Men, Animals, and Aggression*, trans. Eric Mosbacher (New York: Viking, 1979), examines the question of aggression in ways that students of its rhetorical displacement ought to find relevant; see, for instance, the wonderful parody of Homeric rhetorical speechifying in the discussion of New Guinea tribal warfare, 196–204. For rhetoric as the study of the economics of attention, M. R. A. Chance's essay "Social Cohesion and the Structure of Attention" provides a behavioral base, in *Biosocial Anthropology*, ed. Robin Fox (London: Malaby, 1975), 93–114. Eibl-Eibesfeldt's *Ethology: The Biology of Behavior*, 2d ed. (New York: Holt, Rinehart and Winston, 1975) surveys the field. An even broader view is provided by Ernst Mayr's *The Growth of Biological Thought* (n. 5 above). Such works as these may lead the reader to look for the sources of rhetorical figuration in the play faces of primates (emphasizing as they do exaggeration, extra tension, and repetition) as well as in the speeches of Isocrates.

7. I discuss this difference, apropos Richard McKeon, in chapter 7.

8. Burke was by way of being not only a protostructuralist but sometimes almost a sociobiologist: see, inter alia, *Counter-Statement*, 2d ed. (Berkeley and Los Angeles: University of California Press, 1968), 45–53; *Permanence and Change*, 3d ed. (Berkeley and Los Angeles: University of California Press, 1984), 167–272; and *The Philosophy of Literary Form: Studies in Symbolic Action*, 2d ed. (Baton Rouge: Louisiana State University Press, 1967), 116–32. The evolutionary ingredient in Havelock's thought is seen best in *The Liberal Temper in Greek Politics* (New Haven: Yale University Press, 1957).

9. Desmond Morris, *Biology of Art: A Study of the Picture-Making Behaviour of the Great Apes and Its Relationship to Human Art* (London: Methuen, 1962).

10. *The Liberal Temper in Greek Politics* (n. 8 above), 30. Havelock's brilliant reconstruction of the rhetorical thinkers whom Plato sought so successfully to discredit is developed, at times, in frankly evolutionary terms. The connection between pre-Socratic and post-Wilsonian behavioral biology is a fascinating one to make for anyone interested in the history and theory of rhetoric.

11. Marshall McLuhan, *Understanding Media: The Extensions of Man* (New York: McGraw Hill paperback, 1965), 193. Perhaps Philip Marchand's evenhanded survey of McLuhan's life and work, *Marshall McLuhan: The Medium and the Messenger* (New York: Ticknor and Fields, 1989), will dispel the critical disdain that has clouded his work for the last thirty years. Like the Italian Futurists before him, McLuhan was talking about a digital technology that had not yet manifested its central aesthetic, the aesthetic he sought to describe. Unlike the Futurists, McLuhan viewed electronic technology against its natural his-

torical ground—classical rhetoric. Anyone wishing to follow the initial McLuhan controversy can begin with Raymond Rosenthal's handy collection, *McLuhan: Pro and Con* (Baltimore: Penguin, 1969).

12. Well chronicled, albeit under another name, in yet another landmark of rhetorical scholarship from this period, Jonas Barish's *The Antitheatrical Prejudice* (Berkeley and Los Angeles: University of California Press, 1981).

13. Richard D. Alexander, "The Search for a General Theory of Behavior," *Behavioral Science* 20 (1975): 77–100. Alexander had also discussed the dangers of ignoring the evolutionary perspective, and the leftover behavioral baggage that it allows us for the first time to understand, in a strongly argued earlier paper, "The Search for an Evolutionary Philosophy of Man," *Proceedings of the Royal Society of Victoria* 84 (1971): 99–119.

14. *The Liberal Temper in Greek Politics* (n. 8 above), 19.

15. Donald N. McCloskey, *The Rhetoric of Economics* (Madison: University of Wisconsin Press, 1985). McCloskey has extended his arguments to narrative in a second, equally entertaining, book, *If You're So Smart: The Narrative of Economic Expertise* (Chicago: University of Chicago Press, 1990).

16. *The Rhetoric of the Human Sciences: Language and Argument in Scholarship and Public Affairs*, ed. John S. Nelson, Allan Megill, and Donald N. McCloskey (Madison: University of Wisconsin Press, 1987).

17. Gunther S. Stent's edition of James Watson, *The Double Helix* (New York: Norton, 1980) includes a great deal of material about the nature of the discovery and the reception of the book, and reprints selected reviews. The book was first published in 1968, by Atheneum.

18. Francis Crick's attempt, as a now-senior statesman, to set the record straight on how one does science, *What Mad Pursuit: A Personal View of Scientific Discovery* (New York: Basic Books, 1988), does not manage to be so entertaining or true to life as his partner's lighthearted chronicle of years before. For a magisterial survey of the arena in which Watson and Crick played their roles, see Horace Freeland Judson, *The Eighth Day of Creation: Makers of the Revolution in Biology* (New York: Simon and Schuster, 1979).

19. Susan Allport, *Explorers of the Black Box: The Search for the Cellular Basis of Memory* (New York: Norton, 1986).

20. Gary Taubes, *Nobel Dreams: Power, Deceit and the Ultimate Experiment* (Redmond, Wash.: Microsoft Press, 1986).

21. Robert Kanigel, *Apprentice to Genius: The Making of a Scientific Dynasty* (New York: Macmillan, 1986).

22. Derek Freeman, *Margaret Mead and Samoa: The Making and Unmaking of an Anthropological Myth* (Cambridge: Harvard University Press, 1983).

23. See the *Chronicle of Higher Education*, 2 Aug. 1989, A5–6.

24. Bruno Latour, *Science in Action: How to Follow Scientists and Engineers through Society* (Milton Keynes, England: Open University Press; Cambridge: Harvard University Press, 1987).

25. James Gleick, *Chaos: Making a New Science* (New York: Viking, 1987).

26. Some literary instances of this analogy have been worked out by N. Katherine Hayles in *Chaos Bound: Orderly Disorder in Contemporary Literature and Science* (Ithaca: Cornell University Press, 1990).

27. The basic opposition is explained with great ease and clarity—albeit with a grudging and unwilling hand when discussing the rhetoricians—by H. I. Marrou in *A History of Education in Antiquity*, trans. George Lamb (1956; reprint, Madison: University of Wisconsin Press, 1982). It is expanded into the Renaissance in Jerrold E. Seigel's *Rhetoric and Philosophy in Renaissance Humanism: The Union of Eloquence and Wisdom, Petrarch to Valla* (Princeton: Princeton University Press, 1968). The historical development from classical to modern times is surveyed in Bruce A. Kimball's *Orators and Philosophers: A History of the Idea of Liberal Education* (New York: Teachers College Press, 1986).

28. Gleick, *Chaos* (n. 25 above), 102.

29. Ibid., 116–18.

30. Charles Jencks, *Post-Modernism: The New Classicism in Art and Architecture* (New York: Rizzoli, 1987).

31. Charles Jencks, *The Language of Post-Modern Architecture*, 4th ed., rev. and enl. (New York: Rizzoli, 1984).

32. Ibid., 50.

33. Robert Venturi, Denise Scott Brown, and Steven Izenour, *Learning from Las Vegas: The Forgotten Symbolism of Architectural Form*, rev. ed. (Cambridge: MIT Press, 1977). Venturi's full repudiation of Platonic aesthetics in favor of rhetorical analysis is contained in his now classic *Complexity and Contradiction in Architecture*, 2d ed. (New York: Museum of Modern Art, 1977).

34. "One of the most convincing historicist buildings of the fifties was Paolo Portoghesi's Casa Baldi, 1959–61, an essay in free-form curves definitely reminiscent of the Borromini he was studying, yet also unmistakably influenced by Le Corbusier. Here is the schizophrenic cross between two codes that is characteristic of Post-Modernism: the enveloping, sweeping curves of the Baroque, the overlap of space, the various foci of space interfering with each other *and* the Brutalist treatment, the expression of concrete block, rugged joinery and the guitar-shapes of modernism." Jencks, *Language* (n. 31 above), 81–82.

35. In 1981, the *Stanford Law Review* devoted a very substantial issue to the critical legal studies movement. Mark Kelman's *A Guide to Critical Legal Studies* (Cambridge: Harvard University Press, 1987) is reviewed at length by John Stick in the *Columbia Law Review* 88, no. 2 (March 1988): 407–32. Roberto Unger's *The Critical Legal Studies Movement* (Cambridge: Harvard University

Press, 1986) is subjected to rhetorical scrutiny by Stanley Fish in "Unger and Milton," *Duke Law Journal* 88, no. 5 (Nov. 1988): 975–1012. Laura Kalman, in *Legal Realism at Yale: 1927–1960* (Chapel Hill: University of North Carolina Press, 1986), has pushed the discussion back one generation by describing the struggle between the "scientific" study of law advocated by the founding dean of the Harvard Law School, Christopher Columbus Langdell, and the "realistic" study advocated by Jerome Frank's pioneering *Law and the Modern Mind* (New York: Coward-McCann, 1930). Langdell, who hated live interaction, whether in classroom or court, argued for two principles: (1) law is a science; (2) "all the available materials of that science are contained in printed books" (11). Against this print-based scientism, Frank argued that principles were often, in the actual practice of law, accompanied by other intuitive factors. Frank was willing to admit rhetoric into the courtroom and class; Langdell, like many before him, would have liked to abolish not only rhetoric but the classroom and court domains where it has always been practiced.

36. For a fuller discussion of "hard" and "soft" defenses in rhetoric, see chapter 7, "The 'Q' Question."

37. Michael Sean Quinn, "Closing Arguments in Insurance Fraud Cases," *Tort and Insurance Law Journal* 23, no. 4 (Summer 1988): 744–811.

38. Ibid., 749. Quinn's footnote here is revealing about the influence of Burkean dramatism. He cites, among others, W. Bennett and M. Feldman, *Reconstructing Reality in the Courtroom* (New Brunswick: Rutgers University Press, 1981); Call, "Trial Story Analysis," *Texas Bar Journal* 50 (1987): 970ff.; and Milner S. Ball, "The Play's the Thing: An Unscientific Reflection on Courts Under the Rubric of Theater," *Stanford Law Review* 28 (1975): 81ff.

39. Peter F. Drucker, *The New Realities* (New York: Harper and Row, 1989), 229.

40. Three exemplary models, on the level of industry, company, and product: (1) John P. Hoerr's *And the Wolf Finally Came: The Decline of the American Steel Industry* (Pittsburgh: University of Pittsburgh Press, 1988) studies in detail the difficulties of moving from a culture based on confrontational rhetoric to one based on cooperative rhetoric. It is an anatomy of what happens when the process Drucker describes *fails to happen*. Hoerr grew up in the Monongahela Valley, the "Mon Valley" of the Pittsburgh steel industry, and he feels the tale he tells as the destruction of his homeland. (2) In *The Big Store: Inside the Crisis and Revolution at Sears* (New York: Viking, 1987), Donald R. Katz tells, with great sensitivity to feeling, emotion, and prose style, the story of the perturbations at Sears since 1979. It is an extraordinary story of what happens to vast enterprises when their managers lack the kind of judgment, the acute, toggling, bi-stable vision, that Drucker recommends. Very interestingly for the rhetorician's purposes, the movement at Sears was countercultural to that of American industry as a whole. It had always been a "Theory X" company and

had to become, was forced to become, a "Theory Y" company. The conversion, as of this writing, continues to be a not-yet-fatal failure. (3) The study by Douglas K. Smith and Robert C. Alexander, *Fumbling the Future: How Xerox Invented, Then Ignored, the First Personal Computer* (New York: Morrow, 1988), deserves a detailed rhetorical scrutiny perhaps more than the previous two books because the product involved embodied a revolutionary informational technique, the very personal computer that has—to bring the matter near to home— occasioned this essay. The failure chronicled was, finally, a failure to see how a technological device might be socialized, a failure to perceive the *rhetorical* essence in what looked like a standard Turing *logic machine*, only in a smaller box.

41. Huizinga's foreword to *Homo Ludens* is dated 1938, but the book was published first (in German) in Switzerland in 1944; first English edition 1949. For a retrospective of his work, see E. H. Gombrich, "Huizinga and *Homo ludens*," *Times Literary Supplement*, 4 Oct. 1974, 1083–89.

42. Johan Huizinga, *Homo Ludens: A Study of the Play-Element in Culture* (Boston: Beacon, 1955), 6.

43. Roger Caillois, *Les Jeux et les Hommes: Le masque et le vertige*, rev. ed. (Paris: Gallimard, 1958); trans. Meyer Barash, *Man, Play, and Games* (London: Thames and Hudson, 1962).

44. David L. Miller, *Gods and Games: Toward a Theology of Play* (New York: World, 1970).

45. It is elaborated in several different ways throughout the essays in Bateson's *Steps to an Ecology of Mind* (New York: Ballantine, 1972).

46. Clifford Geertz, "Deep Play: Notes on the Balinese Cockfight," in *The Interpretation of Cultures* (New York: Basic Books, 1973), 412–53.

47. Alan Dundes and Alessandro Falassi, *La Terra in Piazza: An Interpretation of the Palio of Siena* (Berkeley and Los Angeles: University of California Press, 1975).

48. See, for example, "Thick Description: Toward an Interpretive Theory of Culture," in *The Interpretation of Cultures* (n. 46 above), 3–30.

49. Richard A. Lanham, *The Motives of Eloquence: Literary Rhetoric in the Renaissance* (New Haven: Yale University Press, 1976), chapter 1, "The Rhetorical Ideal of Life."

50. Richard Sennett has illuminated this interface very suggestively in *The Fall of Public Man* (New York: Random House, Vintage, 1974); he describes eighteenth-century European culture as essentially dramatistic and rhetorical, and nineteenth-century culture as essentially serious and purposive. His analysis of dress codes in the grip of such a pervasive figure/ground oscillation is especially apt to our discussion here.

51. As a sampler of such efforts, see "Games, Play, Literature," *Yale French*

Studies no. 41 (Dec. 1968), ed. Jacques Ehrmann. One of the best literary studies from this point of view is Michel Beaujour's *Le Jeu de Rabelais* ([Paris:] L'Herne, 1969). V. A. Kolve has used this range of thinking in *The Play Called Corpus Christi* (Stanford: Stanford University Press, 1966), and Martin Stevens has developed an illuminating argument based upon it in "Laughter and Game in *Sir Gawain and the Green Knight*," *Speculum* 47 (1972): 65–78. I argue in *The Motives of Eloquence* (n. 49 above) that an oscillation between a rhetorical and a serious, a ludic and a purposeful, conception of human life lies at the stylistic and structural center of Western literature. And I develop game theory in its mathematical form as a critical tool in *"Tristram Shandy": The Games of Pleasure* (Berkeley and Los Angeles: University of California Press, 1973).

52. For a start, see Morton D. Davis, *Game Theory: A Nontechnical Introduction*, rev. ed. (New York: Basic Books, 1970). Anatol Rapoport has written two general introductions: *Fights, Games, and Debates* (Ann Arbor: University of Michigan Press, 1960) and *Two-Person Game Theory: The Essential Ideas* (Ann Arbor: University of Michigan Press, 1966). See also R. D. Luce and H. Raiffa, *Games and Decisions: Introduction and Critical Survey* (New York: Wiley, 1957); "Games and Decisions," part 3 of *Mathematical Thinking in Behavioral Sciences: Readings from "Scientific American,"* ed. David M. Messick (San Francisco: W. H. Freeman, 1968), 83–106; Martin Shubik, *Game Theory in the Social Sciences: Concepts and Solutions* (Cambridge: MIT Press, 1982).

53. Robert Axelrod, *The Evolution of Cooperation* (New York: Basic Books, 1984). Douglas Hofstadter's jacket comment rightly calls it "a fascinating, provocative, and important book."

54. Computer simulation goes back further than the roughly twenty-year period I am trying to survey. See, for example, Martin Shubik and Garry D. Brewer, *Reviews of Selected Books and Articles on Gaming and Simulation*, RAND Corporation Report R-732 -ARPA (Santa Monica, Calif.: RAND, 1972).

55. Walter J. Ong, *Orality and Literacy: The Technologizing of the Word* (London and New York: Methuen, 1982). Eric Havelock, in his last book, *The Muse Learns to Write: Reflections on Orality and Literacy from Antiquity to the Present* (New Haven: Yale University Press, 1986), 25, argues that the modern conversation on this point came into focus in 1963, at just about the beginning of the period we are considering: "Within the span of twelve months or less, from some time in 1962 to the spring of 1963, in three different countries—France, Britain, and the United States—there issued from the printing presses five publications by five authors who at the time when they wrote could not have been aware of any mutual relationship. The works in question were *La Pensée Sauvage* (Lévi-Strauss), "The Consequences of Literacy" (Goody and Watt, an extended article), *The Gutenberg Galaxy* (McLuhan), *Animal Species and Evolution* (Mayr), and *Preface to Plato* (Havelock)." Havelock's earlier *The Liberal Temper in Greek Politics* (1957), especially its stunning first and last chapters, had really set the stage for the whole later debate.

56. Ong, *Orality and Literacy* (n. 55 above), 68.

57. Robert Pattison, *On Literacy: The Politics of the Word from Homer to the Age of Rock* (New York: Oxford University Press, 1982), 41. Others have disputed the "technological determinism" of Havelock and Ong. See, for example, Sylvia Scribner and Michael Cole, *The Psychology of Literacy* (Cambridge: Harvard University Press, 1981).

58. A version of this polarity can be found in Jane Healy's *Endangered Minds: Why Our Children Don't Think* (New York: Simon and Schuster, Touchstone, 1990), which I discuss in detail in chapter 9.

59. "In particular, the hard dying hope that there can again be (assuming there ever was) an integrated high culture, anchored in the educated classes and setting a general intellectual norm for the society as a whole, has to be abandoned in favor of the much more modest sort of ambition that scholars, artists, scientists, professionals, and (dare we hope?) administrators who are radically different, not just in their opinions, or even in their passions, but in the very foundations of their experience, can begin to find something circumstantial to say to one another again. ... All we can hope for, which if it were to happen would be that rarest of phenomena, a *useful* miracle, is that we can devise ways to gain access to one another's vocational lives." Clifford Geertz, *Local Knowledge: Further Essays in Interpretive Anthropology* (New York: Basic Books, 1983), 160.

60. The "Lorenz attractor" is named after Edward Lorenz, whose pioneering work on the impossibility of long-range weather forecasting is generally thought to have begun modern thinking about nonlinear, "chaotic" systems. When Lorenz plotted the data from his initial observations, they drew a butterfly-shaped double spiral which never repeated itself but always stayed within certain bounds. See Gleick, *Chaos* (n. 25 above), 11–31, esp. the illustration on 28.

61. For a penetrating analysis of just what that Greek debate really was about, see G. B. Kerferd, *The Sophistic Movement* (Cambridge: Cambridge University Press, 1981).

62. William G. Ouchi reflects this attempt directly in the title for his study of Japanese management: *Theory Z: How American Business Can Meet the Japanese Challenge* (Reading, Mass.: Addison-Wesley, 1981).

63. For a discussion of the digital computer as a "Turing logic machine," see Andrew Hodges' *Alan Turing: The Enigma* (New York: Simon and Schuster, 1983). Hodges combines a clear and detailed explanation of Turing's work with a sensitive reconstruction of his life. Hodges tells the birth-of-the-computer story from the English point of view; the American story (von Neumann as hero as against Turing) is recounted in Herman H. Goldstine's *The Computer from Pascal to von Neumann* (Princeton: Princeton University Press, 1972). J. David Bolter, *Turing's Man: Western Culture in the Computer Age* (Chapel Hill: Uni-

versity of North Carolina Press, 1984), discusses the cultural and philosophical implications of the electronic logic machine Turing invented. The limitations of electronic logic have been mapped by Hubert L. Dreyfus's satirical history of artificial intelligence, *What Computers Can't Do: The Limits of Artificial Intelligence* (1972; rev. ed., New York: Harper and Row, 1979). (The introduction to the revised edition, which describes the reception of the first edition by the AI community, ought not be missed.) Dreyfus expands his discussion of computer use into management and teaching in *Mind Over Machine: The Power of Human Intuition and Expertise in the Era of the Computer*, with Stuart E. Dreyfus (New York: Free Press, 1986). First Amendment issues of freedom of access presented by electronic technologies are discussed in a detailed and balanced way in Ithiel de Sola Pool's *Technologies of Freedom* (Cambridge: Harvard University Press, 1983). A good general introduction to the digital revolution is Stewart Brand's *The Media Lab: Inventing the Future at MIT* (New York: Viking, 1987). Michael Heim has focused some of the philosophical issues in *Electric Language: A Philosophical Study of Word Processing* (New Haven: Yale University Press, 1987). K. Eric Drexler's *Engines of Creation* (New York: Anchor, 1987), considers digital technology on both microatomic and macrosocial levels in an attempt to look into at least the middle future. The birth and growth of the computer industry has evoked a number of histories and analyses, starting with Ted Nelson's *Computer Lib/Dream Machines* (Redmond, Wash.: Microsoft Press, 1974; rev. ed. 1987), which picks up again the typographical manipulations pioneered by the Italian Futurists at the beginning of the century. Nelson has continued his discussion of electronic text, and described his prophetic "Xanadu" project, in *Literary Machines* (Sausalito, Calif.: Mindful Press, 1990). By far the best of the American computer chronicles is Steven Levy's *Hackers: Heroes of the Computer Revolution* (Garden City, N.Y.: Anchor Press/Doubleday, 1984). The genesis of the computer in the domain of game and play has never been better described than here. The more existential angst that also inhabits this domain comes to the fore in Tracy Kidder's *The Soul of a New Machine* (Boston: Little, Brown, 1981). George Gilder's *Microcosm: The Quantum Revolution in Economics and Technology* (New York: Simon and Schuster, 1989) describes the great scale-change in economic thinking brought on by silicon technology.

From time to time in these essays, I discuss the computer as creating a new kind of drama. Brenda Laurel's *Computers as Theatre* (Reading, Mass.: Addison-Wesley, 1991) develops this argument in a different way, arguing for the computer screen as an essentially theatrical experience in itself. The next step from the computer as drama leads to what is now called "virtual reality," which allows the viewer to enter an actual electronic three-dimensional space and act in it. Myron W. Krueger has updated his pioneering discussion of this phenomenon in *Artificial Reality II* (Reading, Mass.: Addison-Wesley, 1991). The best general introduction to the current state of play is Howard Rheingold's

Virtual Reality (New York: Summit, 1991). From virtual reality, the next step is to artificial life created through digital information flowing in silicon; Steven Levy's new *Artificial Life: The Quest for a New Creation* (New York: Pantheon, 1992) tells this story from the beginnings.

Two recent books have cast an interesting light on one sociobiological aspect of computer communication: the territorial aspect of networked digital information. Clifford Stoll's *The Cuckoo's Egg* (New York: Doubleday, 1989) tracks a now-famous case of network espionage; Katie Hafner and John Markoff's *Cyberpunk: Outlaws and Hackers on the Computer Frontier* (New York: Simon and Schuster, 1991) describes the attempts of several "peripheral males" to penetrate, via computer hacking, the heartland territory controlled by their elders. Both books are about how computers, which annihilate territory, create what are in effect territorial disputes about information.

64. The basic manifestos of Futurism have been handily collected by Luciano De Maria in *Marinetti e il Futurismo* (Milan: Mondadori, 1973). Marianne W. Martin has studied the period in *Futurist Art and Theory, 1909–1915* (New York: Hacker, 1978). The splendid catalogue of the Venice exhibition "Futurismo & Futurismi," organized by Pontus Hulten, is now the place to begin in illustrating the period (New York: Abbeville, 1983).

65. Crick, *What Mad Pursuit* (n. 18 above), 156.

66. Edward O. Wilson, *Biophilia* (Cambridge: Harvard University Press, 1984), 60.

67. Shirley C. Strum, *Almost Human: A Journey into the World of Baboons* (New York: Random House, 1987), 106.

68. The locus classicus here is Beatrice Warde's *The Crystal Goblet: Sixteen Essays on Typography*, ed. Henry Jacob (London: Sylvan, 1955).

69. Burke, *Counter-Statement* (n. 8 above), 209.

70. Hypertext is a nonlinear means of electronic expression in which the textual surface is given a third dimension by embedding further kinds of information beneath the surface. A changing symbol or typeface lets the reader know that a hypertext is concealed beneath that text. And of course there are texts behind those texts. The reader's path through such interreferentiality soon becomes totally nonlinear and, if not totally unpredictable, certainly "chaotic."

71. Rudolf Arnheim, *Visual Thinking* (Berkeley and Los Angeles: University of California Press, 1969), 243–44.

72. I don't come by this quotation from Susanne Langer's *Philosophy in a New Key* honestly; Stewart Brand quotes a report from the MIT Architecture Machine Group (the forebear of the Media Lab) which quotes the passage, in *The Media Lab* (n. 63 above), 140.

73. Michael Baxandall, *Giotto and the Orators: Humanist Observers of Painting in Italy and the Discovery of Pictorial Composition, 1350–1450* (Oxford: Clarendon Press, 1971).

74. I discuss this reconstruction briefly in chapter 1, and again in chapter 8.

75. Walter J. Ong, *Rhetoric, Romance, and Technology: Studies in the Interaction of Expression and Culture* (Ithaca: Cornell University Press, 1971), 53.

76. See Carol Dana Lanham, "Freshman Composition in the Early Middle Ages: Epistolography and Rhetoric before the *Ars dictaminis*," *Viator* 23 (1992): 115–34.

77. See *Computers and Community: Teaching Composition in the Twenty-first Century*, ed. Carolyn Handa (Portsmouth, N.H.: Boynton/Cook, 1990). John M. Slatin has explored the pedagogical implications of teaching hypertexts in two suggestive papers: "Hypertext and the Teaching of Writing," in *Text, Context, and Hypertext: Writing with and for the Computer*, ed. Edward Barrett (Cambridge: MIT Press, 1988), 111–29, and "Toward a Rhetoric for Hypertext" (Paper delivered at Hypermedia '88, Houston, Sept. 1988). Myron Tuman takes issue with both Handa and Slatin in *Word Perfect: Literacy in the Computer Age* (London: Falmer, 1992). I discuss Tuman's work in chapter 9.

78. Aristotle, *Rhetorica,* trans. W. Rhys Roberts (Oxford: Oxford University Press, 1959), 1408b.

79. Quintilian, *Institutio oratoria*, trans. H. E. Butler, 4 vols. (Cambridge: Harvard University Press, Loeb Classical Library, 1921), 8.3.58.

80. [Cicero], *Ad C. Herennium*, trans. Harry Caplan (Cambridge: Harvard University Press, Loeb Classical Library, 1954), 4.10.15.

81. Plutarch, "The Education of Children,"*Moralia*, vol. 1, trans. Frank Cole Babbitt (Cambridge: Harvard University Press, Loeb Classical Library, 1927), 7.A-B.

82. "For art is only perfect when it looks like nature and Nature succeeds only by concealing art about her person." Longinus, *On the Sublime*, trans. W. Hamilton Fyfe (Cambridge: Harvard University Press, Loeb Classical Library, 1965), 22.1.

83. Charles Horton Cooley, *Life and the Student* (New York: Knopf, 1927), 103.

84. Augustine, *On Christian Doctrine*, trans. D. W. Robertson, Jr. (Indianapolis: Bobbs-Merrill, Library of Liberal Arts, 1958), 120. The modern philosopher Michael Polanyi has developed this point into a theory of knowledge in *Personal Knowledge: Towards a Post-Critical Philosophy* (1958; New York: Harper and Row, Torchbook, 1964). Thus he argues for the centrality of touchstones: "Connoisseurship, like skill, can be communicated only by example, not by precept" (54).

85. I discuss an earlier version of this spectrum in *"At* and *Through:* The Opaque Style and Its Uses," in *Literacy and the Survival of Humanism* (New Haven: Yale University Press, 1983), 58–86.

86. This argument is a central thesis in Morse Peckham's landmark study,

Man's Rage for Chaos: Biology, Behavior, and the Arts (Philadelphia: Chilton, 1965).

87. E. H. Gombrich, *Art and Illusion: A Study in the Psychology of Pictorial Representation*, 2d ed., Bollingen Series 5 (New York: Pantheon, 1961), figs. 247–48; and see index s.v. Constable, *Wivenhoe Park*.

88. The Universal Studios tour in Los Angeles uses exactly this strategy: it shows you how the trick works and then plays it on you and scares the dickens out of you anyway. You know it is a trick and yet it seems totally real.

89. I have illustrated this point from a variety of classical and Renaissance texts in *The Motives of Eloquence* (n. 49 above).

90. Sahlins poses and answers the question in *Culture and Practical Reason* (Chicago: University of Chicago Press, 1976).

91. See chapter 7 for a fuller discussion of this "Q" question.

92. See George H. Mead, *Mind, Self, and Society* (1934), ed. with intro. by Charles W. Morris (Chicago: University of Chicago Press, 1962).

93. George Steiner, *In Bluebeard's Castle: Some Notes towards the Redefinition of Culture* (New Haven: Yale University Press, 1971), 71.

94. "The life of the law has not been logic; it has been experience. The felt necessities of the time, the prevalent moral and political theories, institutions of public policy, avowed or unconscious, even the prejudices which judges share with their fellow men, have had a good deal more to do than the syllogism in determining the rules by which men should be governed." Oliver Wendell Holmes, quoted in Sheldon M. Novick's *Honorable Justice: The Life of Oliver Wendell Holmes* (Boston: Little, Brown, 1989), 158.

4

The 1988 Duke conference at which I delivered the first version of this paper was described by its appointed summationer as a "pep rally for the New Left." It certainly felt like that. Lynne Cheney, then director of the National Endowment for the Humanities and self-appointed leader of the humanities' New Right, sent advance copies of her report on the state of the humanities in America[1] to the conference participants, as if firing a warning shot across the enemy's bow. Several of us read the report and returned her fire in our presentations.

My paper was supposed to supply the keynote, but I don't think it did so. It didn't fit the race/gender/class political agenda. Defining the "Great Books" debate in terms of Left and Right proved too much fun for both sides for either to notice the obsolescence of that confrontation. As I have argued in the preceding essays, the real change we must confront and understand is not a new selection of canonical great books but, as our expressive radical moves from print to screen, a new conception of human reason and how Western culture creates and transmits it. There are political implications aplenty in such a switch, but they don't emerge from debates between "Westerns" and "Western culture."

It has been discouraging to watch the profound disinclination of the "theory world" to acknowledge its rhetorical roots and branches. Perhaps any new academic movement in a competitive intellectual bureaucracy must exaggerate its newness to inspirit its adherents. But in this case, the failure to recognize the return of the rhetorical paideia for what it is has led to a needless "foundationalist" debate. We could

clarify this debate by returning, ad fontes, to that ancient quarrel between the philoso-
phers and the rhetoricians which we are now reincarnating.

Equally discouraging have been the efforts to defend the codex book as the bas-
tion of Western culture, as if defending the wrapper would protect what is in the box.
In 1977, Congress established the Library of Congress Center for the Book, and the
Modern Language Association of America has embraced the subsequent yearly rally-
themes, such as "Explore New Worlds—Read," our motto for 1992. I'm not quarrel-
ing with these pious exhortations. I wish people would read more; it is good and good
for them, and besides that, it makes them more like me, an addictive reader all my
life. But these efforts to galvanize the codex book in the face of encroaching electron-
ic expression miss the two basic points that should underlie such a campaign.

The first is the "Q" question, which I consider in chapter 7. Before we fix on the
*book as the center of humanistic culture, shouldn't we have a better idea of **what***
***books do to and for us**? This is, after all, the fundamental issue confronting human-*
istic inquiry today. We should worry about what is in the box. Then we can better
answer the second vital question: Having decided what we want to protect, how do
we make sure it survives the movement from book to screen? Books will endure for a
long time but, as we shall find several scholars arguing in chapters 8 and 9, a power-
*ful tide is carrying us from printed to electronic expression. To defend the book **just***
***for the form of the codex book** is to focus on the box and not the contents. America*
does not lack, after all, for examples of industries and bureaucracies that have trained

themselves around a particular technology and perished with it. Why should the Amer-
ican academy share this fate? If we fail to understand the expressive environment of
our time, we will have failed in our duty as transmitters of culture, whether we think
the culture to be preserved consists of Dead White Males or Live Female Revolution-
aries of Color.

*I continue to think that it is the **convergence** of technology, the arts and letters,*
and the democratizing of higher education that poses our paramount cultural and
*educational **explanandum**. I don't think this convergence either can or should be*
politicized into the current Left and Right. Its political implications run much deep-
er than this, and neither side seems predisposed to think much about them.

My interest in the lower-division curriculum began in 1952 when, as a naive
sixteen-year-old Ford Foundation Scholar, I entered the Directed Studies Program
at Yale. It hit me so hard I never got over it, and I have spent more years than I want
to reckon trying to recreate for my own students the magic that I found there. Some
of those years were the ones I spent as director of the UCLA Writing Programs, and
it was there that I hoped to create the curriculum I describe at the end of this essay.
Alas, it was not to be.

The Extraordinary Convergence:

Democracy, Technology, Theory,

and the University Curriculum

n a mid-September weekend in 1988, a number of scholars met at Duke University and the University of North
Carolina, Chapel Hill, for another session of the oldest
class in American education, the Seminar on the Future
of the Liberal Arts. Our class had, over the decades, fea-
tured many distinguished seminarians but a repetitive syl-
labus: Does the center of liberal education lie in methods or texts? If methods, intuitive or empirical? If texts, ancient or modern? In an age of
specialization, how specialized should liberal education be? Should it have
a core curriculum common to everyone and, if so, what kind? How democratic can liberal education become without trivializing itself? What, if anything, is a liberal education good for? And why, if we have such a dynamite
product, is it often so hard to sell?

This discussion began (if matters so deep can be said to begin) with the
Yale Faculty Report of 1828.[2] President Jeremiah Day and his colleagues
addressed all these issues, and their answers don't differ much from ours.
They argued that students should know a lot, as Professor Hirsch has recommended,[3] and that they should think a lot, as the Association of American Colleges panel has urged.[4] President Day's group stressed the final
responsibility of each student for his own education, as did a subsequent
Yale panel in 1972.[5] Day's committee argued that a liberal education should
not be specialized or preprofessional but broad and humane, and these
expansive sentiments have found echo in the Rockefeller Commission's
Report of 1980, where we read that "the essence of the humanities is a spirit or an attitude toward humanity."[6] The 1828 group argued that a core curriculum is essential; so have many since, from John Erskine's Great Books
course at Columbia after World War I and its descendants at Chicago, Yale,
and elsewhere, to recent pronouncements by ex-Education Secretary William
Bennett and the *Wall Street Journal.* And just as Yale in 1828 thought the
proper time to move students from general education into their favorite spe-

cial subject was the junior year,[7] so do we. Like us, they were concerned to democratize access to higher education, and they sought to achieve this goal, as do we, by raising admissions standards. And of course they debated the canon, their Ancients and Moderns differing in language, but not in argument, from ours.

The curricular historian Frederick Rudolph has some harsh words for the 1828 patriarchs: "They embraced the uses of the past, but they withdrew from the uncertainties of the future. ...Their respect for quality, for standards, for certain enduring definitions of human worth, was class bound. They were blinded to much that was insistent and already out of control in American life."[8] Just so. But here we were debating the same issues 160 years later. Why hadn't we found some answers? Had nothing changed in this endless debate?

I think three things have changed. Three new conditions, or clusters of conditions, have emerged—social, technological, and theoretical—and their convergence suggests a new kind of "core" for the liberal arts.

The social pressures are the easiest to summarize. First, the radical democratization of higher learning. In the early nineteenth century only one or two in a hundred Americans attended college, and they were almost all male, white, leisure-class, native English speakers; now half do, and they are often none of these. This change has been a gradual one but the quantitative change has now become a qualitative one. American minorities hitherto excluded from higher education have demanded access to it, and a new influx of immigrants has joined them. The immigrants who created modern America came in successive waves that left time for assimilation, and they came into an agrarian and then into an industrial society. Today's immigrants come from dozens of cultures and languages all at once, and into an information society that rewards linguistic competence more than willing hands. Over 600,000 immigrants came to this country in 1987—probably more than to all the other countries in the world put together.[9] And we have more in prospect: "In industrial countries the population is growing slowly and aging rapidly; in developing countries—China excepted—the population is growing fast enough to double in less than a generation, and 40% of the people are under age 15."[10] If we want to use that youthful energy, large-scale immigration and the linguistic and cultural adjustments it brings with it will be with us for a long time to come.

Liberal arts education has been built on the word, and in America on the English word as spoken by middle-class, white, native speakers. We have thought of ourselves, up to now, as a monolingual country and have always, after each wave of immigration, become one again—notoriously so, in fact.

That monolingualism has now been destabilized. We will have to rethink our entire enterprise. If we grow into bilingualism—English and Spanish— as well we may, that will present its own particular problems in the university, as it has for some time done in the schools. It may also present its own unique opportunities, as Greek and Latin once did working against one another in classical culture. If you want a numerical marker for this change, here's one from the place where I earn my living: for several years now, undergraduate enrollment in the University of California at Berkeley and at Los Angeles has been more than 50 percent nonwhite.

To this situation, add a further development. These new immigration patterns, permitting for the first time substantial numbers of entrants from non-Western lands, have brought to America a new citizenry for whom the "Western tradition" that informs our traditional humanities curriculum is alien. Judeo-Christian culture stands now subject to a polite but puzzled reappraisal. And other, very different reappraisals of the liberal arts are being made from very different points of view by women and by blacks.

This linguistic and cultural revolution will force an answer to a major question that has been on our agenda since 1828: How can we democratize the liberal arts without trivializing them? Up to now, our answer has been the 1828 Yale answer: don't really democratize them; it can't be done; proceed as we always have—what else can we do, eternal verities being our principal product?—and let all these "nontraditional" students learn our ways as best they can. Political and economic pressures have now become too insistent for this. We are required to find really new ways to widen access to the liberal arts without trivializing them. Digital technology and rhetorical theory offer the new ways we need.

The second social pressure is for systematic public accountability. Since government, whether federal, state, or local, pays for much of our labors and those of our students, it demands an accountability that Arnoldian sweetness and light were not formerly asked to supply. And students in the private sector have become more discriminating—or at least more price-conscious—consumers of educational services as well. We face now a genuinely new, more searching and quantitative, invigilation. We claim to teach culture, civic virtue, and advanced symbolic processing. When asked to prove it, we have always begged the question: of course we are vitally important, even though, since we do what we do "for its own sake," we can't tell you why. But the issue is now being forced. George Steiner has been pressing it for years, to our stifled embarrassment, juxtaposing the pretensions of Western culture to the hundred million people that same culture has slaughtered in the twentieth century. And now the government, with less elegance and learning, is asking the same question: If the liberal arts do supply these need-ful qualities, as you claim, let's have some proof; show us some statistics. If we can't or won't comply, then resources now given to us will be allocated elsewhere.

The liberal arts, like higher education as a whole, have operated hereto-fore on our version of the "General Motors rule" ("What's good for Gener-al Motors is good for the country"). What's good for the arts must be good for the country. To doubt this only proves you a Philistine. Now we are asked, shocking though it be, to do some cost accounting. We shouldn't be surprised at this. Every other sector of American professional life is being held accountable in new and detailed ways for its practices. Why not us? With our customary GM complacency and with a conception of costs that would disgrace a child's lemonade stand, we will find this required account-ing more than an incidental bureaucratic aggravation. It will force us to rethink the heart of our enterprise, to provide at last a straight answer to another vital question we have been dodging since 1828: What are the lib-eral arts good for?

Third, educational sequence. Students now often come older to the uni-versity, attend in broken times often more than one institution, and take more than four years to graduate; more of them work, and work more. This fragmented, discontinuous pattern is now more norm than exception. To it we may add the conceptual dislocations they feel hourly as they change class-es from one disciplinary universe to another. Yet our thinking about the undergraduate curriculum continues to assume the four-year, upper- and lower-division, linear sequence and ignores the conceptual bewilderment it imposes on students. This assumption, as we shall see, blinds us to the only kind of core curriculum—a third key item left over from the 1828 agenda—that is possible today.

None of these social pressures—democratization, accountability, or edu-cational sequence—is unprecedented, but surely we must reckon their inten-sity and combined force as something really new. The second emergent con-dition I'll consider, the pressures of electronic digital technology on the liberal arts, is in itself truly a new thing under the sun.

◻   ◻   ◻

Imagine a student brought up on computers interacting with the volatile text I've described in earlier chapters. She is used to moving it around, play-ing games with it, illustrating and animating it. Now let her follow Arnold's advice and sift a dubious classic like, say, *Love's Labor's Lost*. Imagine her charting the rhetorical figures, displaying them in a special type, diagramming and cataloguing them, and then making hypertext animations of how they work. She'll use another program now on the market to make her own production, plotting out action, sight lines, costumes, etc. And then a voice program to suggest how certain lines should be read. Or she can compile her own edition, splicing in illustrations of cheirographia from the contemporary manuals. Or make it into a film. Or simply mess around with it in the irreverent way undergraduates always have, mustaching the *Mona Lisa* just for the hell of it.

All of these machinations upon greatness are pedagogical techniques that open literary texts to people whose talents are not intrinsically "literary," people who want, in all kinds of intuitive ways, to operate upon experience rather than passively receive it. Codex books limit the wisdom of the Great Books to students who are Great Readers—as, to be sure, all of us who debate curricular matters were and are. Electronic text blows that limitation wide open. It offers new ways to democratize the arts, ways of the sort society is asking us to provide. If groups of people newly come to the world of liberal learning cannot unpack the Silenus box of wisdom with the tools they bring, maybe we can redesign the box electronically, so that the tools they have, the talents they already possess, will suffice. We need not necessarily compromise the wisdom therein.

I don't think that the Great Books, for example, the classical tradition now defended with Luddite determination, will suffer by electronic presentation. Just the opposite, in fact. (And, we might reflect, because they are mostly in the public domain, the great books will be the first to be digitized.) We have, ever since the Newtonian interlude banished rhetoric, sifted out the rhetorical ingredient from our classical texts. Yet all these texts, the Greek and Roman ones entirely, the medieval and Renaissance ones in Christian partnership, were created out of a rhetorical tradition and can be understood only in light of it. We have had so hard a time selling the Great Books partly because we have systematically travestied their greatness, strained out—both in commentary and in translation—half of what makes them great. They weave their spell out of the ancient quarrel between the philosophers and the rhetoricians, and we have cut that quarrel in half and broken the spell.

Here, as so often, the humanities have *created* the "humanities crisis" they have spent the last century maundering on about. The bit-mapped, graphics-based personal computer is, as I have argued in chapter 2, intrinsically a rhetorical device. In its memory storage and retrieval, in its dynamic interactivity, in the dramatic rehearsal-reality it creates, in the way game and play are built into its motival structure, it expresses the rhetorical tradition just as the codex book embodies the philosophical tradition. The computer's oscillation between reader and writer reintroduces the oscillation between literate and oral coordinates that stands at the center of classical Western literature. The electronic word will allow us to teach the classical canon with more understanding and zest than ever before. We don't need to worry about its impending destruction, or deconstruction. Western Lit is in no danger from Westerns. They are both going interactive.

Indeed, by devising new ways to unlock the Western tradition for *nontraditional* students, we may find out more about what its wisdom is and does, begin to answer that other pressing question, what are the arts and letters good for? Up to now, the liberal arts have always, when pressed, been able to define their essence by appealing to their expressive means. Literary scholars read books and write them. Musicians compose music and play it. Artists paint pictures. Taking away this physical definition of the liberal arts—defining them by pointing to the physical objects they create, or that create them—compels the arts to define their essence in a new way.

The powers of digital technology both to teach nontraditional students and to document how they learn are being explored in a world the academic liberal arts have ignored, the world of applied-learning technologies developed for business, government, and the military. The developers of these interactive laserdisc "texts" and computer-managed instructional programs, because they do not share our commitment to the codex book, and because they must document the success of their efforts, have approached digital pedagogy without crippling preconceptions. They are redefining what a textbook is, among other things, and completely renegotiating the traditional ratio of alphabetic to iconographic information upon which it has been based. Their *logos* has already become bi-stable.

They capitalize on another democratizing insight that traditional humanists have ignored. When the arts are digitized, as they all now have been, they become radically interchangeable. A single digital code can be expressed in either sight or sound. Even the most traditional musicians are coming to acknowledge that the basis for the creation, notation, and performance of music has become digitized. It is not simply that notation and printing—the notoriously expensive bottleneck in that art—is now almost a do-it-yourself affair. Musical instruments themselves have been transformed. The clavier keyboard is now a unitary input device for all kinds of musical output. One digital "horn" creates the sounds of every instrument in a wind ensemble. Visual and musical signals are routinely translated into and out of one another for sampling and editing. If you sit down to a weighted-action electronic keyboard, you confront, in addition to the familiar eighty-eight in white and black, wave forms graphically displayed, a library of sounds on disk, and a computer to play, and play with, them. Such instruments, and such a manner of composition and performance, call upon talents quite different from those demanded when our mothers cajoled us into doing our Czerny exercises. The neural mix seems almost totally new, in fact. One software program, cheap and widely available, allows anyone, with no training whatsoever, to compose music by drawing with a mouse and then translating the sketch into its musical equivalent. (No, the music produced isn't horrid.) Digital synthesizers and samplers allow sounds to be created and edited as visual patterns. Musicians can now even choose with a keystroke which temperament (among other performance parameters) they wish to observe, from conventional equal temperament to the just intonation of Harry Partch. Digitization has rendered the world of music-making infinitely more accessible than it was, accessible to people who before had not the talent or the resources to make music and hear how it sounds.

The metamorphic pressures on painting are equally Ovidian. Even as pixeling a written text onto an electronic screen radically destabilizes and volatilizes it, so painting on an electronic screen launches the image into an existence forever *in potentia.* Electronic painting exists to be transformed by the viewer. The image you see is but one readout of a digital code that can produce hundreds more. Apply a contrast-enhancement program and you have a different picture; a Fourier transform and you get yet another. The Arnoldian ideal of fixed perfection simply dissolves. Again, as with literature, the entire supporting structure of criticism must be recomputed.

This digital revolution offers the most extraordinary opportunities to *teach* the arts in new ways, from kindergarten to graduate school. The criticism/creation dichotomy automatically becomes, in a digital world, a dynamic oscillation: you simply cannot be a critic without being in turn a creator. This oscillation prompts a new type of teaching in which intuitive skills and conceptual reasoning can reinforce one another directly. The digital interchangeability of the arts through a common code—that old Platonic dream that everything returns to mathematics—allows us to translate one range of human talents into another. Our sense of how teaching *in* the arts, and *about* the arts, ought to proceed is metamorphosed, again with truly Ovidian intensity and insouciance, by this convertibility. Academic humanists, so far as I can discover, have hardly begun to think about these opportunities, but they will help us answer the social pressures of the time.

Digitization of the arts radically democratizes them. The woman who wrote the program that translates a drawing into music did so because she wanted to open up musical composition to people who had no training in or talent for it, but loved it nevertheless. Digitization makes all the arts interactive, opens them up potentially to the full range of talents that humankind possesses. The people who developed the personal computer considered it a device of radical democratization from its inception. It was a way to open levels of symbolic transformation, and the work and information that went with them, to people hitherto shut out from this world. This democratization is a perfect instance of the new thinking society is demanding of the liberal arts.

I have remarked in passing that digitizing the arts requires a new criticism of them. We have it already in the postmodern aesthetic. The fit is so close that one might call the personal computer the ultimate postmodern work of art. The Italian Futurists at the beginning of the century attacked the codex book and its conventional typography, and in their "Teatro di Varietà" bullied the silent Victorian audience into interactivity. Duchamp and Stella exhibited, or tried to exhibit, their celebrated urinal in order to move the definition of art from the masterpiece to the beholder. John Cage opened music-making to everyone by converting everything into a potential musical instrument. The repetition and variation of motifs drawn from a treasure-house of standard forms (a routine postmodern rhetorical tactic from Andy Warhol to Charles Moore) is done by the electronic arts with ridiculous ease. Electronic interactive fiction finds rehearsals in printed postmodern fiction.

One of the computer's most powerful gifts of interactivity is the power to change scale. Absolutely altering one boundary-condition of the visual arts, it has put scaling into continual dynamic play as a choice for both beholder and creator. Scaling is an analytic as well as creative tool of extraordinary power, and it is available to anyone "reading" images on a graphics computer. You just click in the zoom box. Scaling is everywhere in the postmodern arts, from Oldenburg's gigantic Swiss Army Knife Venetian Galley and Rosenquist's gigantic billboard paintings to the music of Philip Glass. Robert Wilson's dramas are extended experiments in the time-scaling of rhetorical gesture, in the revelations of very, very slow motion. Everywhere such experiments strive to make us aware of how scale determines the world we live in, and gives us an unprecedented power to domesticate it, live in it comfortably. A major term in the liberal arts has been factored out of the masterpiece aesthetic and radically democratized, and has found a direct digital counterpart.

The most powerful influence of the computer on modern thinking, I would argue, is not statistical or scientific but humanistic. Rhetorical, in fact. Precisely as the rhetorical practice of declamation put dramatic rehearsal at the center of classical thought, the computer has put modeling at the center of ours. It is difficult to overestimate the influence of this across-the-board dramaticality in the world of contemporary affairs. And again we find a counterpart in that range of postmodern art which constitutes itself from self-conscious happenings.

My long discussion of Christo's *Running Fence* in chapter 2 addresses directly the questions first formulated by the 1828 Yale committee: How do we democratize art without trivializing it? How do you factor out the powers of the masterpiece and make them available to an untrained audience? If the liberal arts teach citizenship, how can they do it for every citizen? As with all of Christo's works, the "work" involved not only building the fence itself but turning into self-conscious art, through hearings and publicity and subsequent films and publications, the four years of arrangements and permits and bureaucratic wrangling needed to legalize the administrative structure, and all the engineering efforts needed to design and build it, and the civic efforts needed to control and comfort the crowds who would view it. Christo converted American industrial enterprise, that is, into a gigantic Happening, a live civics lesson. *Running Fence* was not intended to allegorize the deficiencies of bureaucracy and so reform them, but only to make people visualize large-scale human organization in a clearer and more self-conscious way, as having its own form, justification, and even beauty. It made its art up out of politics.

But to act in, and thus to "appreciate" *Running Fence*, no one needed a credential in connoisseurship. They had only to be what they were, do what they did to earn their living and play their social roles—but to look at all this in a new way, to look AT it rather than THROUGH it. Christo too was creating the pedagogical technique society now requires of the liberal arts, a new liberating art that could offer art's defamiliarizing power to a wider audience. It was not intended to be immortal (like all Christo's work, it was soon taken down) but to teach the opposite lesson, a reverence for transitory, *mortal* enterprise. *Running Fence* was also extraordinarily beautiful, because the beauty was needed to teach the integral lesson, show the dynamic relation between beauty and purpose that Christo has given his career to illustrating.

◻   ◻   ◻

I have been edging sideways toward the third of my three emergent conditions. To it I have despairingly—like an outfielder throwing his glove at a ball soaring overhead into the stands—given the name of "theory." The ball I'm throwing my glove at represents, if I have drawn its many parts together correctly, the revival of the classical system of education, the rhetorical paideia, of an applied rather than a pure, an interactive rather than a passive, conception of the liberal arts. This system of education prevailed in the West from the Greeks onward, until it was set aside by Newtonian science. It is now returning in the many guises I have described in chapter 3. It includes precisely the emergent social conditions I have been describing, as well as the postmodern digital aesthetic that is replying to them. Indeed, rhetoric itself may be viewed, like them, as an attempt to democratize genius for those not, by nature or society, gifted with it, to explore how far contrivance might supplement talent. A fit between the rhetorical paideia and the social and technological conditions that are helping to revive it makes intrinsic sense. It is not simply an accident.

This revival of our traditional paideia includes those parts of contemporary literary criticism and cultural studies which have rediscovered that all arguments are constructed with a purpose, to serve an interest—a rediscovery symbolized by Terry Eagleton's reflection, at the end of his literary-theory survey, that we might as well call the whole subject "Rhetoric."[11] And it includes a great deal more. Taken together—wrapped up into that ball soaring above this essay's outstretched glove—these theoretical efforts to make sense of our time amount, as the revival of rhetoric should, to a curricular revolution, a new didacticism. We might call it *experimental humanism*.

Rhetoric persuades by taking for its engine our evolutionary heritage as primates—our need for pure play and competitive hierarchy—and slipstreaming behind them some act in the practical world. On this plate lies the main bone of contention over which the philosophers and the rhetoricians have been fighting all these 2,500 years. The philosophers believe that human motive is purpose-driven, and play and game derivative functions; the rhetoricians—forced to get results in the world of affairs—have always inverted this pattern. Sensible use, commonsensical reason, took charge, when these rarities could take charge, because the evolutionary deities of game and play, or the politicians and rhetoricians who manipulate them, had prepared the way.

We now find ourselves in yet another rehearsal of this ancient quarrel between the philosophers and the rhetoricians. We pit sacred texts against topical ones, ultimately meaningful ones against ultimately meaningless ones, Plato against Isocrates, finally—you can fill in the other contrasted pairs of proper names yourself—pitting Almighty God against what one eminent theorist has called "the pleasures of the bottomless." The history of Western thought suggests that if we wait until this dispute is resolved before devising a responsive liberal arts curriculum, we shall wait a right good while. But Western education has never had the leisure to wait.

Henri Marrou argued that, in this historic quarrel, although Plato won the battle, rhetoric won the war, actually formed the curriculum. I must disagree. The rhetorical paideia did not resolve this struggle, or simply teach the rhetorical side of it, but built the debate itself into Western education as its operating principle. Rhetoric as a theory has proved so exasperating and unsatisfactory precisely because it oscillated from one world view to the other. Rhetorical man was a dramatic game-player but he was always claiming that the ground he presently stood upon was more than a stage. Rhetoric's central decorum enshrined this bi-stable oscillation: the great art of art was the art of hiding art, but you had better start out with some art to hide. In behavior, you should always be sincere, whether you mean it or not. This root self-contradiction, as Baldesare Castiglione saw when he gave it the Renaissance name *sprezzatura*, causes trouble only when you take it out of time. *In* time, as a perpetual oscillation, it works fine. Generations of thinkers have bemused themselves, as we do today, by taking the oscillation out of time, stopping it to point out how immiscible the two ingredients are, how moral and formal judgments can never mix. This is how Peter Ramus, in the middle of the sixteenth century, started our humanities crisis. The rhetorical paideia that is now returning puts the oscillation back into time, handles the problem the Renaissance way. Experimental humanism, with its often outrageous didactic, seeks to reanimate that oscillation. It represents not a nihilistic repudiation of the Western intellectual tradition but a self-conscious return to it.

The primary social pressure on the liberal arts—this at least has not changed—has always been a deep hunger for secular wisdom, for some cybernetic control of the forces that threaten to destroy us. This the rhetorical paideia, in the bi-stable form I have described, has always tried to supply. An educational system of this sort does not deny our need for absolutes; it domesticates and controls that need. In its natural oscillation, the rhetorical paideia is deeply irenic, would keep the peace by preventing us from filtering the self-interest and self-consciousness out of our most profoundly disinterested convictions and then committing atrocities in their name. It would control purpose, as Gregory Bateson counseled in his landmark article on the Treaty of Versailles, by showing us its roots in play and game.[12] A rhetorical education, while reminding us of the inevitable circumstantiality of all human judgment, shows us how we can control and offset that circumstantiality. G. B. Kerferd remarks, in his book on the Greek Sophists, that it is not two-sided argument per se that distinguishes rhetorical education but the insistence that the *same person* take both sides, first one then the other.[13] Civility requires the acceptance of imposture. That necessary lesson in toleration and self-understanding undergirds civic education in a secular democracy. It is the lesson that Americans are asking us once again to teach them. How, using the technological and theoretical resources we have just been pondering, might we do so? What would a liberal arts curriculum responsive to these emergent conditions look like? Let me briefly sketch a possible pattern.

It would depart, in my view, from a reversal of the basic structural polarity of the undergraduate curriculum. Undergraduate education has systematically separated the first two years and the last, the upper and lower divisions. Ever since the upper division coalesced around the disciplinary major, it has predominated. The lower division has languished, a low-rent dumping ground without a rationale of its own. If I am correct that the convergence of social, technological, and theoretical emergent conditions constitutes a return to the classical rhetorical paideia, then this dominance is about to reverse itself. Rhetoric has always been a *general* theory. That is its reason for being. It is centripetal, not centrifugal. It draws all subjects into its political and social center rather than spinning them out into separate, apolitical integers, as the modern curriculum has done. Rhetoric's natural home is the lower division not the upper. If we are in the midst of a systemic change from specialized inquiry to general thinking, then the felt seriousness of the curriculum will shift from the upper division to the lower.

Our educational history is littered with the corpses of lower-division programs. Because the lower division occupied a crucial position as climax of secondary preparation and necessary basis for the major, its conceptual vacuum has proved chronically painful, and we have filled it with one program after another, but never with real success. These usually Edenic programs have seldom outlasted their original visionary creators and they have rarely proved popular with either students or teachers. Both groups always knew that the "serious" world lay in specialized inquiry and hastened to join it. General programs in the liberal arts have failed because they have been, for the last hundred years and more, working against the intellectual orientation of higher education, an orientation built upon the reductive specialized inquiry inspired by Newtonian science and the complexities of the modern world. In that scheme of things no core curriculum could be found because none, by design, could exist. Because that orientation is now changing, we may be able to build a lower-division program which, since it no longer stands at variance with the felt center of its time, will endure.

The structure for this program is already in place and funded: the *infra dig* freshman composition program. We need only expand from that base. I am now going to vex sophisticated souls by saying a word about my former line of work, freshman comp, because it bears directly upon our agenda. The way we have trivialized the teaching of composition is precisely the way we have trivialized the liberal arts themselves. We teach comp only as the art of transparent expression of pure, apolitical, extrahuman truth. We remove the rhetoric, the human interest, from it. As with our typography, the ideal is a crystal goblet. The utopian world implied by this Edenic view of human communication is precisely the world of unchanging and nonnegotiable secular truths that Thomas More enshrined in his *Utopia* and that the liberal arts have used as a lodestone ever since. In it, the basic rhetorical impulses of competition and play are outlawed in favor of plain Edenic purpose. Style gives way to an insubstantial something we have learned to call "substance." In this fashion the liberal arts deny their own reason for being. They conceive themselves as teaching a utopian, Socratic lesson about the primacy of substance over style, and yet their own substance, their words and sounds and shapes, are denied and repudiated by such primacy. The liberal arts have for four hundred years been trying to pull the rug out from under their own feet, and more often than not they have succeeded. The liberal arts have made their own problems. That crucial oscillation between play and purpose which constitutes their creative center has been taken out of time and shut down. No wonder we academic humanists have a hard time explaining what we do.

Rhetorical education works in the opposite way. Stylistic decorum measures how we look alternately AT and THROUGH a text (or a painting), first accept it as referential and then refer it to a reality beyond. This same measurement is then mapped onto behavior as a social decorum. Every stylistic balance models a social one. In the rhetorical scheme of things, formal and moral judgments, though immiscible, are held in manageable alternation. A system of education like this spins out from its center in bi-stable decorum a stylistic-behavioral allegory. As I argue in "The 'Q' Question" (chapter 7), here is where we must look if we are to answer that long-standing question about what the arts are good for, about how moral and formal truths can be related to one another in human life. This bi-stable conceptual core, and its lessons, ought to stand at the center of the composition course, as they should at the center of the liberal arts more largely conceived.

The logical course to follow this composition course will build upon the digital interchangeability of the arts. It should develop what for the first time we now can develop, a genuine rhetoric of the arts, a comprehensive discussion of their means and ends. Such a discussion will not distinguish between the fine and applied arts, because digitization has intermixed them beyond recall. It will assume the digital presentation of the arts as a second norm and contrast its dynamic genius with masterpieces of fixed presentation, in this way reflecting the oral/literate axis around which the Western liberal arts have always circled. Such a course should provide students of the humanities with a general framework within which they can locate all their further work in the liberal arts—and, I should say, not only in the liberal arts. It will embody, that is, a genuine core for this core curriculum.

The third course in this sequence would aim to teach the discipline of two-sided argument I spoke of earlier. The real way to open the American mind would be to show it that democratic government requires allegiance to genuine two-sided argument, to the psychological and social discipline required when you learn to speak on both sides of any question, put yourself in your opponent's shoes. This discipline is no mystery; it forms the secular basis of individual tolerance and humane understanding. And, obviously enough, it enfranchises our public system of justice, of a trial by jury in which competing dramatic reenactments are staged and one is determined to be referential, and in case-law becomes so. This moment of determination, when the contingent becomes the absolute, is the moment of that oscillation we have found again and again in the emergent conditions we now face—the oscillation from a "reality" to the circumstances that have created it and back again.

We can study it in an infinity of manifestations, theoretical and historical. Surely, for example, it has created the pivotal oscillation of English constitutional history, wherein the monarchy, that needful absolute, has had to be repeatedly reinvented and reabsolutized by the most preposterous myths, only to be repeatedly compromised and qualified by good sense or violence. And we have, in the legislative and executive branches, built this same oscillation into the center of our own American constitution. If you want to teach citizenship in American democracy, you don't build your educational system on Hirsch's collection of canonical facts, or Bennett's collection of canonical texts—or on Allan Bloom's collection of Platonic pieties either. You build it, as the educational system that was invented to sustain democracy built it in the first place, upon a bi-stable alternation between the contingent and the absolute. The only true absolute, in a secular democratic education, is the obligation to keep that oscillation going, preserving a bi-stable core for the Western tradition that is not timeless but forever in time. The ways to do this are as infinite as the particular courses such a curriculum would create but the center remains the same.

A sequence of this kind, a new core curriculum in language, the arts, and democratic politics, is doable right now. It needs no further study. The electronic technology required is for sale in the marketplace, and cheap. Is, in fact, pixelating around looking for its natural home. The administrative structure is there. We could do it right now.

How would it affect the upper division of specialized inquiry? Our thinking about the core curriculum has been based on the conventional upper-division, lower-division separation, the linear four-year progression, and the common faculty, that were assumed by the Yale Report of 1828. Because times are different now, that *way of thinking* will no longer work. We need a new *conception* of a "core" for the entire four years. Let me borrow one from an original book by the architect Robert Venturi and his associates, called *Learning from Las Vegas*.[14] Venturi took his Yale seminar out to Vegas for a design exercise. From the ordinary judgmental point of view of a modern city planner, there was only one ideal solution: level the place and start over. So too for Hutchins and his associates at Chicago, and "core curriculum" planners ever since, there was only one solution to the marketplace curriculum: abolish it and establish a new, ordered, linear sequence in its place. Ideally, a St. John's College, four years of lock-step courses teaching the classics the way the classics, by Zeus, used to be taught. Venturi suggested, instead, that the seminar suspend judgment and look at Las Vegas, since it consisted largely of signs, as a system of signs. What did it do? How did it do it? Could a semiotic compass of some sort be devised to find one's way around in such a world? Perhaps, having mapped it, to enjoy it?

From similar thinking emerged the eclectic aesthetic of postmodern architecture. This aesthetic sought not to tear the city down and "renew" it but to teach us how to see it and—at our own pace and in our own way, by ourselves and in small groups—to mend it. It taught this lesson by designing eclectic buildings as self-consciously didactic exercises in how to look at the stylistic repertoire found in American cities. I suggest we use this interactive aesthetic, based on beholder as well as beheld, as an educational pattern.

Imagine the lower-division sequence I have sketched as a building like this, a continually remodeled and adaptive self-conscious work of art. The sequence ought to provide for an undergraduate a way to view the educational city as it is, a curricular compass for navigating in the academic marketplace and constructing a personal order there. We are not going to change, probably we *should* not change, the way disciplinary inquiry proceeds or teaches. Humankind is naturally specialist. But we can set up an *integrative* pattern with which specialization can alternate, a lower-division program that can help students find their way in the specialized lands through which they must voyage. Here, too, a lowly structure lies ready to hand as a place to begin, the "writing across the curriculum" courses so common now in American universities. These courses can examine the "rhetoric" of the specialized disciplines, show students the boundary-conditions within which "absolute" disciplinary truths are created, map them on a basic rhetoric of the arts and sciences.[15] Renew, that is, the vital oscillation between absolute and contingent which disciplinary specialization has all but shut down. (I discuss these curricular possibilities at greater length in chapters 5 and 6.)

Such a pattern of courses, such a new "core curriculum," would once again put the lower division and the upper division into fruitful oscillation, bring this dead administrative sequence back into time, into a generative bi-stability that reflects its theoretical premise. Our present disciplinary structure, as Gerald Graff's *Professing Literature* makes clear,[16] is built upon defusing conflict by separating the opposing parties, if they bicker long enough, into separate departments so they no longer have to talk to each other. Built, that is, upon shutting down the root oscillation of the liberal arts. We must start it going again, and if we cannot do so in the separate disciplines, we can show our students how to do it for themselves. If art can lie in the beholder, why not the liberal arts curriculum that studies it?

This lower-division program ought to be organized not as an academic department but as an "intrapreneuring" unit, a quasi-independent division that pioneers changes in a large bureaucracy. It should, for a start, experiment with different patterns and terms of faculty hiring. If our theoretical thinking blurs the distinction between critic and creator, perhaps our hiring policies should follow suit. Not all the creative thinking in the liberal arts is taking place in university seminars. The primary intellectual contracts for the next century—between word and image, between page and screen, between goods and information, between high art and low, between the society's need for symbolic processing and who is to supply that need—are all, in fact, being negotiated off-campus. It might be a good idea for us to get to know those folks, maybe even hire one or two of them.

This intrapreneuring unit also should experiment with new administrative patterns. If our present labor practices in the liberal arts are a scandal, the poverty of our organizational thinking is even worse. Along with enrichment of this thinking should go—another first—some real cost accounting. This unit might train a new kind of academic administrator as well, one whose skills at refereeing the career game are complemented by a larger strategic vision.

And, finally, it should foster *systemic* thinking. Education by discipline sets up every discouragement possible, for both student and teacher, to systemic thinking. The massive bureaucratization of learning that has taken place in America since World War II has intensified this discouragement. Attempting a large view of *anything* is automatically suspect. Implicit in the argument of this essay, and in every development in the arts I've alluded to, is a return to systemic thinking for liberal education. The classical rhetorical paideia was the original training in systemic thinking: it treated liberal arts education as a system, from early childhood to the forum and law court. We must recover that systemic view and the responsibilities that go with it. We now can recognize the infrastructure of literacy upon which the liberal arts depend as a social construct; there is nothing inevitable about it and we can no longer depend on middle-class customs to sustain it. The intrapreneuring lower division ought to think of this entire system as within its charge. It will have, for openers, the world of electronic "text" and "textbook" to redefine and recreate, and the liberal arts curriculum with it. The arts and letters cannot be taught by means of a technology that stands at variance with the technology that creates and sustains the general literacy of its society. To make sure that a technological gap does not open ought to be a primary charge to this new academic unit.

Such an endeavor contravenes what many feel to be the true center of the liberal arts—their "purity," their distance in time and place from the ordinary world of human work and pleasure. But the "humanities crisis" that has been our routine cry for a century and more is one we have manufactured ourselves by distancing ourselves from the world. Claim to be above the struggle, specialize in "values" that others have to embody, and then wonder why the world sets you aside. Implicit in the revolution in the liberal arts I have tried to describe is a return to a systemic and systematic involvement in the social purposes of our time.

◻   ◻   ◻

I began by asking whether anything new has appeared on our agenda. Obviously I think something has. The extraordinary convergence of social, technological, and theoretical pressures indicates this beyond dispute. We have until now considered these pressures as problems, threats to our traditional essence. I suggest that we view them, instead, as telling us what that essence is, and how we might embody it in answerable practices that will bring our students, all of them, up to the height of our times.

If my analysis of these three emergent conditions is correct, our times could hold for the liberal arts the very centrality we have so long sought. This centrality won't be given to us; we shall have to create it. We can do this. But we cannot do it by ignoring everything new and exciting and promising that has happened to the liberal arts in the twentieth century—as does, to instance an egregious example, the clone of the 1828 Yale Report issued by the National Endowment for the Humanities on the eve of the conference that occasioned this essay. We should not lose heart because the current public conversation about the liberal arts has been so ignorant, short-sighted, and pedagogically sterile. The long-term march of events, the extraordinary convergence, is there for anyone with the eyes to see it—and it ought to fill us with excitement, with hope, and with resolution.

NOTES

1. Lynne V. Cheney, *Humanities in America: A Report to the President, the Congress, and the American People* (Washington, D.C.: National Endowment for the Humanities, 1988).

2. Excerpts from the Yale Report of 1828 are published in *American Higher Education: A Documentary History*, ed. Richard Hofstadter and Wilson Smith, 2 vols. (Chicago: University of Chicago Press, 1961), 1.275–91.

3. E. D. Hirsch, Jr., *Cultural Literacy: What Every American Needs to Know* (Boston: Houghton Mifflin, 1987).

4. *Integrity in the College Curriculum: A Report to the Academic Community* (Washington, D.C.: Association of American Colleges, 1985).

5. *Report of the Study Group on Yale College* (1972).

6. Commission on the Humanities, *The Humanities in American Life* (Berkeley and Los Angeles: University of California Press, 1980), 3.

7. Hofstadter and Smith (n. 2 above), 1.284.

8. Frederick Rudolph, *Curriculum: A History of the American Undergraduate Course of Study since 1636* (San Francisco: Jossey-Bass, 1977), 75.

9. *Wall Street Journal,* 6 June 1988, A1.

10. Ibid.

11. Terry Eagleton, *Literary Theory: An Introduction* (Minneapolis: University of Minnesota Press, 1983).

12. Gregory Bateson, "From Versailles to Cybernetics," in *Steps to an Ecology of Mind* (New York: Ballantine, 1972), 469–77.

13. G. B. Kerferd, *The Sophistic Movement* (Cambridge: Cambridge University Press, 1981), 84–85.

14. Robert Venturi, Denise Scott Brown, and Steven Izenour, *Learning from Las Vegas: The Forgotten Symbolism of Architectural Form,* rev. ed. (Cambridge: MIT Press, 1977).

15. This enterprise has been undertaken on a theoretical level by the POROI group at the University of Iowa. See chapter 3 n. 16 above.

16. Gerald Graff, *Professing Literature: An Institutional History* (Chicago: University of Chicago Press, 1987).

5

I began to think about how electronic texts would affect textbooks because I write textbooks, and I began to think about how university administrative structures might be affected because I used to be a composition administrator. The two strands of thought came together when the Council on Library Resources invited me to a series of meetings convened to ponder the role and path research libraries should pursue in an electronic universe. I found the meetings stimulating and felt privileged to attend them. The conversation I heard there prompted this paper. When I delivered a small portion of it, on electronic information, to the national meeting of the American Council of Learned Societies in 1990, I was surprised to be told that my remarks (inoffensive as I thought them—indeed, ineluctable and undeniable) scandalized the meeting. I still can't understand why, but perhaps the reader will be more perceptive. The world that really ought to be scandalized, or at least galvanized, is the world of print-textbook publishing.

Electronic Textbooks and

University Structures

A couple of months ago I happened to hear the chancellor of my campus discuss the future of big institutions like UCLA. He was speaking to a small group of university presidents and provosts and library directors—I was invited through a fluke, as a one-shot sacrificial humanist—and he spoke with candor. He said a number of surprising things about the financial and political realities of university life, but what piqued my curiosity was his insistence that the university should prepare its undergraduate students, seriously and directly, for the world they will actually live in, and the lives they will in fact live out. I was struck not so much by the originality of this exhortation—although it *was* new coming from the chancellor—as by the extraordinary changes that would be required if anyone took it to heart. There's not much chance that anyone will, of course, but I couldn't help asking myself what would happen in my neck of the woods—teaching in the arts and letters—if someone did.

The students we teach are going to do most of their writing and much of their reading on an electronic screen. They are going to live—they live now—in a world of electronic text. The last ten years have brought altogether remarkable changes in this regard. The two predominant learned professions, medicine and law, now rely on electronic databases. The basic bibliographical tool in medicine, the venerable *Index Medicus,* has become the worldwide and phenomenally successful *Medline* on-line information system. On a recent tour of the National Library of Medicine, I saw in their media lab numerous examples of how interactive video systems are being used for medical training and expert-systems diagnosis. In the practice of law, the electronic word has come more slowly but is destined to predominate even more than it does in medicine. The December 1989 issue of *The American Lawyer* carried a supplement on law libraries that described the move from paper to screen. In one large firm's library, the "periodicals remaining in the library should be sold and replaced with their CD-ROM equivalent" in the coming year; "in the space made available by disassembling the periodical shelving" computer workstations would be constructed. Another firm now uses an electronic expert-system created through a database of senior partners' briefs and work papers. Yet another law librarian reports that updating their training videotape from its 1980 form meant teaching lawyers how to use not the one database of 1980 but over forty in 1989. The very "concept and feel" of legal publication has changed from print to electronic text.

Most of our students, though, will work not in law or medicine but in the world of business and government. If we look at the world of "training," as applied education for business, government, and the military has come to be called—with typical humanistic invidiousness, "training" being inferior to the higher-toned "education" that humanists provide—the dominance of digitally displayed information is even stronger than in the learned professions. The military establishment—an enormous force in American education since the Second World War, and one the university world has always ignored—has moved to interactive videodisc as its primary technology. The deep changes in the *logos*, in words as our primary expressive medium, which have not yet fully reached the university world, are everyday reality there. The training world has much to teach us in the university, though we show no inclination to learn it. This world, we might reflect, is enormous—more money is now spent in it, and more students educated, than in all of American higher education put together. It constitutes, in fact, the university world's long-delayed "Japan," the main competitor which may finally force some changes in our own institutional practices. And it is a competitor that already has an over 50 percent market share.

If we glance from business toward the arts, we find an electronic revolution of at least equal magnitude occurring there. More than half of the music performed in the United States now is digitally based. In the entertainment business where many UCLA students expect to find their living, for example, the creation and production of music have been revolutionized. Musical instruments themselves have changed, the nineteenth-century Romantic orchestra collapsing into a generic electronic keyboard, horn, and drum pad. Musical notation, for so long a great bottleneck, has been taken out of the hands of skilled engravers and put on the average electronic desktop. And both composers and performers have been given an enormous repertoire of recorded sounds to play with, reformulate, and mix, a vast library—usually built into, or bundled with, an electronic keyboard when you buy it—that reminds one of the *topoi* of ancient rhetoric, the stock of

ready arguments a classical speaker would regroup into a newly tailored oration. These "samples," as they are called, are "revised" visually, on an electronic screen, as waveforms which can be manipulated by eye and hand
before being returned to sound.

If you spend much time in this world of rock music and video, you'll
find that those folks inhabit a genuinely different world from people of my
generation, fond as we may be of all the arts. They think of sounds and
shapes as interchangeable, and they assume as everyday fact an electronic
smithy where all the signals of the sensorium can be refashioned at will.
When I was growing up, the kid who used to dismantle old radios was a
very different type from the kid who took piano lessons from Miss Fidditch,
and both were very different from the infuriating guy in the front row of
geometry class—in my class his name was Bill Hoover—who invented proofs
that weren't even in the *teacher's* book. Not any more. A new set of types is
emerging that mixes the old categories of self—another rhetorical commonplace—very differently.

Let me give one example. I went not long ago to what was billed as a
"MIDI keyboard show." That is, a trade fair for manufacturers of pianolike
electronic keyboards that interface with computers to synthesize artificial
sounds or mix prerecorded real ones. The actual range of products demonstrated, however, went far beyond this. One demonstration was of two people together composing a short rock-video in real time. One played a MIDI
keyboard while the other manipulated a complex video and graphics device,
and together they assembled sound, image, and word like two jazz players
improvising. They combined, as naturally as breathing, effects that the university world does its best to keep apart. They were living out Cage's dic-
tum that everything returns to opera.

In the visual arts, to which one naturally segues from music in such a
world, digitization has had the same enzymatic effect. Anyone who wants
to work as a graphic artist must contemplate using an electronic screen. From
advertising to architectural drafting to cartography, each of the visual arts
now possesses an electronic base. And yet, on one campus of the University of California system, when I recently had occasion to inquire into its offer-
ings in the studio arts (one of its strong points, I was told), there wasn't a
single course in digital graphics of any sort. Fine Artists presumably do not
do this sort of thing. But the fine arts are doing it all the time now. And arts
that we usually think of as media-based to begin with—film, most obviously—are facing a revolution every bit as profound as that facing written
text.

A profound revolution in educational techniques is occurring as well.

If we truly want to prepare our students for it, though, I don't think we should send them to our local ed school for two years' worth of pedagogical methods. It would make more sense to send them to the firms that are creating the new multimedia programs, firms like the Voyager Company or Lucasfilm. That's where the real revolution in educational technology is taking place, the revolution we would attend to if we wanted to prepare our students for their world rather than ours. Yet again and again, people working in all these areas of the "real world" for which we are now to prepare our students say the same thing: "No one is trained to do not only the work, but the *kind of work,* we need them to do."

Now I must pause for a moment to acknowledge the objections to what I have said that already must be rising in the breast of every right-thinking humanist. For many humanists, perhaps the majority, would deny that education ought to prepare our students for the world we live in now. "Surely humanists should be the ones to defend, instead, the traditional culture based on the great books, the culture that transcends time and place and will provide a rock-solid platform of ethical values upon which students can stand in a changing world"—should defend everything, that is, which we mean by "education" as against "training." Or, reading the signs on the other side of the current political boulevard, "Surely humanists should be the ones pointing out the deep internal contradictions of late-capitalist consumerist culture. Surely we should not be teaching our students to accept this world and work in it, but to reject it and subvert it." These two "surely" arguments are the most common humanist responses to the educational world we live in now. I have not forgotten them and will return to them by and by. But before I do, let me map the changes that electronic text implies for university and disciplinary structures and procedure.

Marshall McLuhan set the agenda for our thinking about electronic media, and for all his prophetic vision he misled us in two important ways. His thinking was based on analogical rather than digital devices, and he focused on broadcast television as the critical media change. Electronic text is a much less sexy affair than the televised global village but it brings with it, as we have remarked in earlier chapters, equally profound changes in the arts and letters, and also in how we organize them as a social activity through a legal system of intellectual property. Interactive digital fiction invites the reader's collaboration. Digital music of all sorts invites, with one degree or another of conscious didacticism, the creative interaction of the listener/composer. (I have a wonderful program called Jam Session that allows me to sit in on various kinds of music from Chopin to bluegrass, adding riffs and chops from the keyboard. Cultural vandalism becomes teaching toy.) Digital artists work in a medium that is dynamic by its very nature; their main problem is how to "print" their work—fix it in a single form—for a secondary nonelectronic distribution.

This volatility metamorphoses scholarly inquiry in the same way. Western poetics and philosophy are transformed, for a start. The Aristotelian categories of beginning, middle, and end, it turns out, are based on fixed texts. Think of all the arguments about coherence and perfection of artistic form that depend on these Aristotelian coordinates. Again, such arguments have been made a general ideal of written expression. All our arguments build toward a conclusion. We find scholarly disputation unthinkable without one—how else are we to separate the true from the false, the good from the bad?

This same volatility dissolves the boundaries between the arts. At the center of this repositioning in the human sensorium stands a major readjustment of the alphabet/image ratio in ordinary communication. We are now using images for a wide range of communication that formerly used written, alphabetic explanation. We can detect this shift in the digital videographic effects used so lavishly on broadcast television, and increasingly in the daily communication and training procedures of business, government, and the military. The cultural prejudices of alphabetic literacy make us interpret this change automatically as a threat and a degradation: people who need a bottle sign to find the liquor store are people who can't read, illiterates. But the changes run much deeper than this routine dismissal. Friedhoff and Benzon title their striking book on this subject *Visualization: The Second Computer Revolution,* and argue that we are coming to depend on visualization as a vital tool for conceptual thought in ways that were simply impossible before the digitization of information.[1] They discuss the importance of computer-graphic illustrations for medical and scientific research, for planning large-scale works of art, and for visualizing the behavior of what we have come to call chaotic systems of all sorts, artistic or scientific. We have to do here not with *ornamentation* of a preexistent rational argument but with an expanded sense of human reason itself.

So, if we want to prepare our students for the world out there, it must be a new kind of preparation for a transformed world. From the vast question of what this preparation might look like, let me select a narrower illustrative focus that I know something about. What would a freshman composition handbook look like if it were a guide to the world of electronic text rather than print? What first principles would it avow, and what practices would it advise? These speculations matter because they involve equally the teaching of literature and of writing, and because they span the spectrum from practical pedagogical details to profound theoretical implications. What happens to one textbook will happen to them all, to some degree to all books as electronic instruction moves into the bloodstream of higher education.

What would such an electronic text look like? Well, we must begin by saying that our handbook cannot be a textbook at all, not a book at all, and that we have as yet no word for the multimedia entity into which it has metamorphosed. And its conception of "text" is so different from print that we probably need another word for that, too. And the "reader" or student—his or her role differs so from that of a print reader that we need a new word here, too. Both "author" and "authority" become softened and diffused as the reading event moves from a one-time exchange to a continuing conversation.

Our new electronic nontext-nonbook will be "published" in a different way, too. It will be a dynamic, open-ended information system, critiqued and updated on a daily basis by its users, both local and distant, both teacher and student. It will be "published" on telephone lines—if the regulatory environment permits it—or through a fiber optic ISDN (Integrated Services Digital Network) of some sort. Systemic textbooks will grow, take on local coloration and emphasis, mutate into new forms of collective cultural enterprise, as they become part of that gigantic structure of 30,000-odd electronic billboards already out there. Not only the idea of single authorship will be knocked for a loop, but royalty payments, copyright law, and academic merit badges for publication as well. These systems will clearly be self-selective for multiple levels of difficulty, and soon for different languages. They will carry, too, a remarkable charge of self-teaching power that will force renegotiation of the teacher-student contract—a renegotiation already reported by those teaching in networked computer classrooms. And their self-contained nature implies that the relationship between primary textbooks and backup library support will have to be rethought.

Anyone who doubts that self-teaching power should take a look at my friend and colleague Robert Winter's HyperCard/CD-ROM programs on Beethoven's *Ninth Symphony*, Stravinsky's *Rite of Spring*, and Mozart's *Dissonant Quartet*.[2] These programs bring with them the complete pedagogical environment needed to understand them. They are self-teaching to a depth and with a power never available before. One can imagine building an entire course around a single one of these programs, or orchestrating a sequence of self-study seminars based upon them. And the test-games built into these programs, and others like them, show how naturally the spirit of game and play arises in such an environment. The final—or semifinal, since in this world there is no finality—the semifinal result will be a motival mixture of game, play, and purpose completely different from the print mixture. The electronic classroom has a different motivational mix from the print classroom. And it has a different sense of "finality" too. How can this not affect, for example, how teachers will grade students, or how students will feel about the boundaries of a class, until now firmly fixed by opening day and final exam?

There will be a final new expressive parameter for the electronic reader as well—the manipulation of scale I discussed in chapter 2. The nonlinear nature of hypertextual information has been universally remarked, but dynamic scaling is at least as important. After you have chosen your typeface and size, you will decide on what scale you are going to read, what levels of generality you need for your particular purpose. We all do this now by skimming books, but in so doing we often miss—I speak as an incorrigible skimmer—crucial elements. Outlining programs only hint at how scaling decisions will affect the reading of electronic text. And every move from single workstation to class network to local and then national network is a scaling decision as well. I would guess that what a "course" will be in the future may rest on a scaling decision made by a student or teacher, working in collaboration.

These delivery systems will teach a very different kind of composition lesson; what will it look like? (I know "delivery system" sounds too much like a rival for UPS, but I haven't come up with a better term.) Herewith, a few oracular speculations.

First, the essay will no longer be the basic unit of writing instruction. The world will not come to an end therefore; the essay was not always the dominant form. In classical times the central expository form was the declamation; in the Middle Ages, it was the letter; now it will be something else, partaking I would guess of both declamation and letter.

Second, we can back off a turn or two on the thumbscrew of spelling instruction, spelling checkers being what they are. And students will be able to do some self-checking in other areas of grammatical correctness and stylistic revision. Electronic text will not revise itself but it can give the reviser some easy ways—global search and replace, visual isolation of single sentences, repositioning of sentence elements—to go about the prose stylist's work.

Third, the nature of punctuation surely will change. The present system was devised—largely by the Alexandrian scholars—as an aide-mémoire for the public performance of a written text. Electronic text offers a much larger repertoire of performative signs—I am thinking of the use on electronic bulletin boards of "emoticons," certain letters and symbols employed as tonal colorizers to indicate the spirit in which to read—and it seems likely that they will become increasingly popular. Again, I don't think the world will come to an end if they do. Think of all the human effort spent on teaching the rules of punctuation: suppose we didn't have to do it! Or at least had some new rules to play around with. Or at the very least, used computer graphics to teach the dynamics of punctuation *dynamically.*

Fourth, writing will be taught as a three-dimensional, not a two-dimensional art. Hypertext does this in one way; computer animation will do it in another. (We are not talking high-end products; you can buy cheap and agile animation programs right now, and fancy 3-D animators for a thousandth of what they cost a decade ago.) Prose as we know it, printed prose, is based on an aesthetic of black and white linear renunciation. We use "figures of speech" but we never let the figures realize themselves in their native iconic form. Ever since Greek rhetoric catalogued the basic figures of speech to recreate in a written culture some of the powers of oral speech and gesture, we have implied patterns—this is what one branch of rhetorical figuration is all about—but we have never let them complete themselves. Now, they can explicate themselves in animations selected by the reader. The text will move, in three dimensions. Given the current state of digital animation programs, I think we'll come pretty soon to three-dimensional modeling of basic argumentative patterns.

And we will add the dimension of color. We talk about the "colors of rhetoric" but our texts are all in "black and white," that phrase itself having come to symbolize the stability of legal writ. Now, the colors of rhetoric can become, indeed, multicolored. And with better compression techniques and gigantic memory storage, we can add sound to our reading as well. Word, image, and sound will be inextricably intertwined in a dynamic and continually shifting mixture.

Clearly, we will need a new theory of prose style to cope with all this. In fact, I would put the matter more strongly: for the first time, we will have a genuine *theory* of prose style, rather than the present folk wisdom and exercises in the psychology of rumor. Only by seeing the enormous area of expressiveness that printed prose *excludes* can you understand how it works, and that area of exclusion is only now coming clear. Think of having a theory of prose style as clear as the periodic table in chemistry! It would do more than any other one thing to clarify, to students and teachers alike, what instruction in discourse is all about. Upon this theory our new electronic nontext-nonbook will be built. I am not talking now about a cobbled-up adjustment to a nonprint world; I am talking about a theory *superior* to any that print allows us to conceive, but which would include print as well as dynamic alphabetic expression.

Fifth, I think this new mixture in the human sensorium will revolutionize that segment of instruction we now stigmatize as "remedial." Some people are better at images or sounds than at words, and some people who have not had the verbal education they wanted or needed can come to it later in life through images and sounds. It will all be one single spectrum of expressivity, with no need to stigmatize any area of it. Behavioral neuroscience is teaching us nowadays a good deal about how the lateralized brain works. Electronic text will allow us to engineer "reading" to fit the brain's needs and ways of proceeding far more adroitly than print's one-size-fits-all approach.

Such a delivery system would condition the teaching of literature, too, would it not? Conventional literary study is pretty much stood on its ear by a changeable, interactive, and nonlinear text that has no final beginnings, middles, and endings, no unchanging dominant tonalities, and no nonnegotiable rules about verbal excess and expressive self-consciousness. And, as I pointed out in chapter 1, much of current poststructuralist theory suffers a sea-change as well. If the reader can adjust the writing by becoming the writer, and to any extent desired, a great deal of the current controversy about the role of the reader can be conveniently shelved. There is as much connection between reader and writer, or as little, as you want to dial in. Is every critic a creator and vice versa? Is textual order a product of our rage for it, more than of the text itself? We can shelve that debate too: contrive whatever mixture you want. Is there a neutral language of conceptual expression or is all expression radically metaphorical? If we cannot settle this controversy finally, we can at least point now to a very broad spectrum of expressivity that includes not only words but images and sounds, a spectrum controlled by a general theory of expressivity (which is what a theory of prose must become). This spectrum runs from least to most metaphorical, and you can locate yourself wherever you want. An identical spectrum exists for the reader as for the text. Mix and match as you like, anywhere along either one.

The late, and now much-disputed, literary theorist Paul de Man spent a lot of time glossing the great American rhetorician Kenneth Burke's apothegm that "every way of seeing is a way of not seeing." Electronic text allows us to see that this version of "blindness" and "insight" is often a matter of scaling-choice. That choice we can now manipulate ourselves; we can dial in a different scale of difficulty, of "readability." That will often defuse, if not solve, the difficulty. If scaling won't work, and we come to an irreducible *aporia*, we can include both alternatives in a toggle switch and move on. Problem solved. Electronic text is intrinsically a bi-stable medium, one made to accommodate exactly this difficulty. Texts, Derrida argued, are not "a store of ready-made 'concepts' but an *activity* resistant to any such reductive ploy."[3] No need to argue that for electronic text—it is manifestly true. The same popular commentary on deconstruction defines it this way: "Deconstruction is therefore an activity performed by texts which in the end have to acknowledge their own partial complicity with what they denounce." Kenneth Burke said the same thing in 1935, but without the political spin of "denunciation" and "complicity": "Even when one attempts to criticize the structure, one must leave some parts of it intact in order to have a point of reference for his criticism. However, for all the self-perpetuating qualities of an orientation, it contains the germs of its dissolution."[4] Electronic text, by its very manipulability, builds in a maximum of the textual self-consciousness such declarations point to. Add all this reflection together (and a lot more one could do), and it is hard not to think that, at the end of the day, electronic text will seem the natural fulfillment of much current literary theory, and resolve many of its questions. Just so, as we saw in chapter 2, the mixture of alphabetic, iconic, and auditory information fulfills so many prophecies in the visual arts, from Italian Futurism and Dada onward. The practice of electronic text seems essentially theoretical.

I've said that the world of "remediation" is as print- and book-centered as the rest of our pedagogical apparatus and may be expected to change. If we move our gaze from this bottom of the curriculum to the top, to the interdisciplinary humanities courses now attracting so much attention from the press, we'll see a similar metamorphosis going on. For the deepest implication of electronic text for the teaching of literature is that literature can no longer be taught in isolation from the other arts. Digitization has made the arts interchangeable. You can change a visual signal into a musical one. You can zoom in on a letter until it changes from an alphabetic sign to an abstract pixel-painting. The digital equivalence of the arts has provided a genuinely theoretical basis for comparing the arts and for teaching them together. The new theory of prose style proves to be a general theory of style for the arts altogether.

Such reflections suggest that the current debate about the humanities curriculum is otiose, based on a print technology at variance with the electronic medium in which artistic activity and its reception will take place. A different educational practice is suggested by this line of thinking, a different kind of core curriculum in fact, dominated by a radically new rhetoric of the digital arts. This *Rhetoric of the Digital Arts* will constitute the "text" for the lower-division undergraduate program I've sketched in the previous chapter. Again, an educational *practice* like this is intrinsically, essentially, self-consciously, *theoretical*. The current debate about the need for a "theory" component in every education in discourse misses this vital point. Our mesmeric interest in the "theorized" race/gender/class curricular debate, rewarding to fight about though it be, has blinded us to the real issues now before us. In any deep sense, we have scarcely begun to think about them.

Computer slang is usually metaphorical and creative, but a new word has popped up recently which is ugly and bureaucratic—"repurposing." It points to the increasing practice of taking an already existing form of electronic information and using it for a new purpose. One might, for example, take the old CLV (constant linear velocity) videodisc of a movie and add a foreign-language translation on the second soundtrack. Or, using a Pioneer 8000 videodisc player, write a HyperCard program that adds commentary and explanation to individual scenes and so converts the film into a teaching tool. Let me finish my discussion of electronic text in its literary aspect by suggesting that we are in for a great deal of "repurposing" of literary and artistic works, and of the theory we use to understand them. Most of this repurposing will be useful and illuminating.

For a start, electronic text allows us to reconceptualize the history of literary criticism; under electronic light, it consists of a series of arbitrary positions taken toward fixed alphabetic information. Great critics have differed ever since Aristotle on the nature of structure, on the relation of literature to the other arts of image and sound, on the desirable place and density of verbal ornament (of the self-consciousness with which typographical clues were to be used to distinguish prose from verse, for example), on the relation of "literary" to "nonliterary" discourse, and so on. All of these expressive parameters are so much more easily adjustable in electronic text that perhaps we shall begin to think our historical differences to have been generated as much by an inflexible technology as by genuine differences of principle. Might electronic text, in making all arbitrary positions adjustable, make them all potentially correct by removing their contradictions with one another? It will be fun, at all events, to watch how things work out. The history of criticism may fall *back into time*, into a continuously roiling present.

Electronic text will also serve as the vehicle for displaying all of Western literature in a new light. Since much of this literature is oral in origin and nature, and self-consciously rhetorical, and since electronic text is both oral and rhetorical to a degree, "repurposing" can reveal to us aspects of our greatest works of art—literary, artistic, and musical—that we have never noticed before. Robert Winter told me that in creating his *Ninth Symphony* program he heard things that he had not only never heard before, but had never *been able to hear* before. I think electronic text will allow us to hear lots of things, in both reading and writing, that we have never been able to hear before.

Let me adduce one example from my own world. I regularly introduce students to the London dialect of Middle English, so that they can read the poetry of Geoffrey Chaucer in its original form. I do it, as does everyone else I know, through a textbook. I supplement it with audiotapes of readings. I diagram the Great Vowel Shift on the board. For my efforts, lasting now for thirty years, I give myself an A for effort but no more than a C+ for results. It would be much easier for the students if they could read the text on an electronic screen and hear it read aloud at the same time. It would be infinitely easier for me if I could explain the vowel shift through a computer-graphics program that put sight, sound, and phonological history together. It would be a great easement if students could take notes on the text by enhancing it in various temporary and noninvasive ways, rather than desecrating the book for all time with a yellow highlighter.[5] It would be easier for me if, when I talked about rhetorical patterning in a particular tale, I could simply ask them to dial in a prearranged program that marked the passages in their text which I wanted them to consider. The computer upon which they would read the text would not weigh as much as the book they now have to lug to class each day. All of these things are possible today; we are not talking about the twenty-first century.

Would this textual pedagogy signal the end of Western Culture As We Know It? Chaucer was an oral poet in many ways, to begin with; he read his poetry aloud to his audience. Electronic text would simply restore that vital "parameter of performance," as we might call it, to Chaucerian study. It would be a different literate/oral mix, and a different image/alphabet mix, but would it inevitably be an inferior one? In some ways it would get us closer to a Chaucerian manuscript, not to mention a Chaucerian court performance, than a contemporary printed text does today.

I think, then, that Western culture, for which "the Great Books" has come to be a convenient shorthand phrase, is not threatened by the world of electronic text, but immensely strengthened and invigorated. I think we shall come to understand our great literary texts, and especially their neglected oral and rhetorical aspects, in ways that we could never before have understood. The Great Books side of our politicized curricular street need not feel imperiled. The Dead White Males, digitally galvanized, will rise again.

What, though, about the other side, the cultural Left, and its critique of late capitalism? How should that critique react to this unprecedented technological determinism? Here we surprise a curious case of cultural convergence. For, if we look at the world of electronic text from the perspective of what we have come to call literary theory, an electronic world comes not as a technological *vis a tergo* but as a fulfillment. The conceptual, even the metaphysical, world that digital text creates—dynamic rather than static, bi-stable rather than mono-stable, open-ended rather than self-contained, participatory rather than authorial, based as much on image and sound as on word—*is* the world of postmodern thought, the world which, as we have seen in chapters 2 and 3, began with Italian Futurism and Dada and is now the focus of theoretical discussions in disciplines all across the human sciences. In introducing our students to electronic text in the practical world of work, it turns out that we also introduce them to the critical issues of our intellectual life. The world of "training" at its most practical turns out to be very like the world of "education" at its most theoretical, whichever side of the theoretical street we happen to walk on.

But if the intellectual, humanistic center of our university world, put in the spotlight by our tenacious debate between Right and Left, is oddly and surprisingly affirmed rather than threatened by the world of electronic text, I'm not sure we can say the same thing for the university's disciplinary and administrative structures. If the arts are finding a common digital base, can the academic disciplines and departments that study them remain indefinitely apart? If the arts and sciences are confronting an emergent discipline we call "visualization," will this scientific /humanist half-breed find itself the bastard at the academic family reunion? If what we hopefully call the "real world" is moving toward the electronic word, can we continue to plan our curriculum around great *books*? Can we, in fact, continue to think of the curriculum in our customary linear terms—preparatory courses, intermediate ones, advanced, prerequisites, the whole big catalogue enchilada?

The arresting experiments in educational multimedia that have been produced so far—Robert Winter's programs for the Voyager Company, George Landow's Intermedia program at Brown, the multimedia programs being developed for IBM, the ABC News interactive videodiscs—are all radically centrifugal hypertexts; they spin a world of information out of a single unitary artistic work or political topic. They bring their "preparation" with them at every point, aim to make the student self-sufficient for information, able to reach back in time and out in space for the "background" needed to understand the "text" at issue. In their structure and rationale, they stand at odds with our heretofore unquestioned assumption that the curriculum ought to be linear if it possibly could. Centrifugal hypertexts ought to work especially well if we can succeed in using one part of the brain to illuminate the others in new ways, so that "remedial" students who are good with sights or sounds but not with words can change media when they get stuck.

It is not too much to suggest that the concept of educational order itself, at every level, will have to be renegotiated. We won't be able, for a start, to cry "Back to the basics!" with simplistic fervor, because the "basics" will have been redefined. The question of access to new educational technologies by disadvantaged groups is certainly a hot topic now, but it has not gone beyond wondering how to buy enough computers for everyone. The real issues are considerably deeper and more complex than that. We really must cease conducting the "literacy" debate on the basis of a print technology which is even now in radical metamorphosis.

And if to digitize cultural texts is to *desubstantialize* them, what of the architectural plan of a university, based as it is on *substance*, the book, the embodied teacher, the chairs we rent out to our students? And what of the only center the multiversity has left, the library? The library world feels *depaysé* today, and rightly so. Both of its physical entities, the buildings and the books they contain, can no longer form the basis for planning. And the curatorial function has metamorphosed, to borrow a phrase from an archivist acquaintance, "from curatorial to interpretive." Librarians of electronic information find their job now a radically rhetorical one—they must consciously construct human attention-structures rather than assemble a collection of books according to commonly accepted rules. They have, perhaps unwillingly, found themselves transported from the ancillary margin of the human sciences to their center. If this be so—and can it be doubted?—how should we train librarians, much less plan the building where they will work? Maybe the novelty of the challenge explains why the number of master of library science degrees awarded in the last ten years has fallen by 50 percent.

We shall also have to renegotiate completely another aspect of our university structure that we have taken for granted—the part which depends on "originality" and defines our major product at the university, "intellectual property." Anglo-American copyright law since the Statute of Anne at the beginning of the eighteenth century has been built on print, arose from print. And since the Sayre case of 1785 (the case that first defined the two extremes of social benefit and authorial profit upon which we still proceed) and the subsequent recodification of copyright law by a Victorian statute of 1842, it has built on a second pillar—the idea of originality, or authorial substance and authority. That, too, as we have observed, is called into question by electronic text. Electronic text and copyright law are steering a collision course at almost every point. In the light of this convergence, ponder all the ways in which the structure of the modern university is based on the idea of originality. Faculty recruitment and advancement, all our individual and collective merit badges, are tied to that no longer unquestioned star.

Another protective umbrella, like copyright so familiar and reliable in the world of print that we scarcely notice it, has started to leak. As de Sola

Pool points out in *Technologies of Freedom*, the First Amendment guarantees of free speech are strongly print-based.[6] These guarantees have by no means been uniformly extended to electronic communication, which tolerates a degree of regulation, by powers both public and private, that we would think intolerable for print. Here, too, basal rethinking lies before us.

And we might go yet further, into the nature of law itself. A recent scholar of law and electronic media has opined, "Our model of law has coincided with the age of the printed word and is an outgrowth of it. Law as we know it would not be possible without the special properties of print."[7] If so—and again I find the point hard to dispute—then the legal changes heralded by electronic text will not be confined to copyright law or First Amendment issues.

The influence of "electronic text," in our now-expanded sense of the term, must then be pervasive. If this is so, why are we not discussing this influence? Surely it is because the university's departmental, disciplinary, and administrative structures work implicitly—and often explicitly—to discourage it. It is almost as if the university's structure had been invented specifically to deny a place for this vital conversation to occur. An extremely thoughtful Research Grants brochure issued by the Council on Library Resources points to the problem. "Despite many claims and assertions, the information structure of the future has not yet taken shape, but the pace of change is such that it is imperative that 'architects' of great skill, who are concerned with the well-being of universities, scholarship, and libraries, go to work with some sense of coordination before a structure is imposed by default."

Where will these "architects of great skill" come from? Where will they be trained? What *department* will they be in? In my own area of the academic world, the humanities, all the basic educational contracts are now being renegotiated—and they are all being renegotiated off campus. If educating our students for the world they will live in, for a competitive global economy and the unprecedented high level of daily symbolic processing that comes with it, is to be a dominant university purpose rather than a routine Chancellor's Exhortation, then we must find ways to bring these new contracts onto campus and to understand them. We must modify our departmental and disciplinary structures so that this vital conversation can occur, and be prepared to modify them much more after the conversation has occurred. I am not sure where the conversation should take place. The library, or library school, seems a logical place. So, from a purely theoretical standpoint, does the freshman composition program, since we are dealing with a revolution in social rhetoric. All the regular academic departments disqualify themselves by their characteristic professional bias. (Certainly this is true, a fortiori, for the English departments.) Perhaps we need a new entity all together.

But we must begin a conversation somewhere, and it must include all the main players in university governance. If we don't begin it, and if we don't move forward swiftly to make basic changes in institutional structure and practice, we mustn't be surprised when American society, public and private, steps in and does it for us. For it is hard not to conclude that what we are doing now is not preparing our students for the world they will live in, and the lives they will live out, but training them, instead, to be the "clerks of a forgotten mood."

NOTES

1. Richard Mark Friedhoff and William Benzon, *Visualization: The Second Computer Revolution* (New York: Abrams, 1989).

2. Robert Winter's HyperCard/CD-ROM programs are produced by the Voyager Company, Santa Monica, Calif.

3. Christopher Norris, *Deconstruction: Theory and Practice* (London: Methuen, 1982), 24; the next quotation is from p. 48.

4. Kenneth Burke, *Permanence and Change*, 3d ed. (Berkeley and Los Angeles: University of California Press, 1984), 169.

5. This kind of annotation is now available in the Voyager Company's "Expanded Book" format; "books" are now being published in this format by Voyager and the format is being licensed to other publishers.

6. Ithiel de Sola Pool, *Technologies of Freedom* (Cambridge: Harvard University Press, 1983).

7. M. Ethan Katsh, *The Electronic Media and the Transformation of Law* (New York: Oxford University Press, 1989), 12.

6

This essay began life as a talk delivered at an Association of American Colleges conference on the undergraduate major. The agenda of the conference made, I thought, two wrong assumptions: that a coherent curriculum necessarily meant a linear one, and that the unity had to be conceptual rather than stylistic. I try here to make a case for a nonlinear, stylistic unity, and the case turns out, like most of the arguments in this book, to be a case for traditional rhetorical education in a new form.

*The question of professional languages, how they are taught and how they are learned, has long seemed to me one of the great unstudied topics. Why is this so? We don't **want** to study them. We don't want to confront our own biases. We don't want to visit foreign disciplinary countries. As a result of this suppressed reluctance, students are deeply confused not only about what style to write in but about what writing itself means and does. Much of the "literacy crisis," as we encounter it at the university level, is created by the faculty and its professional linguistic structures. Professional languages, as we use them now, constitute the main barrier to curricular coherence.*

Strange Lands, Strange Languages,
and Useful Miracles

*I*t is generally agreed that we find incoherence and muddle everywhere we look in American undergraduate education. Students take their random walk through a great K-Mart of the human spirit and end up with a handful of requirements fulfilled and perils passed. As the Association of American Colleges report of 1985 put it, "As for what passes as a college curriculum, almost anything goes. We have reached a point at which we are more confident about the length of a college education than its content and purpose."[1] And we no longer agree about the length, either, since the standard four-year tour of duty has become a thing of the past. For a while, it was the lower division that was stretched shapeless; the major at least retained the pattern it had given the curriculum since it cohered at the beginning of the century. But now the major has succumbed to the same fissioning it was designed to cure. As the AAC report puts it, "The absence of a rationale for the major becomes transparent in college catalogues where the essential message embedded in all the fancy prose is: pick eight of the following" (2). Departments now present to majors the same smorgasbord offered, at a different level of magnification, by the lower division.

It appears equally obvious, though perhaps not equally remarked, that the incoherence of the modern curriculum, major and minor, reflects faithfully the incoherence of modern thought. The anthropologist Clifford Geertz has written perceptively of the "radical variousness of the way we think now."[2] We all find ourselves trapped in our own specializations, both by the structure of the university we work in and by the very prosperity of modern inquiry. The "I really must read that" books fall down upon us thick as snowflakes in Siberia, and promising interdisciplines immediately become specializations of their own.

This situation is not unprecedented. The Spanish philosopher Ortega y Gasset posed the question in *Mission of the University* in 1930, when he declared that the main purpose of the modern university is *generalization,* and dissemination of these generalizations through teaching; specialized inquiry was to take place elsewhere. Well, we have gone another way, but the spirit of generalization as a cure for curricular incoherence lives on today in lower-division distribution requirements and proposals for a core curriculum. These lists of nonnegotiables usually come in one of two forms, an agenda of required texts or one of required abilities. Thus the AAC report calls for training in "inquiry, abstract logical thinking, critical analysis," in "literacy: reading, writing, speaking, listening," and in seven other areas, concluding with "study in depth" (15–24). Sidney Hook has given a shorter list of six basic student "needs" in a recent article,[3] and the NEH has recommended a fifty-hour curriculum of general cultures, concepts, and foundations.[4] Not to mention Bloom and Bennett (the two "Killer B's" of the Stanford curriculum debate), who advocate a return to the basic Greek texts, especially to Plato.

I've spent my scholarly life under the spell of such yearnings, and still feel drawn to them. The ideal undergraduate curriculum, as we all know, is the one each of us followed, and I spent my first two undergraduate years in a planned core curriculum, the Directed Studies Program that flourished at Yale during the early fifties. Since it did indeed make me what I am today, it is hard for me to quarrel with its wisdom. Furthermore, all my intellectual marbles are invested in the game of traditional Western culture. The now maligned Great Books are the ones I like the best, the ones I teach (I paid my devoirs to the *Iliad* only last year), the ones I write about, and the ones written in languages that I can at least pretend to understand.

But in spite of my fondness, I cannot persuade myself that this traditional curriculum is any longer workable, or would bring the longed-for coherence were it imposed. Clifford Geertz, in the article from which I quoted earlier, makes the needful point:

> The hallmark of modern consciousness, as I have been insisting to the point of obsession, is its enormous multiplicity. For our time and forward, the image of a general orientation, perspective, *Weltanschauung*, growing out of humanistic studies (or, for that matter, out of scientific ones) and shaping the direction of culture is a chimera. ...The conception of a 'new humanism,' of forging some general 'the best that is being thought and said' ideology and working it into the curriculum, will then seem not merely implausible but utopian altogether. ... the first step is surely to accept the depth of the differences; the second to understand what these differences are; and the third to construct some sort of vocabulary in which they can be publicly formulated.[5]

We cannot impose upon the curriculum a unity or coherence that is not deeply felt by the world of inquiry itself. We have been trying, God knows, ever since Erskine started his Great Books course at Columbia during World War I. But it turns out that most students don't want to take General Education courses and most professors don't want to teach them. The difficulty of this endeavor is movingly illustrated in Harry Ashmore's recent biography of Robert Maynard Hutchins.[6] Hutchins, surely the most energetic advocate of curricular coherence America has ever seen, flailed about him at Chicago for a good while, but academic specialization pressed upon him and reasserted itself after he left. The Directed Studies program, in altered form, still survives at Yale, but in its original design it proved a great destroyer of careers.[7] The same dislocational dangers threaten the undergraduate major as well. If a discipline is fragmented and fissionated, a curriculum that presents it as a tidy traditional unity will be felt immediately as false and hollow. The bright students will, as always, find their way to where the action is, disorganized and deconstructive though it may be.

What are we to do, then? Our intellectual world is too various and volatile to accept an imposed conceptual coherence even if we could agree on one to impose—and of course we can't, one person's *Republic* being, as we have come to learn, another's *Thoughts of Chairman Mao*. I would like to suggest a less ambitious way to save the curricular world and induce a universal harmony into it, one that departs not from conceptual unity but from the ostensibly secondary matter of professional languages. Students don't encounter great ideas, or even Great Books, directly. They encounter them, whatever the field, in language, and in a context of a professional language and a professional structure. Harken back for a moment to the third of Geertz's modest hopes, the need to "construct some sort of vocabulary in which [our differences] can be publicly formulated." How might we do at least this much? How might we mediate between professional languages and the ways of life, of being in the world, that they embody?

We might begin by reflecting that a student's linguistic life at a modern university differs fundamentally from our own as departmentalized teachers. A modern university student is like a visiting anthropologist who changes countries as she changes classes, every fifty minutes. We departmentalized teachers are the "natives" in this scenario, each of us speaking a professional language which does indeed, as with Shakespeare's dyer's hand, color all that we do and are. In this ethnographic map of the university (as Geertz might put it), life is much easier for us than for the students. We stay in our own country. We know it is the best country, indeed the inevitable country for anyone of intelligence and taste—else why would we have chosen to dwell there? We also know that in other department-countries the inhabitants speak a barbarous jargon. But is that not natural? They are, after all, barbarians. What else would you expect them to speak? We ourselves speak the natural language of God, and it is our sacred obligation to teach that language to all students who pass our way.

For the students, life is not so easy. They must learn three or four natural languages of God at least; they must learn a bureaucratized, difficult, highly Latinate language, rich in impersonal and hence guiltless passives, called "soc-sci"; they must learn a mathematicized language, studded with charts and graphs, called "nat-sci"; and they must learn a computer language or two—which we might consider, I suppose, the natural languages of the gods-in-the-machine. And if through some curricular shipwreck they should stray into English Department territory and land on the island called Critical Theory, they will have to master a language of priestly complexity and anarchistic terror, one composed of magical spells, secret handshakes, ritualized genuflections before freshly deified Continental heroes, and more words for "text" than the Eskimos have for "snow." Naturally enough, student-travelers wandering in this world often don't write very well, and sometimes indeed go crazy, breaking into a hyperkinetic babble of "I mean," "like you know," and "I goes and he goes," which they schizophrenically and quite pathetically claim to be a "language of our own." It is not surprising that students, in such a world, come to hunger for a major subject and select one prematurely, simply to find a place of rest and belonging, a constant conceptual universe and a professional language which they can begin to master. Who wants to be—*horresco referens*—an "undeclared freshperson"?

What kind of stylistic training might equip students for this polyglot voyage? Would it not be the same education that might equip *us* as we attempt to understand our colleagues in other fields, at least to "formulate our differences," even if we cannot agree on a common conceptual universe? For a start, it should teach the sensitivity and adaptability needed to move from one discourse-community to another. It will have to be some sort of rehearsal education, one that imagines particular occasions and then tries to formulate a discourse appropriate to them. Whatever the pedagogical techniques—learning to write essays or lab reports, practicing oral presentations for business or arguments for a law court, rehearsing a political speech—the question would remain the same: Here is a situation; what discourse is appropriate to it?

Such a paideia would differ from our current practices in elemental ways. It would not, for example, place so much stress on originality of thought and expression. Rather, it would recommend mastery of a received body of basic argumentation which could then be assembled into a mixture to fit the occasion. These arguments would be presented as *general* arguments, arguments which could fit any human dispute. And, to make them available when occasion served, they would have to be memorized. We would be creating what you might, without too much stretching, call a general vocabulary of argumentation, a shareable machinery for common conceptual thought. If we all learned it, we would all approach argumentation in the same way.

A system like this would supply us with some preformed arguments, and types of arguments, and with templates to preform language as well, a body of "figures of speech" as we might call them, which taught us how to amplify or shorten an argument as needed—to find the right "brevity" for the occasion. Such templates would allow the auditory and visual machinery of the brain to reinforce our argument, color it with delight, find an aesthetic decorum to fit the argumentative one.

This kind of education would make us very self-conscious about styles. We would be able to "find our footing" (a phrase Geertz uses for anthropological acclimatization) in new departmental lands much more quickly. We would probably find the new languages spoken there less off-putting because part of a larger conceptual structure with which we were already familiar. And so we could attend more immediately to the arguments themselves—and these, too, would ring familiar from our memorized arsenal of basic argument types. We would register a gain, that is, in *comparability*. We would also gain an important tool, one very important for critical thinking: we would always be able to move from style to argument and back, and to scrutinize whatever characteristic movements of this sort predominated for the department/field/country in question. We would gain a feeling for the characteristic expressive tonality of a particular professional world.

It might very well be that, after we had voyaged in strange language-lands for a while, the languages would fall into basic patterns or templates. There might be a formal or "high" group and an informal or "low" group, and some middle group in between. We would be taught versions of these templates for speaker, audience, and speech itself, and a repertoire of suitable allegories to go with them, so that high, middle, and low could refer, like a shorthand, to social class, intellectual or emotional nature of the subject, complexity of moral response, and so on. We might even devise other basic categories along the lines of age, occupation, and even hormonal balance. We would then have housed in our memories a conglomerate social template that we could match against a new occasion, and so keep from putting our foot wrong.

Such an education would be an education specifically designed for survival in our intellectual time, an education in diverse and ever-changing discourse communities. It would be less a master plan—a linear core curriculum—than what the French call *bricolage*, a series of ad hoc decisions with a particular purpose in mind. What would this paideia do for us, or to us? Well, the "self" developed by it would obviously be the actor's self, performative, social rather than central—"central" meaning *really us*, halfway between the ears—a self good at reading the social surface and providing what was decorous for that time and place. An education, that is, in courtesy—which is decorum as applied to the self. And the "society" that such an educational technique both implied and created would be a self-consciously dramatic one, one centered on the social surface, one where political wisdom began with dramatic criticism. In this implied world, ceremony would be very important, and the motives of game and play that attend it. It might not, when you come to think of it, be a bad education for a society that boasts linguistic and ethnic diversity outside the university and professional diversity within.

If we decided that an educational practice of this sort was a good idea, we would not have to go far to implement it. For I have been discussing not a scheme I thought up myself but the basic education in the Western world for most of its history—the paideia that goes under the now-discredited name of *rhetoric*. The Great Books paideia is usually called "classic" or even "classical," but it differs from the real classical curriculum in essential ways. The Great Books course that John Erskine proposed in 1917, and subsequently taught as a general honors course, was a two-year course that met once a week to discuss one great book in a two-hour seminar. This was the course Mortimer Adler and Robert Maynard Hutchins recreated at the University of Chicago.[8] Discussion, in such a course, must remain at a very high level of generality—one great book per two hours of seminar does not make for detailed analysis. Of the minute attention paid to the verbal surface in the classical curriculum, to stylistic analysis, nothing remains—nor could remain, since all the Greek and Latin texts were read in translation. Of the intense drill in rhetorical performance, in declamation, in the imaginative recreation of historical and psychological circumstance, nothing remains. Of the intense drill in written styles, nothing remains. Of the training in memory, nothing remains. Of the training in argumentation from a standard body of topoi, nothing remains. In fact, nothing remains of the classical tradition of rhetorical education except the classical texts themselves, read now as a decontextualized history of disembodied great ideas. No wonder Plato could reign supreme in such a world.

The real classical curriculum, the one followed from classical Greece onward for more than 2,000 years, was the one I have just outlined, the *rhetorical* paideia. It was, above all, a theory of *general* education, a centripetal system rather than our present centrifugal one. We discarded it when Newtonian science came on the scene, but perhaps we may have a use for it again.

There is some evidence, beyond our pressing need for a general system of education that allows us to talk to one another, that the real classical curriculum is returning to the world of learning and the professional tower of dialectical babel. It is this return that I have discussed in chapter 3. Most of our learned professions are now getting on for a hundred years old, and they are beginning to become self-conscious about themselves. They are beginning to realize that they have a history and that it is germane to their present endeavors. They are beginning to become self-conscious about their own professional languages as well. Geertz's essays often emerge as meditations on what we might call the rhetoric of anthropology. Donald McCloskey has written a brilliant analysis of *The Rhetoric of Economics*. Legal studies has been pondering its own rhetorical stance as never before, first under the pressures of plain-language laws and then under the alternative lash of critical legal studies. McCloskey's research group at Iowa has published a fine collection of essays on *The Rhetoric of the Human Sciences*, across the board. The many attacks on the language of critical theory, as it has come to be called, represent yet another self-conscious gaze upon a professional language.[9]

I have argued elsewhere in this book that critical theory itself, if translated into plain language, looks a lot like what the Western world has always called "rhetoric." This theoretical gaze, which has now spread to all the human sciences, if looked at in a historical light represents in fact the return of the rhetorical paideia after its long Newtonian banishment. If this is the case, it is ironic that the NEH critique voiced by Mrs. Cheney and others on the cultural right has attacked the world of theory so sharply. For that world represents what the NEH truly seeks, what Geertz has wanly hoped for—a way for us to talk to one another. To be sure, the theory world wants to admit this no more than the other side; one wants to be a unique and original soul, after all, not a reincarnation.

Insofar as the modern university curriculum is as I have liverishly described it—a series of countries speaking separate languages, among which the students migrate in rotation every hour on the hour—it is a very rhetorical society and will create in our students a very rhetorical self and sense of society. If we wish to create a community from it, we need only revive the traditional rhetorical paideia. It will do just fine. It was created, after all, to provide precisely such training. We should reinstate a rehearsal pedagogy, teach our students once again to recognize and use rhetorical figures, analyze prose, do stylistic translations, synthesize from modern social and neurological science a new nomenclature of personality types, update the topics of arguments, and put all this to work on the discourse in each of our discourse communities. Students would learn to write the professional dialects but also (here McCloskey's *Rhetoric of Economics* provides a perfect model) how to deconstruct them, to show each how its rhetoric creates the boundary-conditions of its thinking. Isn't this, in fact, how the writing-across-the-curriculum courses now popular on many college and university campuses must and do move?

There is nothing difficult about such a curricular reform. It lies within our powers to do it and we have 2,500 years of rhetorical history and pedagogy to guide us. But aren't we all more than a little afraid to follow the logic of our own analysis? We would all welcome a rhetorical system that allows us to diagnose the university curriculum in a new and illuminating way, but what about the kind of student this system will create? A radically dramatic student looks too much like the deconstructive nihilist who haunts the NEH critique from the Right. And what about the curriculum? Will it not, under our analysis, remain in pieces? (Indeed, does not the analysis explain *why* it will remain in pieces?) We would like to create the opposite kind of student, students with real, that is to say central, selves, who write real, that is to say original and heartfelt, prose. We would have, that is, some way to teach our students the deep and constitutive sociability that the rhetorical tradition provides, without making them the cynical connoisseurs of language that rhetorical training tends to produce. We want both Rousseau *and* Quintilian, the Romantic central self with its unique originality *and* the role-playing rhetorical self that makes society possible. Can we formulate a curriculum that enhances both? I think we can, but to learn how, we will have to take another look at traditional rhetoric—and at the deep contradiction that animates it.

For in my description I have not done full justice to the rhetorical paideia. I have described accurately how it worked, and works, but it has never gone about its work with a whole heart or with any accurate sense of what it was actually doing. This is because it has from the beginning been burdened with a Platonic conscience that denied the main tenets of its belief at every point. Plato's quarrel with rhetoric came from rhetoric's very adhocness, its absence of fixed coordinates like a central self and an externally sanctioned society that, on some ultimate front stage, was not dramatic at all. Plato wanted a final and referential language transparent to truth, a type of thinking that derived from reality itself as in itself it really is. And the Killer B's want these same things—no *bricolage* for them. So do all those who have been mounting the orthodox case for the Great Books. Thinking in the rhetorical world is not like this; it is like kiting checks, not like balancing books, even Great ones. In the rhetorical world, every chain of reasoning depends on a previous chain of reasoning that you have just deposited but which hasn't cleared yet. A depositor of theoretically perfect agility can keep this up forever. That was not good enough for Plato: he wanted balanced books. How rhetoric got its guilty Platonic conscience is a fascinating tale too long to tell here, but we must notice its effect on rhetorical education because the effect remains profoundly with us—explains, in fact, the root disagreement at the heart of the current curricular debate.

As a result of this guilty conscience, the great works of classical rhetoric, the scriptures of the paideia, are fundamentally self-contradictory. Their training and doctrine is built on a social self and a dramatistic society but their value judgments are all made, finally, in reference to a central self and an externally sanctioned, nondramatic social reality which is really out there and full of real events and good old-fashioned, back-to-basics historical fact, *wie ist eigentlich gewesen.* The entire rhetorical tradition is deeply self-contradictory in this way, beginning with Aristotle. Rhetorical education regularly invokes two opposite kinds of reality, a self that is first social and then central, a society that is first dramatic and then externally sanctioned, a physical reality that is both "decorous," that is to say created by the discourse which describes it, and at the same time "out there" and independent of the language describing it. The tradition includes, that is, *both* deconstruction *and* the reconstruction of the Killer B's, held in a perpetual oscillation.

This self-contradiction explains both the extraordinary longevity of the rhetorical paideia and its resurrection in so many postmodern guises today. Rhetoric was never allowed, if I may borrow an idea from the great American rhetorician Kenneth Burke, to become fully itself. It was always an uneasy combination of the two basic concepts of the self, central and social, of the two complementary basic conceptions of society, of language as transmission and language as creation, of thought as rule-governed and thought as coaxing chance. The history of rhetoric is at heart the history of how these two conceptions of human life contended with one another.

We can call these two views by several names. Eric Havelock and Walter Ong find this a technology-driven difference, that between *oral* and *literate* cultures. But we can, taking a historical perspective, call it a version of the perennial quarrel between rhetoric and philosophy, or between dialectic and rhetoric, if you prefer those terms. I have called them, since I began thinking about these matters in terms of Matthew Arnold's phrase "high seriousness," the rhetorical and the serious views of life, and tried to suggest that they were opposed theoretical extremes which can be justified by the needs of inquiry alone. Or, we can base our terms on neuroanatomy and talk about left brain and right brain, or about the locus of memory in less schematic terms, or about behavior as hard-wired or as culturist, though I confess I am incompetent to dress the problem in these particular sets of clothes. The crucial thing is not, however, how the opposites are named but how they are related.

We have, it turns out, a Renaissance model of how this relationship maps out. Baldesare Castiglione, in *The Book of the Courtier*, presents an ideal courtier whose self encounters the world in a new way, a way for which he had to invent a new word. This new self was composed of a social self and a central self in oscillation, the frequency and magnitude of the oscillation being a matter of rhetorical decorum. The central self would always be created by a series of social selves, the social self always controlled by a central self that was in the occasion but not of it. Neither self could be seen except from the vantage point of the other. Self-consciousness was consequently volatile and yet not unstable—what, in the psychology of vision, is called a bi-stable illusion. Castiglione invented a term for this dynamic conception of human identity: he called it *sprezzatura*. If we conceive of a rhetorical education as creating this bi-stable self, we can comprehend how crucial *to prepon*, decorum, really was. For that ultimate judgment-call, an estimation built on but transcending rule-governed behavior, was always a judgment about what form of *sprezzatura* was appropriate—how rapid the frequency, how wide the wave form, of the oscillation should be.

It should be clear that the root-disagreement over the curriculum is between the two opposed poles of this oscillation. The deconstructionist insists on a dramatistic conception of human life with no absolutes; the reconstructionist, on an absolute conception with no drama. Both sides ensure that they will never agree because *they formulate their positions outside of time.* If we put the two into time, into oscillation, the unsolvable opposition *simply dissolves.*

Why, then, have we so long resisted this model of human reality, and a curriculum based upon it? Why do we continue to ignore a solution to our problems that has existed at least since the Renaissance—well, since Cicero, whom Castiglione leaned on ... well, since the Greek rhetoricians Cicero leaned on?

First, this volatile stability disconcerts us. Although we can get used to it—the rhetorical paideia would not have lasted two millennia and more if we could not, if we did not in fact internalize it very deeply—such bi-stability remains acutely troubling to think about. That we can see one version of ourselves only while inhabiting the other violates deep-seated feelings about the wholeness of human vision. That every front stage *only exists* when seen from a back stage, and vice versa, is something that at a very profound level we simply do not want to admit.

Second, we are delivered by bi-stability into a perpetual restlessness, since the frequency and wavelength of this change is up to us, is verily what human culture is all about. This range-finding stands at the center of any culturist theory of interpretation. It is a strain-gauge of cultural sophistication, I suppose. Self-consciousness is burdensome enough, but to have to choose your *degree* of it, and then vary that choice from time to time, constitutes a real interpretive challenge.

Third, we as academics, as professional inquirers, instinctively resist this solution because it does promise to be precisely that—a solution. The two polar positions I have sketched are the two that the professional inquirers in Western humanistic culture earn their living arguing about. The adversative stance we take to them—one side must be right, the other must be wrong—comes so naturally that we don't even think about it. A bi-stable model like the matrix I chart in chapters 1 and 3 threatens to resolve the debate, or at least to create a framework to contain it, and so to shut the debate down. The nature of our work would change, and some of us might be put out of work altogether. We resist self-consciousness about our discipline, its history and its language, because we don't *want* to see our own boundary-conditions. If the price of this reluctance is humorlessness on the one hand and peanut-butter prose on the other, well, so be it. We resist seeing ourselves, in other words, as our students see us; we don't want to play "native" to their "visiting anthropologist." We might learn things we don't want to know.

Once we get past these obstacles to conceiving the root problem of the curriculum, a bi-stable resolution suggests itself immediately. And getting past these obstacles is possible, indeed inevitable, if we are to understand the behavioral logic of any self-conscious, that is to say fully literate, culture. You revive the classical rhetorical paideia, but with a clear idea of the indispensable bi-stability underlying it. If you want to know how discourse communities cohere—how undergraduate majors are related, and the subgroups among them form a whole—you must know what the rules are and how to join them, you must play a role in their drama. Social self, dramatic society. And you have a set of analytic tools available for that task, tools polished for you by 2,000 years of use. But in this act of joining a professional specialization, choosing a "major," the rehearsal-reality that you have set up becomes, by the very energy with which you participate in it, a referential reality. Suddenly, you are part of that professional community, using its tools for a job of work. You are looking THROUGH its language not AT it. Your self-consciousness falls away from you and you get on with the job. If you persist in it, you become the job.

There is nothing complex or strange about all this. This is the process of revision, for a start, whatever you are revising. Familiar to us all. It is the oscillation from critic to reader and back that we all rehearse every time we read a work of imaginative literature. We need to show our students that when we perform this oscillation, it is a behavioral allegory. A lot goes with each stage in the bi-stable illusion—an all-embracing theory of the self and of society—and the oscillation is how we hold these two immiscible states together. It is also how we hold together the moral and formal lessons of art in a single coherent expression. That complex act of will is what the complex, unstable, protean, adaptable, Western self is all about.

I can't give you a specific lesson plan or core curriculum or plan for an undergraduate major to go with this oscillation. Its great virtue lies the opposite way, in its being adaptable to any curriculum. As with the genetic code, a simple rule-governed formula can generate endlessly different organisms.[10] If you have a general ideal of what you are doing, you can use anything to realize it. We don't need to fight about Great Books vs. Relevant Books— that fiery argument is pointless. The nonnegotiable center lurks somewhere else altogether, neglected by both sides.

The argument about the Great Books promises to be otiose in yet another way. If our students don't read the Great Books, it will be less because they disdain greatness than because they won't be reading books of any sort. They will be reading electronic text, which throws the fixed text of the Great Book out the coach window as resolutely as Becky Sharp disposed of Dr. Johnson's *Dictionary*.

I have discussed this change in several places earlier in this book. Here we need note only that electronic text *embodies* the bi-stable oscillation between basic world views that I have been talking about. The fixity of print encouraged us to take this opposition out of time. Electronic display encourages us to put it back into time. The very technology through which we display words will embody the bi-stable orchestration of the world which those words will illustrate and discuss. We are accustomed to being told that the computer is a neutral tool; as far as text is concerned, and the humanistic education which rests upon it, nothing could be further from the truth. The computer will affect every element of humanistic inquiry, move it from the single stability of print to the bi-stability of the oral world from which rhetoric first emerged. The bi-stable theoretical revolution that solves the immovable curricular confrontation is also a technological revolution.

I have been trying to present a new way of conceiving the root problem of the human sciences, a new way that is also a very old one. Perhaps it will look a little less outré if we bring to mind a parallel change occurring in the physical sciences, a revolution that usually goes under the name "chaos theory." Insofar as it has been given me to understand this revolution—and that is not very far—it tries to deal with complex systems as they occur in the world not in the laboratory, and *as they occur in time.* That is what the system of classical rhetoric has always tried to do with the complex systems of conceptual thought. Now that we are beginning to put the Newtonian linear system to one side, perhaps we can do the same with the curriculum, and the systems of language instruction, built upon it.

In the Clifford Geertz essay I have twice quoted—it is called "The Way We Think Now: Toward an Ethnography of Modern Thought"—there occurs a sentence that I confess has haunted me ever since I first read it. There is, he says, no hope for "an integrated high culture." And then: "All we can hope for, which if it were to happen would be that rarest of phenomena, a *useful* miracle, is that we can devise ways to gain access to one another's vocational lives."[11] Contriving that "*useful* miracle" could restore coherence to the entire undergraduate curriculum. I am afraid that I really am going to be bold enough to suggest that the bi-stable conception of man and society transmitted to us by the rhetorical paideia constitutes this "useful miracle."

Rhetorical education, for most of Western history, was *education itself,* the aggregate process. It was the origin of, the great example of, *general* education. It shouldn't surprise us, therefore, that it offers a general theory of behavior. But its generality lies in the dynamic oscillation that controls its axial self-contradiction. Shut that oscillation down, choose either view alone—and that is what the current curriculum debate does—and the generality vanishes. Electronic text, happily, sets the vital alternation going again, and by so doing rescues us from the paradoxes generated by print.

By keeping this oscillation going, training our students to think self-consciously in terms of it, will we not equip them with a conceptual tool of general explanatory power, with a curricular compass they can use to create their own general education, their own core curriculum? For in any utterance, even as more largely in any discourse-community, and in any behavior, not only in the flux and reflux of thought, this oscillation takes place. Like it or not, we cannot rearrange our curriculum into a fixed linear order that will structure the students' academic experience; except in a few rare places, that is no longer possible. But a much simpler solution suggests itself, a nonlinear and hypertextual one. Could we not use the freshman English course to provide our students with the curricular compass that a bi-stable rhetorical training provides? A genuine rhetoric of the digital arts? Could we not reinforce it in our humanities courses, since the Western master-pieces we read there are built around the oscillation I have been talking about, the Thucydidean alternation of narrative and speech, of transparent story and opaque rhetoric, which in alternation directly allegorizes the complex Western self? Could we not make it the center of writing-across-the-curriculum courses to follow such a general humanities course, in order to show students how to join a particular discipline? Show them that the secret to working in a discourse-community without being blinded by it is to know how to look AT its professional language as well as THROUGH it, to recognize that one can do the second only because one can do the first? And, finally, could we not teach our students the aesthetics of electronic text that embody and illustrate so clearly this bi-stable process?

None of these changes would require major structural alterations. As I've argued at the end of chapter 4, the needful bureaucracy is already in place. To think of ourselves as using it in this new way is to think of ourselves as providing that direct connection between thinking about language and thinking about life which has formed the axis of humanistic education from the beginning. If we could bring it off, it would be a "useful miracle" indeed.

NOTES

1. *Integrity in the College Curriculum: A Report to the Academic Community* (Washington, D.C.: Association of American Colleges, 1985), 2.

2. Clifford Geertz, "The Way We Think Now: Toward an Ethnography of Modern Thought," in *Local Knowledge* (New York: Basic Books, 1983), 161.

3. Sidney Hook, "*The Closing of the American Mind*: An Intellectual Best-Seller Revisited," *The American Scholar* (Winter 1989): 134.

4. Excerpts of the NEH report are printed in the *Chronicle of Higher Education*, 11 Oct. 1989, A16–20.

5. Geertz (n. 2 above), 161.

6. Harry S. Ashmore, *Unseasonable Truths: The Life of Robert Maynard Hutchins* (Boston: Little, Brown, 1989).

7. I once was interviewed for a job by a dean who had taught in the program

for a long time. I asked him how he had liked it. "It was the best teaching I ever did—and it set my career back ten years."

8. See Frederick Rudolph, *The American College and University: A History* (New York: Vintage, 1965), 455–58; Ashmore (n. 6 above), 98–99; Daniel Bell, *The Reforming of General Education: The Columbia College Experience in Its National Setting* (New York: Columbia University Press, 1966), 12–15. For a general survey of this period in American higher education, see Frederick Rudolph, *Curriculum: A History of the American Undergraduate Course of Study since 1636* (San Francisco: Jossey-Bass, 1977), 245–89. Of the absurdity of calling the Great Books a "classical" curriculum, there has been, to my knowledge, no discussion whatever.

9. Full references to works mentioned in this paragraph may be found in chapter 3, esp. nn. 15, 16, and 35.

10. As the current experimentation with "artificial life" so strikingly shows. See Steven Levy, *Artificial Life: The Quest for a New Creation* (New York: Pantheon, 1992).

11. Geertz (n. 2 above), 160.

7

What I have called the "Q" question emerges every time technology changes in some basic way. In each case, we have to ask ourselves, "What are we trying to protect? The old technology itself or what it carries for us, does to us?" The answer usually returned when considering the movement from book to screen has been the first. The book itself is sacred. Let's protect it. The codex book creates the vital central self. The codex book defines human reason. Our cultural vitals are isomorphic with the codex book. Its very feel and heft and look and smell are talismanic. We must have an agency of the federal government to protect it.

As I have said several times already in this, well, in this book, I am hardly against books. I have spent my life reading them, writing them, buying them, and walling my house with them. But I don't think the codex book provides the real center we want to protect. And defining that center is now an exigent task, which I try to begin in this essay.

The reader might be amused by the genesis of this seemingly heterogeneous essay review. I had agreed to review one of the books I discuss, but kept putting off writing the review. Meanwhile, I was reading all kinds of other books, reading them for amusement and distraction in a time of personal troubles. I woke up one night, literally in the middle of the night, realizing that all these books I had been reading bore upon the root problem I was trying to address in my scholarly life—the "Q" question. I sat down before the computer at sunup and wrote the essay in a single day.

The "Q" Question

t the beginning of book 12 of the *Institutio oratoria* Quintilian confronts what is for him a crucial question. Is the perfect orator—whom he has, for the eleven long books preceding, sought to form—a good man as well as a good orator? Begging the essential question of the entire *Speculum principis* genre, and hence of Western education from that day to this, he replies, "Of course! Such a man is the very one I seek to describe, the *vir bonus dicendi peritus* that Cato has defined." And then, sliding back a little to the question he has just begged, he reflects that if oratory serves only to empower evil (*si vis illa dicendi malitiam instruxerit*) then what has he spent his life doing? And not only that, what has nature done to us, if she allows something like that? Turned language, man's best friend, into a potential enemy? To confront this question honestly would imperil his entire endeavor and so, with that genial resolution which illustrates his sweet nature throughout the *Institutio*, he assumes the answer he wants and then goes on to bolster it with inventively adapted Platonism.

The problem itself, which I shall call the "Q" question in honor of its most famous nonanswerer, has underwritten, and plagued, Western humanism from first to last. We have a paideia, a "discipline of discourse," to translate Isocrates' *hē tōn logōn paideia*, which, from his day to ours, we all like to teach and always, in one form or another, have taught. But no one has ever been able to prove that it does conduce to virtue more than to vice. In fact, as we know from our first department meeting, much evidence points the other way. So, like Quintilian, we first deny the problem resolutely, and then construct something that I shall call "the Weak Defense." The Weak Defense argues that there are two kinds of rhetoric, good and bad. The good kind is used in good causes, the bad kind in bad causes. Our kind is the good kind; the bad kind is used by our opponents. This was Plato's solution, and Isocrates', and it has been enthusiastically embraced by humanists ever since.

This permanent postponement of the problem works well enough for us, but not for the locus of so much rhetorical theory and practice, the law courts: there the advocate cannot prejudge the case lest he threaten both justice and his own livelihood. This unavoidable confrontation explains, perhaps, why Isocrates thought the legal aspect of rhetoric so *infra dig*, and why so many commentators have thought Cicero's *De oratore*, which does confront the issue from time to time, so much more one-sided an argument than it is. It certainly explains why Quintilian, when he comes to address the advocate's dilemma in book 12, hides in another patch of up-market flummery. The law's answer to the "Q" question is generally taken to be "No!" And yet jurisprudence in the West from the Greeks onward has offered the opposite answer, a "Yes!" which I shall call "the Strong Defense," and which Samuel Johnson summarized with his usual absence of cant as, "Sir, you do not know it to be good or bad till the Judge determines it." The Strong Defense assumes that truth is determined by social dramas, some more formal than others but all man-made. Rhetoric in such a world is not ornamental but determinative, essentially creative. Truth once created in this way becomes referential, as in legal precedent. The court decides "what really happened" and we then measure against that. The Strong Defense implies a figure/ground shift between philosophy and rhetoric—in fact, as we shall see, a continued series of shifts. In its world, there is as much truth as we need, maybe more, but argument is open-ended, more like kiting checks than balancing books.

Much as we want to evade it, however, the "Q" question is coming after us these days. It presses on us in the university, for the university is like the law courts: it cannot dodge the "Q" question. It must design a curriculum. And it is, more and more insistently, being asked to design one that situates and justifies the humanities. To do that, you must answer the Question, or at least self-consciously beg it. For clearly it applies not only to rhetoric, but to all teaching of the arts and letters, to everything we call the humanities. To design a humanities curriculum (or even, as we more often do, to decline to design one), you must know how you get from a theory of reading and writing to a curriculum, and that requires having a theory of reading and writing in the first place. Requires, that is, answering the "Q" question. So we humanists are being pressured from without. But we are also being pressured from within. For the implications of the "Q" question have been worked on, if not always out and not always with Johnson's absence of cant, by the postmodern critique that began in the arts when the Italian Futurists attacked the codex book and all that it represents at the beginning of the century.

Several recent books have reflected these pressures, external and internal. Coming from a number of fields which the university's disciplinary structure does its best to keep apart, they have re-posed the "Q" question in divergent ways. The answers given to it fall, with a nicety that can help clear the mind, into the two defenses sketched above. By reflecting on these books as a group, we can perhaps begin to look beyond the customary evasions to some more persuasive explanation of what the humanities are and do.

Perhaps the most celebrated answer to the "Q" question in modern times—we might, in fact, argue that this answer started "modern times"—was supplied by Peter Ramus. He begins his *Arguments in Rhetoric against Quintilian* by attacking it head on:

> And so first of all let us put forward the definition in which Quintilian outlined for us his ideal orator. ... "I teach," he says, "that the orator cannot be perfect unless he is a good man. Consequently I demand from him not only outstanding skill in speaking but all the virtuous qualities of character." ...
>
> What then can be said against this definition of an orator? I assert indeed that such a definition of an orator seems to me to be useless and stupid. ...
>
> For although I admit that rhetoric is a virtue, it is virtue of the mind and the intelligence, as in all the true liberal arts, whose followers can still be men of the utmost moral depravity.[1]

I am quoting Carole Newlands' recent translation, which appears with the Latin text of 1549 and an extended introduction by James J. Murphy (in which he tells us that Quintilian himself brings up the "Q" question twenty-three times!). For the debate about the humanities and the humanities curriculum in which we currently find ourselves, a more splendidly useful and well-timed volume can scarcely be imagined. To read it is to learn how the "humanities crisis" started, how the conception of language as value-free and ideally transparent underwrote the modern world.

Ramus separated the traditional five parts of rhetoric into two divisions, giving invention, argument, and arrangement to philosophy, and leaving "style and delivery [as] the only true parts of the art of rhetoric" (90). Ramus also separated thought from language: "There are two universal, general gifts bestowed by nature upon man, Reason and Speech; dialectic is the theory of the former, grammar and rhetoric of the latter" (86). Rhetoric and grammar thus become cosmetic arts, and speech—and of course writing—along with them. Reason breaks free of speech and takes on a Platonic self-standing freedom. Add to a free-standing reason the Ramist zeal, one might almost say obsession, for dividing the seamless web of learning into self-standing and self-sealing divisions, divisions that later became academic disciplines, and we can see anatomized the two crucial elements that separate the traditional rhetorical paideia from the modern curriculum. Ramus, or the broad cultural change that he focused, not only settled the "Q" question by breaking rhetoric down the middle, but also reversed the centripetal flow the rhetorical paideia had built into its heart. In the traditional rhetorical curriculum, all subjects exfoliated out from the *ars disserendi*. This central focus meant that the arts were perpetually shifting position and overlapping one another. Such shifting is what Ramus hated the most: "For arts ought to consist of subjects that are constant, perpetual, and unchanging, and they should consider only those concepts which Plato says are archetypal and eternal" (99). And the self-contained discipline meant the possibility of a real textbook. As Father Ong, whose work has allowed us to accept Ramus as a major figure, puts it: "A Ramist textbook on a given subject had no acknowledged interchange with anything outside itself. ... [I]f you defined and divided in the proper way, everything in the art was ... complete and self-contained."[2]

We can hardly make too much of this decision. Value-free language and the possibility of a self-contained discipline make possible both modern science and that mapping of humanistic inquiry onto a scientific model which has created modern social science as well. And they create a concomitant problem, one Richard McKeon, in a discussion to be noticed later, finds characteristic of our own time: they render problematic the relation of thought to action. Thought now had its own disciplinary arena. Knowing could now be a self-enclosed activity all by itself, pursued "for its own sake," a claim that simply makes no sense in the rhetorical paideia, tied as it was to public action.

Restricting rhetoric to style and delivery, Ramus solves the "Q" question by definition. Rhetoric is a cosmetic, and bad girls wear makeup as well as good ones, probably better. The rhetorical paideia, as Quintilian described it, existed to hold rhetoric and philosophy together. Ramus rips them apart. By so doing, he makes possible a secularity in education that, for all the Platonic objections to it, the rhetorical paideia never permitted. Envaluation was everywhere in rhetorical education. From now on, ethics would have a special "department," religion first and then philosophy, where it could be studied in and for itself. And the Ramist division, by dividing the curriculum into separate subjects and texts, separated intellection and values in yet another way. The rhetorical paideia was built upon the student's experience through time; no treatise illustrates this better than Quintilian's. But once disciplines and texts supervened, the student's development would always be at odds with the boundaries of disciplinary inquiry. Thus began the world we have now, where students change intellectual worlds every hour on the hour. Thus also begins another adjustment of inquiry to abstract schema rather than human experience: Ramus divides up rhetoric, and the range of learning to which he applied his attention, to facilitate inquiry.

If you separate the discipline of discourse into essence and ornament, into philosophy and rhetoric, and make each a separate discipline, it makes them easier to think about. Thus begins modern inquiry's long history of looking for its lost keys not where it lost them but under the lamppost, where they are easier to find. The consequences of these Ramist decisions, as the texts I will now notice illustrate, extend from how we interpret Renaissance education to how we read our own, from how we write about economics to how we manage big corporations, from the Platonic zeal of Allan Bloom to the supercilious treason of Anthony Blunt.

◻   ◻   ◻

Arthur F. Kinney, in his ambitious *Humanist Poetics: Thought, Rhetoric, and Fiction in Sixteenth-Century England*,[3] describes the rhetoric-centered world Ramus upended. Kinney started out to write a book on Renaissance English fictions but came to something much broader, an attempt to understand the English Renaissance as animated by rhetoric, not by philosophy. "What may at first be startling, but is nevertheless essential to understand, is that philosophy was displaced by rhetoric among humanists and humanist educators. ... Reason, as man's distinguishing characteristic, was to be realized primarily through speech. *Oratio* is next to *ratio*, as Sidney puts it in the *Defence of Poesie*. ... [I]n the beginning was always the Word. We can see this wherever we look" (7). The texts Kinney discusses—*Utopia, The Courtier, The Adventures of Master F. J., Euphues,* Sidney's *Arcadia,* Greene's romances, Lodge's tales, and Nashe's *Unfortunate Traveller*—all grow directly out of rhetorical education. The rhetorical neophyte's endless training in epistles, themes, and orations invites him "to frame narratives and characters in conflict: the authentic roots of western fiction, they set the imagination leaping. ... The line between a developing rhetoric and a developing poetic for fiction thus becomes perilously thin" (22). Kinney traces these and many other ways in which the rhetorical paideia of the English Renaissance led directly and specifically to the kind of literature it produced. Kinney restricts himself to fiction, but the mapping to all of Elizabethan literature is easy enough to do once we know the moves. To have shown us how to do it, in such informed detail, removes a long-standing task from the Renaissance agenda and represents a very considerable scholarly and critical accomplishment.

But Kinney is after bigger game. He wants to confront the fundamental implications of the rhetorical paideia as a philosophy of education, and this means confronting the "Q" question. It stands at the center of his book, and by that I mean not only at the center of his argument about Renaissance education but at the center of his textual interpretations as well. Here, in my view, he is less successful in what he sets out to do. In his reading of both the educational philosophy and the literary texts, he follows Quintilian's procedure almost exactly. He poses the "Q" question; he says that he sees its difficulties; he then takes refuge in Plato, in "good rhetoric," in the Weak Defense. Finally, when the unsolved question threatens to get out of control—as it does in every text he examines—like Quintilian he begs the question, usually in a ringing phrase.

In his opening discussion of rhetorical education, for example, Kinney poses the "Q" question by quoting Sextus Empiricus: "For the orator, of whatever sort he may be, must certainly practise himself in contradictory speeches, and injustice is inherent in contradictions; therefore every orator, being an advocate of injustice, is unjust" (26). And then, by way of Cicero, Isocrates, and Puttenham, he comes to Plato. "Plato seems to have been the first to foresee this, to sense the endangering possibilities. In rescuing a rhetoric for a usable poetic while confronting such dangers openly, he established grounds for a fiction that might reliably teach. He gave philosophic and rhetorical validity and purpose, that is, for More to create Utopia, Castiglione his Urbino, or Sidney Arcadia" (27–28). But Plato did nothing of the sort. He did not confront the rhetorical paideia. Much of his work, as Eric Havelock has pointed out, exists not to confront it directly and "openly" but to distort and obscure it. If Kinney had confronted this Platonic critique (and it is hardly restricted to Havelock), he could not have rescued his "usable poetic." Plato allows as "good rhetoric" only the kind that enhances an argument we already know, from a priori grounds, to be true. As with Ramus, reason is one thing, and primary; rhetoric is another, derivative and cosmetic. Permitted in the service of truth, it is otherwise an abomination. Whether Tudor educational theory, which Kinney correctly describes as being rhetorical to the core, adopted in theory this Platonic nonanswer to the "Q" question is a very doubtful proposition, though Kinney argues it.

What stands beyond question, however, is that Tudor education could not carry it out in practice. In practice, rhetorical education is education in two-sided argument, argument where the truth is decided by the judge or jury, where truth is a dramatic criticism handed down on the forensic drama which has been played out according to the rules laid down by a rhetorical education. Such an education stands fundamentally at odds with any absolute or a priori system of thought, and no amount of Platonic evasion, at first or second hand, can conceal this. The current religious fundamentalists of the "moral majority," with their fear of "secular humanism," as they call this interior logic, understand the danger. The Renaissance humanists understood it too. However frequent their euphoric flights about the unlimited powers and malleability of man, they knew that rhetorical education, in practice, saw man as limited, not unlimited, living in a world of play, not of ideal forms. Such an education inevitably involved the full range of human motive, our agonistic contentions and impulses of pure play as well as the ostensible purposes, or arguments, at issue.

Kinney fails to understand that the Strong Defense is required here, and he completely fails to imagine how one might construct it. This is a crucial failing, and it leads him repeatedly astray when he comes to read literary texts—*Utopia, Praise of Folly, Arcadia*, the fictions of Gascoigne, Lyly, Greene, and Lodge. Kinney keeps talking about "redeeming" rhetoric, but when rhetoric empowers literature, it is unredeemable. That is what rhetorical literature, I am tempted to say Western literature, is all about. I will argue later in this essay that a failure to confront the "Q" question disempowers humanistic study in general. Kinney's failure to see how rhetoric works in particular texts provides, for the Renaissance, a paradigmatic illustration of this disempowering.

Because the most acute reenactment of the Strong Defense in the Renaissance, and perhaps ever since, is Castiglione's in *The Book of the Courtier*, it is especially interesting to notice what Kinney makes of that. Castiglione resolves the immiscibility of rhetoric and philosophy, of truth and Truth, by creating a cultural ideal he calls *sprezzatura* that puts the two into a perpetual oscillation.[4] The conversations in Urbino model the continual "conversation" which is human culture in a rhetorical, interpretive universe of discourse. Truth and truth are put in a continually reversing figure/ground relation that answers the "Q" question by putting it back into time. Castiglione implies a literary, as against a philosophical, answer to the basic humanistic question. Kinney completely misinterprets this argument, which is a vital one for his thesis:

> The twin motives that inspire and govern *Il Cortegiano* (and in turn govern us) are, then, the inductive establishment of the pure human-

ist community and the securing of its permanence. Such impulses resemble those of Hythlodaye. The fatal difficulty is that, in so shaping Urbino, Castiglione insists on realizing perfectibility in an imperfect society whose flaws are caught in a discernible time and place. Yet, confronted by the problems of mortality, Castiglione has, by a courageous act of the imagination, made his men and women *im*mortal, impervious to time, by rendering them into the verbal art of a book, *Il Libro*, of the courtier.[5]

Philosophy and rhetoric, taken as the two great opposites of the Western cultural conversation, can be harmonized only by reversing the Platonic effort, by putting them back into time. Kinney's Platonizing makes sure that he misses the point. But once you have decided the "Q" question as he has, the point could not be there in the first place.

That the "Q" question takes so central a place in Kinney's effort to account for Renaissance literary rhetoric has an importance beyond the particular texts he seeks to explain. What stands at issue is how we read Western literature in general. Depending on which answer we bring to the basic question, we shall confront two different literatures. This becomes a matter of some moment when a series of self-teaching Great Texts is urged as the answer to all our educational and cultural problems.

The "Q" question, as posed by Renaissance rhetorical education, has been addressed in another recent book, Anthony Grafton and Lisa Jardine's *From Humanism to the Humanities: Education and the Liberal Arts in Fifteenth- and Sixteenth-Century Europe*. "The subject of this book," they tell us, is "the sense in which the *bonae artes* are 'good.'"[6] They are interested, more narrowly, in the gap Kinney discusses between the claims the Renaissance made for rhetorical education and the actual practice of it. They offer a rich set of case studies from original documents which no one interested in humanistic education, Renaissance or modern, should fail to ponder.

Grafton and Jardine view the failure to ask the "Q" question as the endemic failing in earlier discussions of Renaissance education: "The few intellectual historians [as against social historians] who have worked on early modern education have been more intent on grinding old axes than on testing new hypotheses. Themselves believing in the preeminent value of a literary education, committed to preserving a canon of classics and a tradition of humanism, they have treated the rise of the classical curriculum and the downfall of scholasticism as the natural triumph of virtue over vice" (xii). In other words, these historians have, with Quintilian, simply assumed that a rhetorical education, and the literary one that evolved from it, brought with it moral improvement and civic virtue. So, when the Renaissance educators pronounced this creed, surely that was what their educational practice produced. Educational practice, that is, was read with the same assumptions Kinney brings to Renaissance texts, and with the same results. Theory and practice are found to agree because the agreement was decided on beforehand. Grafton and Jardine read with a more jaundiced eye, and find that rhetorical education, in practice, did not support the claims made for it. It educated scoundrels as well as statesmen, and it served as a class badge for both. And if the meticulous patterns of rote repetition and memorization, verbal analysis, and dramatic rehearsal which made up the core of rhetorical education in Latin had any real connection with producing either scoundrels or statesmen, rather than unthinking parrots and poseurs, no one then was able to demonstrate it.

Erasmus, to take but one example from their discussion, "maintains that there is an intimate and vital relationship between the piety of his intentions ... and the systematic works on humanistic eloquence" (139). But the connection is never demonstrated. Instead, as we have seen Quintilian do, Erasmus resorts to iteration: "The fact that Erasmus returns again and again in his letters to the connection between his publishing activities in the secular sphere and his scriptural and doctrinal studies suggests that the welding of profane learning to lay piety requires a certain amount of intellectual sleight-of-hand" (144). The "sleight-of-hand" is simply to repeat, as Quintilian does twenty-three times, what you cannot prove, and such repetition has been the basic defense of humanism ever since, the generator of the endless tautological justifications of the humanities that have accompanied our requests for handouts, private or public, ever since.

Erasmus also uses that other staple evasion of the "Q" question, the great literary text itself:

> In the *Methodus* Erasmus lays careful emphasis on the proper procedure for "disciplined" reading. He argues in detail that the only way to draw the true message from the Bible is to read it as a good humanist would read a classic pagan text: as the record of Christ, that incomparable orator, and Paul, that incomparable theologian, addressing specific audiences and dealing with specific issues. By keeping the context always in view, by bearing in mind the speaker's and writer's situation, the student will be able to avoid the doctrinal errors and evasions that the scholastics—those insensitive readers—have committed.
>
> ...
>
> What Erasmus does not explain (what from his point of view as a humanist pedagogue requires no explanation) is how the young the-

ologian can be sure that simple, straightforward reading will produce guaranteed right doctrine. (146–48)

This "great text + right reading = moral truth" equation, this "convenient confusion" of the methodical with the morally sound, as Grafton and Jardine style it, has—as evidenced in Gerald Graff's history and Allan Bloom's revivalist tract to be considered below—caused trouble right up to the present moment.

Perhaps the most provocative discussion in the book is the chapter on "Pragmatic Humanism: Ramism and the Rise of 'the Humanities.'" Ramus did not think he had split rhetoric from philosophy, only separated them so that, in due course, they would find their natural unity *in forum, in Senatum, in concionem populi, in omnem hominum conventum.* It is a touching faith that, as Grafton and Jardine make clear, did not always work out in practice. This great curricular Judgment Day when all things that humanist specialization has rent apart will come together, though we continually believe in and plan on it, continues to elude us.

On the one hand, we have the "humanism" of their title, the kind of liberal education which is moral in its essence, which answers "Yes" to the "Q" question. Ramus replaces that with the second key term of their title, the "humanities." The *ars disserendi* was to be converted into a series of techniques that anyone could use to get ahead in any field. "It opened the prospect that the purpose of education was to purvey information and skills, not to be morally improving: Ramist teaching might make you a good grammarian or a good mathematician; there was no guarantee that it would make you a good person" (170). "A committed Ramist finds himself free to pursue the *ars disserendi* simply as a route to high government office, without worrying about being a *vir bonus* (a good man)" (189). This represents "the final *secularisation* of humanist teaching—the transition from 'humanism' to 'the humanities'" (168).

This pattern of root self-contradictions has lived, then, to the present day, and its *Nachleben* is part of the story Grafton and Jardine tell. They begin by talking about Eliot and Leavis and their assumptions and, even closer to home, about the pressures that Mrs. Thatcher (she is not named but alembicated into an impersonal passive) exerted on English universities in recent years:

Where, it is asked, is the marketable end-product in the non-vocational liberal arts faculties that justifies the investment of public money? Where indeed? This book is offered in part as a contribution to our understanding of the long history of evasiveness on the part of teachers of the humanities—an evasiveness which has left them vulnerable to the charge of non-productiveness, irrelevance to modern industrial society, without those teachers themselves having deviated from their commitment to the liberal arts as a "training for life." (xiv)

They pose the question rather than simply evade it. But, alas, they don't answer it, or even begin to. Instead, they end their courageous study with laconic regret:

[W]e watch as our most gifted students master the techniques and methods of textual analysis, the command of ancient and modern languages (which they can transpose effectively to new and developing disciplines), but in the main discard that over-arching framework of "civilised values" by which teachers of the humanities continue to set such store. Whether we like it or not, we still live with the dilemma of late humanism: we can only live in hope, and practise the humanities. (199–200)

◻   ◻   ◻

How energizing it is to turn to the new collection of Richard McKeon's essays that Mark Backman has edited, and for which he has supplied a superb introduction: *Rhetoric: Essays in Invention and Discovery.*[7] Unhappily for America, our two greatest rhetoricians, Kenneth Burke and Richard McKeon, are for most people very hard to understand. Of the two, Burke, the Great Amplifier, is far the easier to follow. McKeon condenses. I have always thought that he took as his model Aristotle's Greek at its most elliptical. For someone new to McKeon, Backman's introduction is worth its weight in gold. Let me give an example. Here is McKeon:

When the philosophic arts are conceived of as arts of being or of thought, rhetoric is not treated as a philosophic art, although it is used extensively in the controversy and refutation which constitutes communication among philosophies. When the philosophic arts are arts of communication and construction, rhetoric is made into a universal and architectonic art. (108)

And here is Backman's translation:

In the curriculum of the schools rhetoric has been assigned a much reduced role when the motive has been to establish discrete disciplines marked by unique subject matters and methods. Conversely, rhetoric has organized the entire course of study when the goal has been to bridge the gap between distinct subject matters. (xix)

McKeon's great theme emerges from these two sentences. He projects the relationship between rhetoric and philosophy, conceived both historically and theoretically, across the breadth of Western culture. From this overarching theme, of the greatest interest (Aristotelian prose and all) to anyone studying rhetoric, I can extract only the principal strand of argument, which focuses on the "Q" question. McKeon distinguishes between two kinds of rhetoric, "verbal" and "architectonic." "Verbal" rhetoric is the cosmetic and ancillary discipline left after the Ramist split occurred. "Architectonic" rhetoric is the overarching paideia Cicero and Quintilian sought to describe. The two definitions describe two basic orchestrations of reality. And from these two orchestrations emerge the Weak Defense and the Strong Defense of rhetoric. If we conceive the world as somehow externally fixed and sanctioned, then rhetoric, and by extension the arts, will be derivative and cosmetic, "verbal." If, on the other hand, truth is what the judge and jury, after a suitably dramatic proceeding, decide it is, then rhetoric is architectonic. McKeon puts it this way: "Rhetoric has replaced metaphysics as an architectonic art, in the past, when the organization and application of the arts and sciences was based, not on supposed natures of things or perceived forms of thought, but on recognition of the consequences of what men say and do" (18). McKeon argued that the reality to which rhetorical terminology referred was continually changing, making standard histories of rhetoric— which assumed that reality was a constant and the terminology changed— derivative functions. The meaning of the terms did change, not because their relations changed but because the reality underneath them changed. It changed, furthermore, in a bipolar pattern: it was either philosophical or rhetorical, or, in Kenneth Burke's terms, "dramatistic." Beneath the continual shifts there is a broad general oscillation between the philosophic and rhetorical world views, and this McKeon took to be the basic plate-tectonic of Western thought.

And so, on a very large scale indeed, McKeon puts our crucial question back into time precisely as Castiglione did, suggesting an answer to the "Q" question that is *sprezzatura* writ large. If we make the Platonic or Ramist assumptions, then to the "Q" question the obvious, indeed the tautological, answer must be "No!" If, on the other hand, we make the rhetorical assumptions, the assumptions built on a dramatistic theory of human reality and a metaphorical theory of language, then the answer, equally obviously, indeed tautologically, must be, as Quintilian has it, "Yes!" How could it be otherwise, since the orator creates the reality in which he acts? He must be at one with it, "just" and "good" in its terms, since it is created for his purpose. Now it becomes apparent that either answer, in its pure state, is logical, true, and useless. And so both sides, once they have returned the answer of their choice, proceed to hedge it. Quintilian brings philosophical coordinates into his discussion continually, so that the basic tectonic oscillation is set in motion without his acknowledging or, most of the time, even knowing it. Ramus, having separated the two, trusts that in practice they will get all mixed up together again. Who cares, since the purpose is not to describe reality but to make inquiry and teaching easier? (Back to finding your keys under the lamppost.)

McKeon is thinking, in a systemic and literally global way, about how to get out of the "Q" question dilemma that has stymied the humanities for so long and made thinking about the humanities curriculum so stultifying an exercise in self-serving cliché and ritualized complaint. As so often with McKeon, however, the range and power of his argument do not immediately communicate themselves, at least to me; the reader is urged to try "The Uses of Rhetoric in a Technological Age," from which I have drawn the following passage, direct:

> The growth of science and communication, the increase of knowledge and the formation of world community, have begun to lay out the field of systematic organization both as a system of communication for a universal audience, mankind, and as a system of operation of an ongoing development and inquiry, technology. It is a field which provides grounding for the intersubjectivity of communications of persons and groups and for the objectivity of conclusions of inquiry and action. It is within this field that the possible worlds, which are discussed in plans and policy, are constructed, and theses which are posited are stabilized into principles. Theses and principles have a history which carries back in tradition to principles that were called eternal and universal but were also derived from theses which posit being in the context of an agent, his environment, and his subject. It is the field of reflexivity and responsibility, which must be explored in rational action concerning rights and justice, laws and conventions, sanctions and obligations, utilities and values, and opinions and truths. The field of the new dialectical rhetoric, of debate and dialogue, is being travelled and cultivated by chance and by art. An architectonic-productive survey of the field of these activities could make its beginning by orienting rhetoric from the oppositions of the past to the understanding and projection of the new processes and needs of the present. (23–24)

He is exploring the interface between absolute and contingent statements, the perpetual frontstage/backstage oscillation of human attention, and trying to distinguish the oscillation as the final integer. We cannot define a front stage, a rhetorical reality, without assuming a back stage or philosophical one. And we never define a back stage without knowing that in another act of attention, or in another time, it will be a front stage.

McKeon is trying, that is to say, to create an architectonic rhetoric which includes "philosophy" as a less than Platonic absolute. "In the emerging community of the world the first problem of philosophy—the new metaphysics or at least the new prolegomenon to all future metaphysics—will expound the sense in which what is on some grounds or in some circumstances true is at other times false and dangerous" (220). And, unlike almost all the professional humanists, but in sync with the postmodern critique in the visual and musical arts, he sees modern technology as a potential ally in this Herculean endeavor. Indeed, in describing what his architectonics would look like, he comes close to restating the postmodern critique itself:

> It should be a rhetoric which relates form to matter, instrumentality to product, presentation to content, agent to audience, intention to reason. It should not make technology the operation of a machine, in which the message is a massage; it should not take its form from its medium. ... It should be positive in the creation, not passive in the reception, of data, facts, consequences, and objective organization. ... In a technological age all men should have an art of creativity, of judgment, of disposition, and of organization. This should be adapted to their individual development and to their contribution to forming a common field in which the subject of inquiry is not how to devise means to achieve accepted ends arranged in hierarchies but the calculation of uses and applications that might be made of the vastly increased available means in order to devise new ends and to eliminate oppositions and segregations based on past competitions for scarce means. (24)

If rhetoric is "an economics of language, the study of how scarce means are allocated to the insatiable desires of people to be heard," as Donald McCloskey argues in the volume noticed next, McKeon is suggesting that technology fundamentally alters this economy, and so the frequency and wavelength of the oscillation that underlies an architectonic rhetoric. His argument is a profound and (still rarer) profoundly forward-looking attempt to confront the "Q" question, not by waffling or resignation, but by thinking the problem through, and in terms likely to bear upon contemporary circumstance.

It may perhaps surprise us that Donald McCloskey's brilliant and witty
The Rhetoric of Economics[8] (Imagine it, a book about economics and rhetoric
that is both brilliant and witty!) refers both to Quintilian's posing of the "Q"
question at the beginning of book 12 and to the Ramist critique of it.
McCloskey's book provides a perfect example of how McKeon's vision might
be implemented. McCloskey's "rhetoric" is what McKeon would call architectonic rather than merely verbal: "Figures of speech are not mere frills.
They think for us" (xvii); and, in a fine pun, "Virtuosity *is* some evidence
of virtue" (71). Such a conception of rhetoric involves broadening the range
of human motive from the economist's Man rationally balancing his possible benefits: "The understanding of individual motivation in economics
could use some complicating" (65). McCloskey would make economists self-
conscious about their rhetoric, in order to teach them that what they do is
"a collection of literary forms, not a science." He argues that social science—
he would extend this to "science" *tout court*—does not use value-free language, that value-free language does not exist, and that we cannot posit a
purely transparent language devoid of distracting ornament, through which
we transact business with pure facts.

McCloskey is attempting, that is, to correct an imbalance that he sees,
as we would expect, as beginning with the Ramist division we have just discussed. To split language and thought, giving us the modernist, "objectivist"
way of teaching, is dangerous for the same reason Ramism was. It is easy to
teach: "Modernism and methodology have intruded into the classroom. The
modernist routine is easy to teach, which is one reason it is taught so widely. This is a pity, because the way we teach becomes the way we think" (178).
Those who oppose this act of self-awareness on the part of social science
view it as one kind or another of "nihilism," and McCloskey makes a great
deal of sense in showing how silly this charge is: "An irrational fear that Western intellectual life is about to be overrun by nihilists grips many people.
They are driven by it to the practice of Objectivity, Demarcation, and other
regimens said to be good for toughening, such as birching and dips in the
river on New Year's Day" (41).

McCloskey's attempt to read economics as literature, to "use the humanist tradition to understand the scientific tradition," brings with it a defense
of rhetoric, and an answer to the "Q" question which he does not appear
altogether to understand. His stated defense is the Weak one: "Rhetoric is
merely a tool, no bad thing in itself. Or rather, it is the box of tools for persuasion taken together, available for persuaders good and bad" (37–38). But
what he succeeds in doing, with his splendid close readings of the rhetoric
of economics in action, is to suggest the Strong Defense we began to see

emerging with McKeon. To read economics as McCloskey suggests is always to be toggling between looking at the prose and through it, reading it "rhetorically" and reading it "philosophically," and this toggling attitude toward utterance is what the rhetorical paideia was after all along. Train someone in it and, according to Quintilian's way of thinking, you have trained that person to be virtuous. "Virtuosity *is* some evidence of virtue." To think of this at/through toggle switch as "virtuous," as implicitly moral, is to comprehend the deeply felt "reasoning" behind Quintilian's evasive answer to his own question and to glimpse, perhaps, the beginnings of a legitimate explanation of, and justification for, what the humanities do—or at least can do.

◻   ◻   ◻

I have been mapping, on my "Q" question grid, various efforts to return to the "architectonic rhetoric" of the rhetorical paideia. With E. D. Hirsch's *Cultural Literacy: What Every American Needs to Know*,[9] we encounter an effort to flee from it. The great enemy for Hirsch is "romantic formalism": "The decline of American literacy and the fragmentation of the American school curriculum have been chiefly caused by the ever growing dominance of romantic formalism in educational theory during the past half century" (110). This is Dewey out of Rousseau's *Emile* by Wordsworth's *Prelude*. Against it, Hirsch calls for an education in the brute facts, as these are imbibed in a good traditional education, the kind that proves in the end much more useful than fancy "progressive" new ones: "For we have learned the paradox that traditional education, which alone yields the flexible skill of mature literacy, outperforms utilitarian education even by utilitarian standards" (126).

This book offers so limited a perspective and such maddening simplifications that it is hard to focus its root self-contradiction as turning on the "Q" question. For Hirsch believes that a positive answer to the "Q" question, the production of individual and civic virtue, comes from the citizenry's sharing the same body of facts, acquired from the same basic, Anglo-Saxon, canonical texts. These texts are self-interpreting, and the facts they contain can float context-free in long quiz sheets that have reminded many readers of the Trivial Pursuit game. That is, Hirsch preserves the same Ramist perspective that has informed his work as a theoretical critic—the belief in an "objectivist" world which is just out there, and a "merely verbal" ornamental rhetoric which is tacked onto the plain words that precisely describe it. He takes the Ramist view and insists, again without any proof, that it produces a "Yes" answer to the "Q" question, rather than the resounding "No" that Ramus himself returned: "What distinguishes good readers from poor ones is simply the possession of a lot of diverse, task-specific information" (61). And good readers of this sort are, he assumes, good citizens.

This is begging the "Q" question in the most embarrassingly simplistic way. Ramus was right about splitting utterance into "facts" and "style," Hirsch would argue, but wrong that this was no guarantee of virtue. The rhetorical man is not always good but the factual man is. We were right all along; the well-informed man is the virtuous citizen. As our civics teacher promised, the world will be saved by the current events club.

The proof Hirsch offers for his case provides proof for the opposite one. It is proof that learning comes only in a context, with a specific purpose. You cannot learn a list of facts and dates because they hone the mind or simply are good and good for you. He opposes the teaching of reading as a value-free activity: "I cannot claim to have studied all the recent textbooks intended to train teachers or educate children in the language arts, but those I have consulted represent learning to read as a neutral, technical process of skill acquisition that is better served by up-to-date 'imaginative literature' than by traditional and factual material" (113). He advocates a contextualized reading, tied to particular texts, the "traditional and factual material." But to do this is to read economics, say, the way McCloskey says it ought to be read, self-consciously. It is to assume that language is intrinsically value-laden and that every "fact" comes with values attached. You cannot assemble a list of neutral facts which every citizen in a secular society can safely learn as a factual bible, a body of knowledge beyond cavil, which once absorbed guarantees public virtue. Put in this plain way, the contention sounds preposterous, but this is what Hirsch claims. And, having claimed it, he then equates it with the rhetorical paideia, which embodies the opposite conception of the world and works in exactly the opposite way:

> The founders of our republic had in mind a Ciceronian ideal of education and discourse in a republic. . . . The Ciceronian ideal of universal public discourse was strong in this country into the early twentieth century. In the Roman republic of Cicero's time, such discourse was chiefly oral, and the education Cicero sought was in "rhetoric" rather than "literacy." But the terms are equivalent. [You can see him begging the "Q" question right here, by making this equivalence.] Literacy—reading and writing taken in a serious sense—is the rhetoric of our day, the basis of public discourse in a modern republic. The teaching of Ciceronian literacy as our founders conceived it is a primary but currently neglected responsibility of our schools. (109)

Hirsch's prime villain, John Dewey, was in fact trying to do exactly this, to reintroduce the full rhetorical paideia into a system which had ossified into the arbitrary memorization of a collection of disconnected common-place facts and opinions. In the rhetorical paideia, facts and opinions are always used for something, enlisted in argument of one kind or another. They are, as Dewey argued, always enmeshed in the rough-and-tumble argumentative purposes of life. The best short statement of this concept of education that I know occurs in Whitehead's essay "The Aims of Education":

> The solution which I am urging, is to eradicate the fatal disconnection of subjects which kills the vitality of our modern curriculum. There is only one subject-matter for education, and that is Life in all its manifestations. Instead of this single unity, we offer children— Algebra, from which nothing follows; Geometry, from which nothing follows; Science, from which nothing follows; History, from which nothing follows; a Couple of Languages, never mastered; and lastly, most dreary of all, Literature, represented by plays of Shakespeare, with philological notes and short analyses of plot and character to be in substance committed to memory. Can such a list be said to represent Life, as it is known in the midst of the living of it? The best that can be said of it is, that it is a rapid table of contents which a deity might run over in his mind while he was thinking of creating a world, and had not yet determined how to put it together.[10]

This table-of-contents curriculum resulted from the Ramist separation of rhetoric from thought, of one discipline from another, and of both from any implicit indwelling values. To this world Hirsch would have us return. To correct one simplification, he would have us return to the simplification that spawned it. Surely it would make more sense to ask what "Ciceronian literacy," the classical rhetorical paideia, was really about and trying to do.

In *Professing Literature: An Institutional History*,[11] Gerald Graff does for the teaching of literature in American universities what Grafton and Jardine do for Renaissance humanism: he contrasts theory and practice. He also does historically for literary study what McCloskey does rhetorically for economics—introduces some therapeutic self-consciousness into it. And, like McKeon, he strives to find some cultural architectonics that can encompass all the current theories of literature competing in the university marketplace today. In all these aspects, it is a long-overdue volume, very well done and welcome indeed in the present debate about the humanist curriculum.

The theory of humanism, which Graff calls the "humanist myth," has two aspects, historical and theoretical. The historical aspect portrays a mythical golden age when the humanities flourished and the sciences, for once, had to eat dirt. From this golden age, we have declined into the present one of mass illiteracy and swinish ignorance, from which we are to be rescued by what Graff calls "MLA Jeremiads," impassioned defenses of the humanities which have the "ritualistic aura of the Sunday rebuke." The theoretical aspect is simply Quintilian's smug answer to the "Q" question, that whatever humanists are doing at the present time makes overwhelmingly for public and private virtue. Graff illustrates in wonderful detail how these eulogistic clichés have protected the most widely differing pedagogies with, in all cases, no proof beyond the psychology of rumor offered to support the splendid claims. At the heart of the "Q" question stands the need to demonstrate a connection between specific reading and writing practices and the moral life. This connection, as Graff documents at length, literary study (like orthodox rhetoric) has never been able to make.

The "practice" of humanism which Graff surveys includes so many different varieties that simply by juxtaposing this perpetual change with the unchanging justifications used to explain them, he illustrates the failure of literary study, and by implication of humanism itself, to supply any convincing self-justification, any real answer to the "Q" question. But he is most convincing in analyzing the stable structure that determines current practice and how it operates. This is the division of literary study into special fields. "The field-coverage principle seems so innocuous as to be hardly worth looking at, and we have lived with it so long that we hardly even see it, but its consequences have been far reaching. Its great advantage was to make the department and the curriculum virtually self-regulating" (7). Field coverage constitutes what the behavioral biologists call an "evolutionarily stable strategy," one that is proof against any demand for adaptation. Simply add another field. And, if the field is the study of nonfieldable studies, simply make a special field out of that. Such ready subdivision constitutes the perfect tool for conflict regulation. Every disagreement can, after suitable preliminary acrimony, be coopted into the fold. The Ramist enfranchisement of disciplinary self-division and self-enclosure can be applied at the level of the discipline itself, with the same fissiparous effect. Instead of a curriculum, we have Whitehead's tentative table of contents.

This "table-of-contents," or as we are now more likely to call it, "supermarket" conception of the curriculum follows directly from the Ramist answer to the "Q" question. No part of the curriculum offers any moral education. That education takes place elsewhere—*in forum, in Senatum, in concionem populi, in omnem hominum conventum*—anywhere but in the curriculum. There, you simply choose the specialization that you want for your own particular purposes. The same stabilizing conflict-resolution strategy used within disciplines applies to the larger curriculum that contains them.

But if you want to return the opposite answer, argue for the discipline of discourse as in some sense a moral education, you cannot accept this supermarket curriculum, and so cannot avail yourself of its handy "Q" question-begging conflict-resolver. You must argue for some kind of general education. There has to be, somewhere, a nonnegotiable kernel of humanistic learning, and we should be able to specify this kernel and insist on it as the nonnegotiable prolegomenon to professionalized advanced study. Therefore to the question, "How do we get from specific reading and writing practices to moral judgment?" we must add a parallel one: "If we claim such a relationship, how do we get from it to a specific curriculum?" The structure of the humanities curriculum is a subset of the "Q" question. If you answer it with "No," you get what we have now. If you answer it with "Yes," you must then decide what curriculum is implied by your answer.

Two basic patterns have been suggested: the Great Books and the course in method. The Great Books argument was first advanced by John Erskine at Columbia in 1917 and then in a different form by Robert Maynard Hutchins and Mortimer Adler at the University of Chicago in the 1930s and after. The best-known contemporary version of the method argument is Daniel Bell's *The Reforming of General Education.* The most widely discussed restatement of the Adler thesis is Allan Bloom's *The Closing of the American Mind,* and E. D. Hirsch's volume, as we have seen, belongs in this camp as well.

Graff discusses the periodic appearances of both these views on the American scene. He points out how traditional humanist theory and practice have assumed that the literary text is self-teaching: "The assumption implicit in the humanist myth and the field-coverage principle has been that *literature teaches itself.* Since the literary tradition is presumably coherent in and of itself, it should naturally dictate the way teachers collectively organize themselves" (9–10). The Great Books curriculum must make the same assumption. The books come context-free. You need only expose the students to them. If they require interpretation, then you must ask what kind, and the "Q" question returns—how do you get from a specific theory of reading and writing to moral judgment? But if they don't require interpretation, then they are context-free and, as Ramus saw, value-free as well, and hence cannot be the source of value.

The alternate "method" curriculum, which we must recognize, I suppose, as some etiolated variant of Dewey's educational argument, returns us again to the "Q" question. The Bad Persons as well as the Good Persons can use the same method. Science, like rhetoric in the Weak Defense, is a neutral tool, equally available to all. Those who defend this curriculum, like Quintilian defending his own program, have found "good" and "bad" versions of method, but the distinction has never been supported convincingly.

Graff concludes his history with an account of the current contention between the Arnoldian "humanists" and the Derridean "theorists," as representing today's version of the quarrel about how to connect discursive practices with moral judgment. He does not take sides in the debate, though he takes each side apart with great skill. Rather, he suggests that, since we cannot resolve this debate, we dramatize it instead—make the students privy to our private debates through team-teaching and other pedagogical techniques. We can recognize in this advice a pedagogical implementation of the *sprezzatura* oscillation that McKeon recommends, and that had always stood at the heart of the rhetorical paideia.

Allan Bloom's *The Closing of the American Mind*[12] does not offer a coherent or informed argument, either historically or theoretically, for the Great Books curriculum, but is instead an "MLA Jeremiad," a thunderous collection of what Graff calls "Sunday Clichés." Its cardinal theme is an apocalyptic restatement of the Adlerian argument for the Great Books curriculum, and its greatest triumph is the most extended, pretentious, and self-satisfied begging of the "Q" question we have seen in a long time. It is a hard book to summarize, since its premises and arguments metamorphose so unpredictably, but what it proposes as a solution for the spiritual debilities of our time (rock music, feminism, social science, the sixties and the changes in university governance resulting therefrom, the democratization of learning and university admission, the decline of the nuclear family, pop culture, nonrepresentational art, deconstruction and other relativisms, etc.) is this:

> Of course, the only serious solution is the one that is almost universally rejected: the good old Great Books approach, in which a liberal education means reading certain generally recognized classic texts, just reading them, letting them dictate what the questions are and the method of approaching them—not forcing them into categories we make up, not treating them as historical products, but trying to read them as their authors wished them to be read. ... [O]ne thing is certain: wherever the Great Books make up a central part of the curriculum, the students are excited and satisfied, feel they are doing something that is independent and fulfilling, getting something from

the university they cannot get elsewhere. ... Programs based on judicious use of great texts provide the royal road to students' hearts. Their gratitude at learning of Achilles or the categorical imperative is boundless. (344)

One is tempted to cite external fact to disprove this preposterous ukase (What, for example, about the alarming drop-out rate at St. John's, which teaches the very curriculum Bloom proposes, or its equally embarrassing failure to produce any of the seminal minds who people Bloom's Ideal U.?), or to consult one's own teaching experience, in which student enthusiasm for the categorical imperative may in fact know bounds; but verily we need go no further than that qualifier "judicious." This means, presumably, "as I, Allan Bloom, do it," and puts us, as Grafton and Jardine saw that it put Erasmus, right back into the lap of interpretation and the "Q" question. Or we might ask why, if the Great Books are "generally recognized" as being the great and self-teaching source of all intellectual authority, a curriculum based on them is "almost universally rejected." And if we can read them as totally context-free (and this is the most extreme statement of the Ramist position one is likely to come across), how can they at the same time be so value-laden?

For Bloom, like Hirsch, accepts the Ramist division but not the Ramist "No" to the "Q" question. The answer for Professor Bloom is that the book of books is Plato's *Dialogues*, and there we learn that the truths the books communicate are Platonic absolutes. Like the Word of God in an absolutist religion, they require no interpretation, no cultural Protestantism. And so he solves the "Q" question, or begs it, by a private act of religious revelation. Because he knows the truth, and where to seek it, like Erasmus he will always read aright. Such biblical teaching is indeed self-validating. And it brings its own curriculum with it, and so solves that question too.

These views are not new. Mortimer Adler protested in a national magazine that Bloom's book was but Adler *redivivus*, and he was right. And Bloom is far from the only humanist to hold them. But Bloom is unusual for the candor with which he expresses them. He doesn't construct any equivocal answer to the "Q" question; he doesn't think that any is needed. He thus has performed a signal service for us, in revealing at devastating length what substructure the humanities presently stand on. As a subset of revealed religion, public or private, solid as a rock; as a subset of intellectual inquiry, incredibly flimsy. He also shows, and for this we should be equally grateful, what version of humanism follows from answering the "Q" question in a religious way. For the book is a spiritual as well as an intellectual confession, and the book's very favorable reception suggests that Bloom's conception of the humanist life is widely shared. What kind of life, in his view, does the ideal humanist lead? What kind of person has a lifetime of the Great Books made of Allan Bloom?

Well, obviously a Platonic absolutist, for a start. The answers are known, right there in the Great Books. The university exists to spell them out. Spelling them out Bloom calls "the theoretical life," and it is the only acceptable, the only truly human life possible.

> Never did I think that the university was properly ministerial to the society around it. Rather I thought and think that society is ministerial to the university, and I bless a society that tolerates and supports an eternal childhood for some [the professors, not the students], a childhood whose playfulness can in turn be a blessing to society. Falling in love with the idea of the university is not a folly, for only by means of it is one able to see what can be. Without it, all these wonderful results of the theoretical life collapse back into the primal slime from which they cannot re-emerge. (245)

The "primal slime" is ordinary nonuniversity life, as the following reflection on the role of the college years suggests:

> He has four years of freedom to discover himself—a space between the intellectual wasteland he has left behind and the inevitable dreary professional training that awaits him after the baccalaureate. In this short time he must learn that there is a great world beyond the little one he knows, experience the exhilaration of it and digest enough of it to sustain himself in the intellectual deserts he is destined to traverse. He must do this, that is, if he is to have any hope of a higher life. These are the charmed years when he can, if he so chooses, become anything he wishes and when he has the opportunity to survey his alternatives, not merely those current in his time or provided by careers, but those available to him as a human being. The importance of these years for an American cannot be overestimated. *They are civilization's only chance to get to him.* (336; emphasis mine)

All human life and value is condensed into the university—everything else is "primal slime," presumably—but not the university as it exists now, Clark Kerr's multiversity of pluralistic interests and contending values, or as it has actually existed in a very checkered and irregular past, but the university as a golden-age collection of "authentically great thinkers who gave living proof of the existence of the theoretical life and whose motives could not easily be reduced to any of the baser ones people delight in thinking universal. They had authority, not based on power, money or family, but on natural gifts that properly compel respect. The relations among them and between them and students were the revelation of a community in which there is a true common good" (244–45). This paradise he locates in the American university of the 1950s. Those of us who were students in that university may well gaze in wonder at Bloom's characterization, even if he does go on to acknowledge that his youthful imagination has made most of it up.

At the top of Bloom's ideal curriculum stands the figure of Plato's Socrates: "The character of the experience Socrates represents is important because it is the soul of the university" (268); "Socrates is of the essence of the university. It exists to preserve and further what he represents" (272). So all that is worthwhile in human life comes down, at last, to studying about the Platonic Socrates with, presumably, Allan Bloom. The combination of personal arrogance, historical ignorance of educational history, and adulatory misreading of Plato which this definition of the university represents simply takes your breath away. But clearly it is not only what Bloom believes the ideal life of the humanist to be; it is what the many thousands of people who bought his book believe humanist inquiry to be all about. Socrates is the secular messiah; we are apostles studying the book that chronicles his deeds, sayings, and martyrdom; and we do so in a monastery that shuts out a fundamentally corrupt and irredeemable world.

Behold what the great Renaissance dreams Arthur Kinney chronicles have come to. The difference between humanist theory and practice that Grafton and Jardine describe could hardly have found a more striking modern representation than this book, a bizarre and scary confession of a closed mind at work rearranging intellectual and educational history, and calling itself, with ultimate intellectual arrogance, the closing of the *American* mind.

We should all be grateful to Bloom for this extraordinary act of humanist self-revelation. For what he says is also, though seldom put with such bold contempt of one's fellow human beings (especially of one's students— what strikes you above all in this book is how the man despises his students, even when they give him the proper adulatory audience), what a great many humanists think they are and are doing. Humanists regularly rewrite the history of universities into a golden-age Platonic academy which puts them centerstage. That is what Graff's book is all about. We regularly preach one way and teach another; that is what Grafton and Jardine's book is all about. We regularly confuse the right kind of middle-class factual knowledge with moral virtue, public and private, as does E. D. Hirsch. We apply to our own writing a Platonic and Ramist theory of language which pretends that it is value-free, as McCloskey's critique of scholarly writing, using economists as an example, so brilliantly points out. We regularly, in the interests of Plato-worship, disembody language and reason, with the narrow-mindedness Mark Johnson points out in an important recent book, *The Body in the Mind*.[13] Our persistent evasion of the "Q" question makes for a great deal of self-centered, self-serving preaching and a great deal of self-satisfied practice. We do sometimes follow that master of contemptuous, self-satisfied self-absorption, the Platonic Socrates, closely indeed.

◻   ◻   ◻

As circumstances would have it, recent history has given us an extraordinary example of how unhumanistic the humanities can be, of an archetypal "No!" to the "Q" question. Barrie Penrose and Simon Freeman begin their *Conspiracy of Silence* thus: "On Thursday, 15 November 1979, the Conservative Prime Minister, Margaret Thatcher, told the House of Commons that Sir Anthony Blunt, the distinguished art historian who was a former Surveyor of the Queen's Pictures, was a self-confessed Soviet Spy."[14] It is a fortuitous coincidence, perhaps, but one a Greek tragedian might have seized upon, that the same prime minister who made this announcement is responsible for the attack on the English humanities establishment which Grafton and Jardine remark. "If," Mrs. Thatcher might have said with her parliamentary disclosure fresh in mind, "humanist inquiry is as morally improving, as essential to civilization as you claim, please explain to me the case of Anthony Blunt." The English universities, Grafton and Jardine suggest, are paying a high price for their inability to answer this question. After all, what could have been more quintessentially humanistic than Blunt's education at Marlborough and Trinity College, Cambridge? Than his brilliant, indeed almost preeminent career, as an art historian and royal curator?

George Steiner, in his penetrating essay on the Blunt case, "The Cleric of Treason" (1980), remarks of the Blunt story, "A cursory look at the tale shows that it is so full of gaps, unanswered questions, and implausibilities as to be almost useless."[15] It is to these gaps, unanswered questions, and implausibilities that Penrose and Freeman address themselves, with as much success as a very cold trail and the Official Secrets Act permit. Their bizarre tale includes some extraordinary snapshots: "the Surveyor of the Queen's Pictures awaking at the Courtauld after a night with rough trade [the working-class homosexual companions Blunt used to pick up at a nearby public lavatory]; then taking seminars with his students, emphasizing the need for art historians to be champions of Truth and Beauty, before slipping away late in the afternoon for a session with Martin [the government agent investigating him for spying]."[16] Or this one: "In November 1972 the Queen met Blunt at the Palace and thanked him for his hard work as a royal servant over the past twenty-seven years. She said that she hoped to see him just as often in his new capacity as adviser. Since there is no doubt that she knew about his work for the Soviets she must have gone through this ceremony with mixed feelings" (477).

The most amazing aspect of the Blunt case was the public reception of Blunt's treachery. A few people attacked him, like the art historian Denis Mahon: "Once you get away with lying on one subject, it spills over into the rest of your life and that is what happened with Blunt, he became a practised liar" (295). But much more characteristic was the response of A. J. P. Taylor to the demand that Blunt be expelled from the British Academy: "I couldn't be a fellow of an academy which uses the late Senator McCarthy as its patron saint. It's not the duty of the academy to probe into the behaviour of fellows, except on grounds of scholarship" (529–30). In other words, humanist inquiry, indeed the whole life of the mind, has nothing to do with the moral life. Even to ask the question is infamous. This is the Ramist answer with a vengeance.

Perhaps the most illuminating example of how the news about Blunt was received is contained in an extraordinary letter written to the *Guardian* in April 1983 by Janet Kennish:

> I was there [at the Courtauld] from 1961 to 1964 and we did not need to assess the Director's political ideals from attention to his lectures; it seems extraordinary now, but, as new students we were casually informed that the Director was also a Russian spy. It was even more specific than that—he was actually said to be "the fourth man involved with Burgess and Maclean." I have no idea who told us, but I believe it was the older students who were merely, and openly, passing on the folklore of the place to new arrivals. After I left, I thought no more of it for many years but when the Blunt scandal became public, my reaction was one of astonishment—but we all *knew*, why did no one else? Should we have told someone? I suppose we didn't take it seriously, and I was naive enough to accept anything that I was told, so awed was I by the esoteric, socially élite atmosphere of the Courtauld in those years. Just another idiosyncrasy of the unfathomable upper classes—you might meet a spy on the Adam staircase. (453–54)

To my mind, this is the most revealing passage in *Conspiracy of Silence*, for it suggests that the "secret" was no secret but a shared hypocrisy, a spontaneous conspiracy, not only on the part of the authorities but of the intellectual classes too, not to ask the embarrassing "Q" question. At this point emerges, now on a broad social scale, the persistent evasion we have been tracing. As Ms. Kennish shows, it is no problem, really, so long as the atmosphere is imposing enough, the stylistic signals are all right, and the ruling classes keep their solidarity. Penrose and Freeman remark, "Half a century later it probably seems odd that Blunt should have been able to find a job so easily in the heart of British intelligence. Yet, it has to be emphasized, the recruiters of MI5 and MI6 had no alternative other than to accept personal recommendations. Recruits were invariably drawn from that closed circle (the public schools—Oxbridge—the City—the Law), membership of which had always been a guarantee of a man's character and patriotism" (236). The assumption that humanist education worked, that the answer to the "Q" question was "Yes," underlay how the British government worked, how the society worked. To doubt Blunt was to doubt the traditional educational system and therefore the entire society. Nobody wanted to do it. If you met a spy on the Adam staircase, you smiled and went on your way. As Penrose and Freeman conclude their book and their argument, "Perhaps it was not so surprising, after all, that Britain had produced Anthony Blunt. Indeed, it might be said that Britain deserved Anthony Blunt" (570).

The "Q" question has been George Steiner's great subject for a number of years. "Unlike Matthew Arnold and unlike Dr. Leavis," he tells us in an early essay, "I find myself unable to assert confidently that the humanities humanize." In "The Cleric of Treason," Steiner asks the "Q" question in its most uncompromising form:

> What *is* certain is simply this: Anthony Blunt was a K.G.B. minion whose treason over thirty years or more almost certainly did grave damage to his own country and may well have sent other men ... to abject death.... Professor Blunt's treason and duplicity do pose fundamental questions about the nature of intellectual-academic obsession, about the co-existence within a single sensibility of utmost truth and falsehood, and about certain germs of the inhuman planted, as it were, at the very roots of excellence in our society.... I would like to think for a moment about a man who in the morning teaches his students that a false attribution of a Watteau drawing or an inaccurate transcription of a fourteenth-century epigraph is a sin against the spirit and in the afternoon or evening transmits to the agents of Soviet intelligence classified, perhaps vital information given to him in sworn trust by his countrymen and intimate colleagues. What are the sources of such scission? How does the spirit mask itself?[17]

Penrose and Freeman seek an explanation in Blunt's life, and find there an actor whom nobody truly knew, an Iago who deceived for the pleasure of deception—and a society that collaborated with the deception. Steiner looks, instinctively, at Blunt's work. The explanation he finds there, I am afraid, is one he constructs himself. It goes this way:

> Like so many of the "radical élite," Blunt cherishes two possibly anti-thetical persuasions. He holds great art to be of matchless significance to man; and he would want this significance to be accessible to the community as a whole. The solution is, more or less unavoidably, Plato's: "guardians," chosen for their intellectual force and their pro-bity, are to ensure the positive, life-enhancing quality of art and are to organize the presentation of such art to their entire society. And this quality and public presentation will elevate collective sensibility to a higher plane. Blunt seems to have felt that something very like this mechanism of authority and diffusion was at work in the autocratic city-states of Renaissance Italy and, above all, in the century of Louis XIV and his immediate successor. ... [H]ow else are the arts, without which man would recede into animality, to be rescued from their iso-lation, from the prostitution of the money market? (192–93)

So, at least, Steiner conjectures that Blunt might have thought. He is trying to find an explanation that will make Blunt a hero along the lines laid down by Allan Bloom, to put him again on the right side, as a "man of the-ory," so that this horrible split will be a mistake or misunderstanding, not a betrayal. Steiner floats another guess: that Blunt wanted to study Lorrain, not Poussin, but the fact that Lorrain's paintings were mostly in private hands and this private ownership prevented his studying them so enraged Blunt that he went over to Russia. This grasps even harder at a straw. And Stein-er knows it, for he broadens his search for an explanation into the nature of humanistic inquiry itself. What he says takes us deeper into the "Q" ques-tion than anyone has gone in a long time.

> The absolute scholar is in fact a rather uncanny being. He is instinct with Nietzsche's finding that to be interested in something, to be total-ly interested in it, is a libidinal thrust more powerful than love or hatred, more tenacious than faith or friendship—not infrequently, indeed, more compelling than personal life itself. ... He is, when in the grip of his pursuit, monomaniacally disinterested in the possible usefulness of his findings, in the good fortune or honour that they may bring him, in whether or not any but one or two other men or women on the earth care for, can even begin to understand or evalu-

ate, what he is after. This disinterestedness is the dignity of his mania. But it can extend to more troubling zones. The archivist, the monographer, the antiquarian, the specialist consumed by fires of esoteric fascination may be indifferent also to the distracting claims of social justice, of familial affection, of political awareness, and of run-of-the-mill humanity. The world out there is the formless, boorish impediment that keeps him from the philosopher's stone.... The more so... when the spell is antiquarian.... [Such a man] has, necessarily, inverted time. For him, the pulse of most vivid presence beats from out of the past. This, again, is a social and psychological estrangement to which we pay too little heed.... The humanist is a rememberer. He walks, as does one troupe of the accursed in Dante's *Inferno*, with his head twisted backward. He lurches indifferent into tomorrow. (197–98)

Here is Allan Bloom's hunger for "spirituality" without the pretentious Platonism or evangelical zeal. Steiner sees that at the core of humanistic inquiry stands the pure formal pleasure of play. No intrinsic connection binds this pleasure to moral judgment. When you leave humanistic inquiry to itself, it folds itself in on this formal pleasure. And as Bloom's book illustrates, when deprived of action it turns rancid. Steiner is brilliant about this: "The practice of devoting one's waking hours to the collation of a manuscript, to the recension of watermarks on old drawings, the discipline of investing one's dreams in the always vulnerable elucidation of abstruse problems accessible only to a handful of prying and rival colleagues can secrete a rare venom into the spirit. *Odium philologicum* is a notorious infirmity" (199). Scholarly asceticism, he argues, "cuts a writer off from 'the great springs of life' and can nurture a pathological need for cruelty." We return to McKeon's paramount question, the connection between thought and action: "Above all, Professor Blunt was able to translate into clandestine performance, into covert mendacity and, possibly, murderousness (the men and women tagged for Soviet vengeance in Eastern Europe), those fantasies of virile action, those solicitations of violence, which bubble like marsh gas from the deeps of abstruse thought and erudition" (200).

An academic autobiography has appeared recently that makes a fascinating contrast with the Blunt story, Sidney Hook's *Out of Step: An Unquiet Life in the 20th Century*.[18] Hook's youth in the Williamsburg section of Brooklyn and his intellectual odyssey at City College lie as far as may be from Blunt's Marlborough and Trinity, Cambridge. And if much of Blunt's real education came from the aesthetical hothouse of the "Apostles," much of Hook's education took shape in that antithetically opposite intellectual hothouse of New York Jewish intellectuals Irving Kristol has described in *Reflections of a Neo-Conservative.* Both Hook and Blunt began as leftists. Both were approached by the Party to be spies (Hook by Earl Browder). Both ended up, to some part of their constituency, traitors to their class. But Hook earned his scorn by turning down the invitation to espionage, by becoming disillusioned with the Communist utopia which Blunt served faithfully, and by becoming a spokesman for free enterprise and an ardent and tireless activist in the open political debate from which Blunt took flight into art history. Both ended up answering McKeon's question about the relation of thought to action, though in very different ways.

And both, again in opposed ways, confronted our key question. Blunt answered it by treachery and silence, and his friends answered it for him by asserting that humanist inquiry had nothing to do with goodness. Hook, in a memorable passage in his life, and in the book, looked it in the face and confessed that he had no answer. The passage comes when he is relating his disgust with the response of American universities, and the American professoriate, to the threats and intimidations of the student left during the sixties:

> Not only did the events of the sixties in American universities lead me to modify the severity of my judgment on the behavior of the German professoriate under Hitler, it led me to reevaluate one of the cardinal principles of my ethical philosophy. I had always believed, and was fortified in that belief by my study of John Dewey, that intelligence was the supreme virtue. I had taken for granted the operation of moral courage. After discovering that it was in such short supply in the academy, I began to wonder whether, as necessary as intelligence was, it was sufficient, and if not, what was the source of moral courage. By sophistical argument I could like Plato try to show that someone who was truly intelligent would also possess moral courage. But I knew this to be empirically false. ... Although I have puzzled over the problems concerning the nature and nurture of moral courage, I am not satisfied that I have found any adequate answers to them. Nor so far as I know has anyone else. (550–51)

We find ourselves with a curious pairing. Blunt, the actor par excellence, the man who created a public identity out of stylistic rhetoric, found at the end of it all the same gulf between humanist learning and moral action which Hook, the man of consummate philosophical principle, came to stare down at the end of his academic career. Rhetoric and philosophy come to the same chasm each of our texts has either made up, tripped over, or fallen down. For Hook, as for Allan Bloom, the university represents, or represented, the last best hope of humankind. Clearly they both idolized and idealized it in their youth. It is extraordinary, and profoundly sad, that Hook can look the failure of that enthusiasm so resolutely in the face. But, like Grafton and Jardine, he remarks the Gorgon by the roadside and then trudges bravely on.

To set Hook beside Allan Bloom is to surprise another suggestive comparison, not only between two different humanities curricula but between two different kinds of humanism. Bloom's conception of humanism is absolutist, religious, theoretical, and asocial. Society exists to serve the university and not vice versa, and the scholar remains a "perpetual child," pure in heart and motive, professing a set of canonical texts (although, since they are self-teaching, they scarcely need professing) in an environment insulated from all political pressures—without, in fact, any social context whatever. The scholar does not act in society except by being what he is. He is, in terms of the familiar Harold Nicolson anecdote, what the culture exists to create. (Harold Nicolson, walking in civilian clothes in London during World War II, was reproached for his lack of uniform. He is said to have replied, "I *am* what you all are fighting for!")

Sidney Hook was the opposite brand of humanist. The truth he served was contingent rather than absolute, secular rather than religious, and texts were admitted to his canon only after screening by a tough street-kid's experienced crap-detector. He devoted his life to political and social activism, and in his conception the university served society as much as society served it. Both Bloom and Hook were horrified at the campus disruptions of the sixties, but Bloom's response is the jeremiad in his book; Hook, characteristically, founded a national organization and pursued the issues it raised until the day he died.

The differences in their humanisms come into clearest focus in Hook's chapter on "God and the Professors." Bloom, as we have seen, was trained by Plato; Sidney Hook was trained by John Dewey. Some of the book's most illuminating moments come when he describes how he took on his teacher's great enemies, Hutchins, Adler, and the neo-Aristotelian Great Books movement, a movement which made in the thirties the same argument that Bloom and a different moral majority are raising today. "The educational philosophy of Hutchins and Adler was an attempt to justify a counterreformation in American education.... Education was to be desecularized; metaphysics and theology were to be instated as prescribed courses in the curriculum of institutions of higher learning. The controlling values and objectives of the lower school were to rest upon the truths of metaphysics and religion, which were declared 'superior' to all other truths, particularly those reached by the scientific method" (341). We are hearing this same argument against secular education and for a religious counterreformation today, and it has not grown in stature or persuasiveness during the intervening half-century. On Hutchins and Adler especially, Hook is simply devastating. Anyone who wonders where Bloom comes from can find out in this chapter. And since Hook went through the kind of fact-heavy education Hirsch would resurrect, his comments on it effectively demolish Hirsch as well.

> The curriculum of Boys High School was still fairly classical in those days [1916]. Latin was a required subject for two or three years, as were algebra, geometry, a year of biology, a year of physics or chemistry, a modern foreign language, three years of European and American history, and four years of English. Some stress was placed on elocution in the English classes. Compared to contemporary high schools, it would be considered an elite school. Some of its distinguished graduates, Clifton Fadiman for one, have written about their educational experience as if it were ideal and contrasted its course of study very favorably with the curricula that were introduced later. The truth of the matter—and I sat in some of the very classes that Fadiman has described in such glowing terms—is that no one learned anything in that school who was not already self-motivated, and not (with the rarest of exceptions) by virtue of the teaching but despite it. The pedagogy was execrable. The textbook was the only authority, and except in some classes where problems were studied (mathematics and physics), excellence in scholarship depended upon the students' ability to regurgitate it....Instruction was not geared to broadening the interests and liberalizing the minds of the students but to the passing of examinations, especially the Regents' tests. (17–18)

It is to these basics—accepted facts in accepted texts—that we are now from all sides urged to return. True, Hook's intellectual confessional is not free of an old man's cranky vindictiveness—his motto sometimes seems to be "Never Forget! Never Forgive!" But when we ask of him the question we asked of Bloom—"What kind of person did this life of humanist inquiry and teaching create?"—the answer, even for those who dislike his politics, must be more reassuring.

◻   ◻   ◻

We return by broad ambages to where we began, Quintilian's seemingly facile begging of his own central question. What genuine argument, or at least observation, might lie behind what appears only permissive optimism? Might he have been arguing, or at a deeper level might he simply have felt he knew in his bones, from a lifetime of experience, that the rhetorical education he had just finished describing vented the discipline of discourse in action, liberated it from the *odium philologicum* that hermetic enclosure in pure formal pleasure creates?

What sets us humanists, the Bloomian persons of theory, above the sordid world of trade, what we like to think defines us as humanists, is the purity of our motives. We do what we do, not for money or power but "for its own sake." Yet this turns out to be a formal, not a moral, pleasure, as Steiner comes to admit, and a formal pleasure that left to itself soon sours, as Bloom's book so embarrassingly illustrates. What rescues the humanities from this poisonous self-enclosure, when they are rescued, is some external circumstance, some problem, that puts this formal pleasure to work. Steiner adduces a perfect example, the way purely formal mathematical and logical talent was put to work by the British to break the German codes during World War II: "All who look back on the days of 'Ultra' and 'Enigma' at Bletchley Park do so with a sense of holiday. For once, hermetic addiction and the raw needs of the time coincided."[19] Practical purpose, the need to defend England, was added to the motivational mix. And a third type of motive, competition, was added to the mixture, for they were trying at every point to match wits with their German counterparts, to decrypt what the enemy was encrypting.

Could this mixture of motives have been what animated and supported Quintilian's optimism? Might the good man, for him, have been the man whose motives were deeply mixed, and who knew how and why? I would argue that this mixture of play, game, and purpose was the characteristic product (if not always the avowed purpose) of the rhetorical, as against the philosophical, paideia. It did not try to purify our motives but to radically mix them. It created not a self-enclosed humanism but one connected at every juncture to what Whitehead called "the insistent present." It aimed, that is, to address what McKeon thought the characteristic problem of our times, the relation of thought to action, the problem that became a problem when Ramus "purified" thought of rhetoric, and thus of action as well.

Humanism, construed in this rhetorical way, is above all an education in politics and management. Can it also be construed as an education in civic virtue? To answer this question, we must revert to what I have called the Strong Defense of rhetoric. The Strong Defense argues that, since truth comes to humankind in so many diverse and disagreeing forms, we cannot base a polity upon it. We must, instead, devise some system by which we can agree on a series of contingent operating premises. The system that rhetoric devised, and which was enshrined in rhetoric as a system of education, was built upon an oscillation very like Castiglione's *sprezzatura*.

The most familiar example of this procedure to most of us is the Anglo-Saxon system of jurisprudence. We stage a public drama, empanel an audience whom we call a jury, and offer contending versions of reality. The jury decides on one. That decision then becomes a different sort of reality altogether, a precedent, a referential reality against which further judicial dramas are measured. The magic moment of transmutation, what drives the system, is the need to reach a decision. Chaim Perelman cites Article 4 of the Napoleonic Code in this connection, an article which says that the judge must render a verdict in every case. As York says in *Richard II*, when he has to decide whether to join Bolingbroke or not, "Somewhat we must do." That decision is made by people, not handed down by God, but the system does all it can to strengthen the decision by arriving at it in a certain way. It is a proceeding of radically impure motives. It is fundamentally a contest, a game. It is full of the formal pleasure—what makes the law so complex is the need for formal pleasure, as much as for exactitude—that renders the proceedings themselves highly satisfying, "full of drama" as we like to say. And these two motives, play and game, are driven and controlled by purpose, by the need to reach a decision: "Somewhat we must do." The Strong Defense does not apologize for this mixture of motives but rather glories in it, for it reflects the motivational structure of humankind, and in so doing holds the greatest promise of enduring effectiveness.

The Platonic and Bloomian condemnation of this political manner of proceeding argues that conceptual truth, arrived at through pure reason, should create our "referential reality"; the "baser [motives] people delight in thinking universal" must be purified out. The Strong Defense would contend not only that this argument is impossible but that it is dangerous; that its decision-making process has no built-in system of error-correction, of cybernetic control when human purpose, rationally arrived at, turns out to be wrong. Such a cybernetic system of error-correction, of continually modifying one arena of motive by another, is what the Strong Defense of rhetoric aims to create and explain. Gregory Bateson tried to sketch out such a system in a prophetic essay on the Treaty of Versailles.[20] Pure rational purpose, Bateson argued, ran out of control, established a positive-feedback system of geometrically increasing error. The formal pleasure of play can control this increasing reamplification of the same signal, and so (though Bateson was not arguing in this direction) can the pleasures of contest. Motive-balancing provides the means by which we can exercise social control over ourselves.

Perhaps now we can comprehend how Quintilian might have felt that a rhetorical education as he had traced it conduced to civic virtue. It trained people in the Strong Defense, in the skills needed to create and sustain a public, as against a private, reality. It did not simply train, it created, the public person. It is the perfect training for the pattern of government Plato hated the most, a genuine, open-ended democracy.

Such a training implies a particular version of humanism: Hook's kind instead of Bloom's, a kind that is always oscillating from the formal pleasure of game and play to the demands of insistent purpose. The rhetorical paideia, the "discipline of discourse" Isocrates bequeathed to us, tried to build a verbal model of this oscillation. It was the oscillation around a fulcrum of self-consciousness that built up the linguistic model, the behavioral allegory, by which rhetorical education trained for the public life, by which it built in self-consciousness about motive as a cybernetic correction to social deliberation. To look at language self-consciously is to play games with it; to look through language unselfconsciously is to act purposively with it. The running debate about decorum as a key term in rhetorical theory is a debate about how this behavioral toggle-switch operates. And rhetoric's long effort to preserve both kinds of attention, and both kinds of language, however self-contradictory in theory the effort may prove to be, attests to its final loyalty to making things happen in the world. To do that, you must forever estimate human motive, and toggle from contemplating the surface of human behavior to taking a role in it. Writ small, this oscillation is the method of the pun; writ large, it is McKeon's architectonic rhetoric. McCloskey has put the two together in the golden apothegm I have already cited: "Virtuosity *is* some evidence of virtue."

We can begin to envisage as well how a theory of reading and writing can become a training in moral judgment. For what links virtuosity, the love of form, and virtue, is *virtù*, power. Formal training in words models the balance of motive that creates power; this is how Isocrates' "discipline of discourse," how "Ciceronian literacy" has always worked. And if we want to view in detail how a curriculum can be developed to do this modeling, we have only to reexamine, more diligently to be sure than we have done up to now, the rhetorical paideia which has dominated Western education for most of its two-and-a-half millennia.

If we can conceive the connection between verbal practices, moral judgment, and education in this way, a deep and abiding irony about the Great Books curriculum—the alternate curriculum to this rhetorical one—begins to dawn. Those canonical texts—Homer, Virgil, Dante, Chaucer, Shakespeare—are rhetorical through and through. The very substance out of which they were created was, as Arthur Kinney's book demonstrates for the English Renaissance, drawn from the standard practices of rhetorical education. The characteristic humanist "right reading," as Grafton and Jardine document so well, was also rhetorical through and through. I have argued myself that the oscillation of self-consciousness sketched above underlies the basic narrative-speech-narrative Thucydidean pattern which informs Western literature from its beginnings until today. What these canonical texts teach—and let us assume them to be as didactic as a Bloomian "man of theory" would desire—is the rhetorical kind of civic virtue I have just sketched.

It really does need saying that the professional defenders of the canon don't understand what makes it canonical. They radically mistake why the Great Books are "great." The primary spokesman for the traditional cultural canon which the Great Books symbolize, former Secretary of Education William Bennett, observed when pressed that he wanted *King Lear* taught today the way it was taught to him—the way, presumably, Professor Bloom might teach it. It is no exaggeration to say that such teaching, such an answer to the "Q" question, radically disempowers humanistic study, fundamentally misapprehends its nonnegotiable core, cuts us off from the wisdom of Western literature we so vitally need.

If we return a "Yes" answer to the "Q" question, then, I think we can explain why we have done so. But what follows from that answer implies a very different definition of humanism from the cloistered virtues and pure motives which humanism at the present day is usually thought to require. If you vote for the cloister, then you can no longer pretend that, though you do what you do "for its own sake," somehow what you do is still essential to moral health and civic virtue. That is the essential fraudulent equation that humanism has perpetrated for too long, that leaves Grafton and Jardine, and even Sidney Hook, finally speechless. No, if the university does not want to serve the society, there is no reason why the society should serve the university. If humanists want to remain perpetual children, then their poetry will, to use Bentham's alliterative pairing, never be any better than pushpin, will indeed be taught as if it were pushpin.

I have said that humanism rhetorically construed is a training in management as well as in politics. The need for a humanistic ingredient in business and government management-practices is front-page news, of course, though it is not being couched in our terms. Japanese industrial practices are beating our brains out because their motivational mix—the final human equation for "efficiency"—is deeper and richer than our own. The American automobile industry has nearly destroyed itself by its blindness to the play sphere, to a wide range of formal pleasures of both design and engineering. The great American companies have separated their vital functions—engineering, manufacturing, sales—with the same Ramist rigor the university has applied to dividing itself into disciplines, and with the same effect: nobody talks to anybody else and the collective purpose evaporates. Instead, American industries perish by slavish loyalty to a "bottom line" that proves the obverse of "practical." About these issues humanism has much to say and something to learn; they, too, should be part of its "canon."

As an illustration of how this cross-fertilization might work, let me discuss a last recent book that revolves around the "Q" question, John Sculley's *Odyssey: Pepsi to Apple.*[21] Sculley began his life as an orthodox hard-charger at PepsiCo, and he ended up as president of Pepsi-Cola. He begins his account with the climax of that career, the meeting at which it was announced that Pepsi had at long last sold more soft drink than Coca-Cola. "It was," he says, "one of those moments for which you worked your entire career. ... All of us started out with that objective, and we never took our eyes off it" (3). This culmination reads as self-satire to humanists, but surely we have unveiled the "purity" of motive Bloom recommends, only now transposed from pure play to pure competition. The PepsiCo corporate headquarters in Purchase, New York, was not called "the campus" for nothing. The social usefulness—the purpose—of producing Pepsi-Cola was taken for granted, and this left smart guys—they were then all guys—like Sculley free to drink deep of the pleasures of pure competition and pure play. His account shows him intoxicated with both, "obsessed" in precisely the way Steiner describes the academic obsession.

Then the guys at Apple Computer broke in on the pure career game that Sculley was playing; he was "the guy from corporate America" they needed to take Apple into the big time. Their prolonged courtship was consummated on the balcony of Steve Jobs's Manhattan condo. In a line that has already become legendary in the computer world, Jobs asked Sculley the management version of the "Q" question: "Do you want to spend the rest of your life selling sugared water or do you want a chance to change the world?" Do you want to "apply" your "pure career" to the moral life?

Sculley decided to change the world, and if he hasn't done that, he has certainly changed Apple. The company he found there differed in almost every way from Pepsi. Sculley calls Apple a "third wave" company and Pepsi a "second wave" one. "Second wave" organizations are hierarchical, focus on stability, institutional tradition, and stable markets; "third wave" organizations are flexibly networked, focus on interdependency, individual entrepreneurship, and growth. The differences, transposed into terms humanists would find familiar, might be thought of as the differences between "modernism" and "postmodernism."

Is not Sculley's "third wave" thinking (though perhaps trite in its terminology) similar to McKeon's description of an architectonic rhetoric, which "relates form to matter, instrumentality to product, presentation to content, agent to audience, intention to reason," which is "positive in the creation, not passive in the reception of data, facts, consequences, and objective organization"? Although both corporations represent the world Allan Bloom describes as "primal slime," perhaps Apple would seem worse than Pepsi to him because its "curriculum," if I may use the word, deliberately tries to mix motives rather than purify them. Mixing the game and play motives that created the personal computer with the purposive world of salable products was what Sculley was brought to Apple to do. Doing it made Apple a completely different world from Pepsi, and John Sculley's acclimatization to the new environment makes for an interesting reading he did not altogether intend.

Without sentimentalizing the life of a volatile corporation, we can say that people working at Apple found that it engaged far more of the human personality than the highly ritualized and spiritualized competitive atmosphere at Pepsi. The people at Pepsi were pursuing a purely theoretical goal and reward very like what Bloom means by "spirituality." The two companies represent, in fact, two model curricula, two possible patterns of university life. Pepsi is the perfectly pure career game; pure competition with a wonderfully symbolic product to lend a laughable justification to it—sugared water with bubbles. Apple, at least at its best, has been trying to mix human motives, not to purify them, to stake its future on a rich mixture of game, play, and purpose, as the most creative for us humans. It answers its version of the "Q" question with the motivational mixture of the older, rhetorical paideia, rather than the Ramist one. It has been trying to expand the industrial canon.

◻   ◻   ◻

The books I have reviewed show, I would argue, that the American university, or at least its humanistic component, stands at a similar crossroads. We humanists are becoming ever more career-oriented in the purely competitive Pepsi way. We are perpetually attracted to the pure think tank, on its idyllic campus, the perennial golden age which Graff describes and Bloom yearns for. We assume the virtue of our product automatically, just as they did at Pepsi, and because we do so, it is coming to resemble more and more, for all its pretensions, not the model of power it pretends to be, but our own version of sugar water with bubbles. Yet the structure of the American land-grant model for a university, the practical place of immediate use as well as the home of pure speculation, where any person can study any subject, however untraditional, offers an opportunity for the opposite pattern, for the radical mixture of motives that Sculley describes at Apple. But, like the Ramist agenda which enfranchised it, the land-grant pattern defers indefinitely the time when its various separate inquiries will be mixed into the moral life. Finding the means to resituate this mixing into the curriculum, giving it both a theoretical and an administrative home, is the primary item on our current agenda. For this mixing of motives, this perpetually fruitful and unstable struggle to build a fully human purpose, is the nonnegotiable center for which all our learned commissions have been searching in vain. If we don't reincarnate it, the humanist establishment in America will both create, and deserve, its own Anthony Blunts.

NOTES

1. Peter Ramus, *Rhetoricae Distinctiones in Quintilianum (1549)* (Arguments in rhetoric against Quintilian), trans. Carole Newlands, intro. James J. Murphy (DeKalb, Ill.: Northern Illinois University Press, 1986), 83–84, 87.

2. Walter J. Ong, *Orality and Literacy: The Technologizing of the Word* (London and New York: Methuen, 1982), 134.

3. Arthur F. Kinney, *Humanist Poetics: Thought, Rhetoric, and Fiction in Sixteenth-Century England* (Amherst: University of Massachusetts Press, 1986).

4. For a fuller discussion of this key term, see chapter 6.

5. Kinney (n. 3 above), 122–23.

6. Anthony Grafton and Lisa Jardine, *From Humanism to the Humanities: Education and the Liberal Arts in Fifteenth- and Sixteenth-Century Europe* (London: Duckworth, 1986), 141 n. 68.

7. Richard McKeon, *Rhetoric: Essays in Invention and Discovery*, ed. Mark Backman (Woodbridge, Conn.: Ox Bow, 1987).

8. Donald N. McCloskey, *The Rhetoric of Economics* (Madison: University of Wisconsin Press, 1985).

9. E. D. Hirsch, Jr., *Cultural Literacy: What Every American Needs to Know* (Boston: Houghton Mifflin, 1987).

10. Alfred North Whitehead, "The Aims of Education," *The Aims of Education and Other Essays* (New York: Macmillan, 1929), 10–11.

11. Gerald Graff, *Professing Literature: An Institutional History* (Chicago: University of Chicago Press, 1987).

12. Allan Bloom, *The Closing of the American Mind* (New York: Simon and Schuster, 1987).

13. Mark Johnson, *The Body in the Mind: The Bodily Basis of Meaning, Imagination, and Reason* (Chicago: University of Chicago Press, 1987).

14. Barrie Penrose and Simon Freeman, *Conspiracy of Silence: The Secret Life of Anthony Blunt* (New York: Farrar Straus Giroux, 1987), ix.

15. George Steiner, "The Cleric of Treason," *The New Yorker*, 8 Dec. 1980, reprinted in *George Steiner: A Reader* (Cambridge: Penguin; New York: Oxford University Press, 1984), 190.

16. Penrose and Freeman (n. 14 above), 419.

17. Steiner (n. 15 above), 191.

18. Sidney Hook, *Out of Step: An Unquiet Life in the 20th Century* (New York: Harper and Row, 1987).

19. Steiner (n. 15 above), 199.

20. Gregory Bateson, "From Versailles to Cybernetics," *Steps toward an Ecology of Mind* (New York: Ballantine, 1972), 469–77.

21. John Sculley, with John A. Byrne, *Odyssey: Pepsi to Apple…, A Journey of Adventure, Ideas, and the Future* (New York: Harper and Row, 1987).

8

The convergence for which the previous chapters have been arguing—an interplay between democracy, technology, and the arts—met with such bemused wonder when I argued it over the last half dozen years, that I began to doubt my own judgment. In the last few years, however, a cluster of books has appeared which, taken together, debate the convergence I have sought to describe. In this chapter and the next I examine these books; they form a remarkably instructive group, for they come at the convergence from very different points of view. Through them one can glimpse a new rhetorical agenda forming. That agenda I sketch in the concluding chapter. Before I begin this last section, though, it may help to restate in plain stages the argument of the preceding essays.

I argue (in chapter 3) that many of the changes we observe in contemporary intellectual life make sense if we consider them as part of a larger single movement, the return of the Western pattern of education in language that I call the rhetorical paideia. This pattern dominated Western education from the earliest Greek beginnings until the Renaissance, when it gave way to what I have called the Newtonian interlude, a radical inversion in language education and the conceptions of self and society that grew out of it. I sketch this change when discussing Ramism in chapter 7. Peter Ramus separated rhetoric from philosophy, giving to rhetoric only the presentational and ornamental functions of language, and beginning a way of thinking about language that I have elsewhere described as the "C-B-S" or "Clarity-Brevity-Sincerity" method.[1] In this world, language is a neutral and transparent conduit for preexistent facts. As Bishop Sprat went on to argue, words and facts should be iso-

morphic, one-on-one. *Ideally, we would not need words at all, since they cause so much trouble and confusion. We would simply exchange wordless chunks of "reality" somehow. One can see how easily this transparent ideal for language mapped onto the aesthetics of print. The "crystal goblet" theory of typography that matured in the nineteenth century was simply a Ramist theory of language transferred to the aesthetics of print.*

Now the much older way of conceiving discourse is returning, often under the guise of an outrageously didactic postmodernity. In the rhetorical tradition, language comes not transparent and neutral but intrinsically colored (hence the "colors" of rhetoric) with ornament and inherently nonneutral, weighted by play or purpose. In chapter 2, I point out how the rhetorical ways of thinking are returning to the visual arts, how they are didactic rather than avant garde, and how they begin to supply an aesthetic for electronic expression. I suggest, briefly (in chapters 1, 3, and 4), that the explosion of what we call "literary theory" can best be seen, like so much of postmodernism in the visual arts, not as new and outrageous but as traditional and didactic.

I argue (in chapters 4, 5, and 6) that the democratization of higher education brings with it structural consequences we have not yet confronted, and that this democratization is intimately connected with the return of a rhetorical pedagogy and with what in chapter 1 I call the "electronic word."

These three areas—democracy, technology, and the arts and letters—I argue (in chapter 4) have now converged into a single cultural development. Both electronic text and the traditional system of rhetorical education, it turns out, fit very nicely into the efforts we are making in America to democratize higher education.

This convergence poses yet again the crucial question for the arts and letters: What are they good for? We have systematically dodged this question, confusing thereby many subsidiary questions, curricular and pedagogical. As I argue in chapter 1, technology now puts this question in a way we can dodge no longer. And, as we would expect if the convergence is a reality, this question is turning up all over the intellectual landscape; that is my argument in chapter 7, "The 'Q' Question."

From our answer to the "Q" question will emerge the guidance we need in how to use electronic technology to preserve "the book" without preserving it in pickle. I have suggested my own answer in several places (especially in chapters 3 and 7); the conclusions that follow from it are these:

*(1) The arguments against electronic technology which I'll review below are seen to be variations on the traditional arguments developed against rhetoric by Platonic philosophy and Christian theology. This perennial argument in Western culture has been chronicled by Jonas Barish as **The Antitheatrical Prejudice,**[2] but his book might just as well have been called **The Antirhetorical Prejudice,** for the arguments it describes are the same. Popular laments like Daniel Boorstin's **The Image,** or Neil Postman's **Amusing Ourselves to Death** (which I discuss in chapter 9), rehearse them yet again.*

(2) The modern difficulties of copyright law, resulting from its basis in print technology, intimately affect and are affected by the other two elements of our triad, democratization and rhetoric.

(3) The current curriculum debate ignores the real problems before us. How uni-

versity structures and professional structures and languages are affected (chapters 5 and 6) has hardly been discussed.

(4) When we have clearly in view the traditional quarrel between the philosophers and the rhetoricians—the quarrel we are currently replaying—we will have a clear view of the fundamental contradiction in Western humanism that has so muddled our thinking about it. And perhaps we may have some clue about how to resolve this contradiction and how the powers of electronic technology might help in the task.

Elegies for the Book

"McLuhanesque"

ad electronic technology invaded a simpler cultural landscape, we might more easily map its spheres of influence. But so many things happened, it seemed, nearly at once, and they all affected each other. First came the big, remote, inaccessible mainframe computer. Dealing with that was easy for the humanist imagination: nurtured in the bosom of the military and the codebreakers, the mainframe was surely the electronic embodiment of Big Brother, folding, spindling, and mutilating the alienated student proletariat at U.C. Berkeley, and all the rest of us too. So, in a sense, it has proved to be, since the networked files of digital information now maintained on all of us for commercial as well as governmental purposes have in a real sense abolished the privacy of private life. At the same time, computers have enhanced the powers of invigilatory efficiency experts who threaten (at least so humanist critics think) to speed up work until the workers drop.

But no sooner had we adequately mythologized this monster than the personal computer arrived on the scene, and promised to liberate us from Big Brother, if not from Big Blue. And so, in a sense, it too has proved to do, since the small computer reflects and enables our individual, idiosyncratic needs and purposes as no device ever has done before. Online networks have immediately become a seminar room for intellectuals—as we might expect. But—as we might not expect—they have built a new expressive genre for the intellectual life of people whom intellectuals would not think to call intellectuals. Special-interest groups, hobbyists, whatever you want to call them, have always embodied that disinterested pursuit of the "life of the mind" that America was supposed to lack. Suddenly, people who love baseball statistics, or genealogy, or classic Komenda-designed Porsches, or Ford 8N farm tractors, or Shaker furniture, or Sandwich glass, or all the hundreds of other subjects upon which Americans do deep research in their spare time, have a social and scholarly forum.

Beyond this, we have come to view the small "private" computer as a new expressive device for the arts and letters, not simply a computational engine but a rhetorical and graphical one as well. With the newer generations of small and very small portable computers, "electronic notebooks" as they have inevitably been called, these trends have been reinforced. We can now carry around with us our personal expressive engines. And an explosion of digital instruments for musical and artistic composition and performance has enfranchised the public imagination in genuinely new ways. We can, then, chart one area of the electronic invasion: a democratic movement from big to small, impersonal to personal, citadel to coat pocket.

This tidy picture immediately blurs when we consider what "electronic technology" means to most people: it means commercial broadcast television. Nothing has been so speedily demonized by culture-critics as TV, and perhaps deservedly so. Certainly no medium has commercialized itself so thoroughly, or dedicated itself so wholeheartedly to pushing the buttons of sex and violence which degrade the human nature. And no single source of entertainment has ever proved so globally narcotic. Electronic technology has come to seem the degradation, not the liberation, of the popular imagination. The condemnations have followed hard upon, predictions of cultural catastrophe falling thick as snowflakes in Siberia.

But here, too, the reversal from top-down, centralized power to bottom-up individualized selection, from broadcasting to narrowcasting, goes forward apace. The biggest change has come from the VCR and (above all) from the camcorder, which together make us all television photographers and producers. The viewer is on the way, through optical-fiber networks entering the home, to selecting from a very wide menu, constructing an individual cultural palette. These choices may not always favor dramatic drivel. George Gilder has argued, in his recent *Life After Television*,[3] that broadcast television is an obsolete technology and that its cultural depredations will soon give way to a much richer culture of optical-fiber narrowcasting. We can, thus, chart a second, more blurred area of influence, but one following the same democratizing pattern as the first.

To further confuse our landscape, we must separate the influences all those thousands of TV-watching hours exert directly on children from the activities, like reading or ordinary social play, which they displace. Jane Healy argues in *Endangered Minds*, a recent study we'll examine in chapter 9, that American students are not developing the neural networks upon which higher-level human thinking depends. Why not? In the critical period when these powers must be developed by talking and listening, the kids are watching TV instead.[4] Such narcotic displacement would be comparable to brain damage caused by chemical narcotics. We should not confuse this narcotizing of American society, horrible as it is, with the mixture of word, image, and sound emerging now through digital multimedia techniques.

Beyond the challenge of separating direct influence from narcotic displacement, another difficulty has blurred our view of digital technology. Commercial television was early and apocalyptically theorized by Marshall McLuhan. McLuhan was hard to understand. As George Steiner pegged him, "The writings of Marshall McLuhan are so compounded of novelty, force of suggestion, vulgarity of mind, and sheer carelessness that one is quickly tempted to put them aside."[5] But difficult prose did not generate the main problem. (A perplexing, visionary prose—as the modern cultural conversation illustrates—much more often helps than hinders the ambitious critic.) At least three deeper problems have continued to occlude McLuhan's commentary on electronic technology, and to confuse our understanding of how that technology influences us.

In the first place, as I've touched upon in chapter 1, McLuhan was talking about broadcast television, an *analogue* technology, but his commentary has been taken to apply to any electronic display, broadcast or narrowcast, analogue or digital. Second, and more unpardonable even than his obscure prose, was his popularity. McLuhan became a cultural guru, a media darling, even a *Playboy* interviewee. How could one take him seriously? "McLuhanesque" became and has remained a standard dyslogistic epithet that critics used to disparage any discussion of electronic media. McLuhan's appeal to the media came, to be sure, from deep within him. As his recent and excellent biographer Philip Marchand points out, McLuhan's characteristic form of expression was *conversation* not *writing*. He was an *oral* man to begin with.[6]

More deeply confusing than either of these premature conclusions, however, was that root distinction upon which McLuhan's thought was based, the distinction between literate and oral cultures. This distinction has met strong resistance wherever and whenever introduced. When Milman Parry originally advanced it, to explain his radical new contribution to the Homeric question, the Department of Classics at Berkeley invited him to leave. He had to finish and publish his work in Paris.[7] Eric Havelock has on several occasions remarked the resistance that his own work encountered. Scribner and Cole and others have attacked the thesis on both anthropological and critical grounds.[8] Through the McLuhan phenomenon (if I may distinguish his work from its media presentations), a very deep and complex cultural argument attained a radical simplicity: electronic technology meant the end of literacy and the return of orality. Since literacy, for most people, *is* Western culture, electronic technology immediately generates formidable opposition.

The oral/literate distinction takes us to the heart of McLuhan's arguments, and now, thirty years after the publication of *The Gutenberg Galaxy*, we can understand why they struck so deep a cultural chord. McLuhan, it is seldom remembered, began as a student of classical rhetoric. He wrote his Cambridge dissertation on the rhetoric of Thomas Nashe. Nashe, in temperament and unconventional prose, resembled McLuhan. His dissertation director said that "I couldn't help feeling that there was a Thomas Nashe inside McLuhan, dying to get out." McLuhan's biographer describes the process:

> McLuhan decided, then, to write his thesis on Nashe. The more he read Nashe, however, the more he kept running into the profound influence of the ancient theory and practice of rhetoric on Nashe's supposedly off-the-cuff, purely journalistic and satirical writing. McLuhan started to read up on this theory and practice. As he did, an astonishing world opened up for him. ...
>
> McLuhan found, for example, why people like Nashe hated the philosophers of the Middle Ages. Nashe was simply involved in a quarrel between the Renaissance followers of a tradition of rhetoric going back to Cicero—the tradition of wisdom as eloquent speaking—and the "schoolmen" of the Middle Ages, who were followers of dialectics—wisdom as pure logic. The quarrel, in fact, had originated in the scorn of Socrates (the dialectician) for the Sophists (the rhetoricians).[9]

The quarrel between the philosophers and the rhetoricians constitutes *the* quarrel in Western culture. McLuhan's argument for electronic media reintroduced the rhetorician's conception of language, and of human self and society, after the three hundred years dominated by the philosophers, with their strongly opposed conceptions of language and social reality. The fuss about McLuhan was, behind its glitzy façade, about something very deep, something bound to set off landmines at every step.

Electronic media were from the beginning, as McLuhan sensed, tied into the underlying intellectual and artistic movement of the twentieth century, the return of the rhetorical world view after an interval so long that rhetoric's very existence (except as a synonym for lying) had been forgotten. As McLuhan well knew, rhetoric was an *oral* phenomenon, returning to an increasingly oral world. Although applied to writing as soon as there was writing, rhetoric was originally a training in public *speaking*, and more largely in an oral culture, in political behavior. To this kind of education the quasi-oral world of electronic media was home ground. And the rhetoric/philosophy distinction, we should remember, is basically an educational one, precipitated out of Greek thought by Plato's *educational* thinking. The curricular framework I've discussed in chapters 4 and 6 reenters our cultural conversation through McLuhan and specifically in the context of electronic media.[10] When we ask how electronic technology affects us, then, we are inquiring, *in terms of* electronic technology, into the most profound division in Western culture. The rhetorical/philosophical distinction, though it grows from the technological distinction between oral and literate cultures, concerns more than technology. It debates opposed theories of human motive, human selfhood, and human society.

It is clear by now, I hope, why the debate about the social harm or benefit of electronic technology has been so muddled. It involved the basic positions of our cultural world as soon as the argument opened in classical Greece, and has done so again ever since McLuhan precipitated it back onto the popular cultural agenda. As a result, when people talk about the baneful influence of electronic technology, often they are really talking about something quite different, about a cultural debate which technology has reintroduced. The deepest debates about TV, about the decline of the book, about the computer as Big Brother or little one, are usually variations on the long-standing debate between the rhetoricians and the philosophers. Since the premises of the two camps differ radically, the contenders always talk past each other.

This talking-past explains the misunderstanding of McLuhan. *The Gutenberg Galaxy* rereads a series of texts from the rhetorical point of view. These texts make a new and different sense from that point of view, just as much of postmodern visual art and music makes new sense once we interpret it, as we did in chapter 2, as a didactic lesson about the rhetorical coordinates of human life rather than an "outrageous" lesson about its philosophical coordinates. (Some time after I had written the "Q" question essay, I realized that I had followed this "McLuhanesque" strategy there.) If, however, you read McLuhan from a philosophical point of view, he is not didactic but "outrageous," just like Duchamp or Andy Warhol or John Cage, who are all, in their different ways, trying to teach the same lesson. The same bafflement emerges from the same argumentative context in all of them.

Around the electronic word, then, around this movement from book to screen, cluster the major humanistic issues of our time. Until we perceive this cultural convergence, and understand that McLuhan was mapping a brand new technology onto the oldest and most foundational of cultural disputes, we will never understand the argument electronic technology has precipitated. As long as "McLuhanesque" remains a dyslogistic epithet, we can never decide what we should do with these marvelous new means of expression that now lie like quicksilver in our hands. Fortunately, a group of studies appearing in the last few years suggests that the argument is once again being pursued in its larger, more promising context.

From Book to Screen

As we've seen in chapter 2, Marinetti declared that the printed book had lost its cultural primacy and argued for a more dynamic alternative. McLuhan reformulated Marinetti's argument in specifically rhetorical terms. Some recent books have now resumed this argument in the light of digital technologies. Attitudes and ranges vary widely, but the focus remains the same.

> We are coming to the end of the culture of the book. Books are still produced and read in prodigious numbers, and they will continue to be as far into the future as one can imagine. However, they do not command the center of the cultural stage. Modern culture is taking shapes that are more various and more complicated than the book-centered culture it is succeeding.[11]

> Television, computer database, Xerox, word processor, tape, and VCR are not symbiotic with literature and its values in the way that print was, and new ways of acquiring, storing, and transmitting information are signaling the end of a conception of writing and reading oriented to the printed book and institutionalized as literature.[12]

> The printed book, therefore, seems destined to move to the margin of our literate culture. ... This shift from print to the computer does not mean the end of literacy. What will be lost is not literacy itself, but the literacy of print, for electronic technology offers us a new kind of book and new ways to write and read.[13]

This common focus emerges from very different cultural appraisals. The author of the first quotation, Renaissance scholar and contemporary cultural critic O. B. Hardison, paints on the widest canvas. *Disappearing Through the Skylight*, he tells us in the preface, "examines five basic and interrelated areas—nature, history, language, art, and human evolution—reviewing the ways in which central concepts in each area have changed since the beginning of the present century. Because the changes have been fundamental, the concepts—and even the vocabularies and images in which the concepts tend to be framed—no longer seem to objectify a real world. It is as though progress were making the real world invisible" (xi). He argues, as I have been doing, that the changes in these five areas are related parts of a single cultural manifestation, an organic state-change Hardison calls a "horizon of invisibility." "Those who have passed through it cannot put their experience into familiar words and images because the languages they have inherited are inadequate to the new worlds they inhabit" (5). In this fashion he seeks to describe the movement from philosophical to rhetorical coordinates.

The cultural terrain he surveys to establish this deep shift in the plate tectonics of culture ranges from Benoit Mandelbrot's work on fractals to an extended critique of postmodern art and architecture (including a discussion of Christo's *Running Fence*); from Dada and "concrete poetry" to "artificial reality"; from current trends in multimedia to artificial intelligence and its implications for human evolution; from "modern" and "modernism" in the arts to "game" and "play" motives in postmodern culture.

From all he surveys, Hardison draws the same lurking question: "Is the claim of humanity to uniqueness disappearing along with the claim of each human to a separate identity shaped by a local habitation and a name? Is the idea of what it is to be human disappearing, along with so many other ideas, through the modern skylight?" (5). He fears that "man—at least man in the old sense of a separate and individual essence—may disappear" (289). Oddly enough, for all his perceptiveness about the present and future, Hardison misreads the past. He never considers that the cultural cataclysm he fears may represent the return of the old as well as the onset of the new. The "humanity" disappearing up the skylight was the "humanity" of a particular time in Western culture. The "natural" scale of the nineteenth-century middle distance, the "reality" that was comfortably "out there," and the "self" comfortably "in here" were not eternalities of the human condition. Maddeningly, he keeps seeing this and then not seeing it. Modern science has moved from observing the world in the middle distance to "observations of the very small and the very distant. ... All of these versions of nature are 'real'" (42). But Hardison thinks one version more real than the others, and more native to humankind, and it is this version which is vanishing up the skylight. Again: "Between the publication of Newton's *Principia Mathematica* in 1687 and Darwin's *Origin of Species* in 1859, science believed it could present man with truth. This was a fantasy" (48). And so now, like a desperate deconstructionist, we are delivered into a time without truth.

This misplaced nostalgia causes Hardison to misread the evidence he has marshalled. We are not going from one exclusive extreme to another, from Newtonianism to relativism, from the pure central self to the pure social self. We are correcting an imbalance, restoring that characteristic Western oscillation between these two states. It has always been unstable, and we have always been tempted to make the mistake Hardison makes, to absolutize one side of the oscillation in order to shut the oscillation itself down and relieve the tension.

You can watch this characteristic misreading in action when he talks about postmodern architecture. Take two examples which he considers back-to-back, the Red Lion Row redevelopment project in Washington, D.C., and the considerably more famous Centre Pompidou, the "Beaubourg," in Paris. Both work the same way, by embodying the very oscillation we are talking about. First, Red Lion Row:

> A bizarre example—and perhaps the most vulgar structure created in America between 1965 and 1985—is the Red Lion Row development in Washington, D.C., five blocks from the White House. This structure—if structure it can be called—appears to be a block of three-story rowhouses restored with such germicidal precision that it looks like a stage set. That is exactly what they are. Behind them rises the real building, an immense, smooth, ominous steel-and-glass structure that stares down on them with equal measures of contempt and surprise, like the owner of a penthouse examining cockroaches on the kitchen floor. (115)

The "real building"—that is the tip-off. The building juxtaposes two kinds of reality, the self-conscious, postmodern "stage set" and the unselfconscious, practical, international-style office building behind it. The eye must hold the two in oscillation, self-conscious and unselfconscious, transparent and opaque, purpose and play. The "real" building is neither the background one nor the foreground one but the oscillation created by the two working against one another. Hardison cannot see that working, and he fails to see it in almost every cultural configuration he examines.

Lest we fail to note the mistake, he repeats it on the next building he considers, the Beaubourg.

> The Pompidou, which opened in 1977, expresses its radical functionalism by exhibiting all of its mechanical services openly. Their bright colors and contrasts of shape, scale, and materials make their anti-aesthetic aesthetic explicit and continuous. Form follows function with relentless literalness. On the building's façade the most striking feature is an escalator that jogs its way up the outside wall with a pause

at each floor. Visually prominent posts and tie-rods help support the building and maintain rigidity in ways vaguely reminiscent of the Crystal Palace. (117)

As I've argued in chapter 2, this building juxtaposes play and purpose by reversing them, making the "purposive" mechanisms of the building into a playful façade and so creating a deliberate oscillation between the two ranges of motive. Rogers and Piano created not a "functional" building but its opposite. Hardison can't fathom the energizing *bi-stability*. The building sets form and function in oscillation, rather than making one triumph over the other.

This failure of perception generates Hardison's cultural pessimism. He notices one change—admittedly a big one—in the oscillation that composes Western reality, and interprets it cataclysmically. One repetition of the wave form tells the whole story. In interpreting the future he ignores the past. He gets the "convergence" right, the conglomerate vision, but doesn't focus the larger pattern of which it forms part. Every time he comes up against the bi-stable center, he flinches. It constitutes the theoretical core of what he seeks to describe but, for all his openness of mind, he cannot understand it.

◻   ◻   ◻

Alvin Kernan's *The Death of Literature*, which appeared in 1990, a year after Hardison's book, deals with the same enzymatic influence of electronic technology on the culture of the book. Like Hardison, Kernan discusses the confluence of electronic technology and a literary theory that proleptically describes it. Like Hardison, he reflects on electronic technology's collision with copyright law. Like Hardison, he feels that a crucial chapter in Western intellectual history has come to a cataclysmic end. And like Hardison, how he reads the past distorts how he foresees the technological future.

And yet, for all these similarities, the two books could scarcely differ more. Hardison surveys a much wider landscape than Kernan's narrow literary pasture, and he maintains a more consistent analytic distance from it. Kernan's book projects so uneven a tone that it seems to have been written by three people. We might call them the Analyst, the Satirist, and the Curmudgeon. The Analyst pursues an argument he first engaged in an earlier book, *Samuel Johnson and the Impact of Print* (1989). He argues that "literature," if by that we mean the print-centered product that matured in the eighteenth century and lasted approximately until the publication of *Finnegans Wake*, has been killed by electronic technology. And along with it goes the book-centered culture it created.

The Satirist finds much to ridicule in the current critical scene. He pokes fun at what Gerald Graff, in *Professing Literature*, calls the "Deconstructionist Two-Step," whereby critics write books that argue for the undependability of all critical reading except their own. He points out, with acuity and humor, that the humanist world's current infatuation with Marxist "empowerment" struggles is built on a bureaucratization of learning supported by the oppressive capitalist system it seeks to overturn. Keep biting the hand that feeds you, his satire suggests, and, as in Margaret Thatcher's England, that hand may feed no longer. He points out that the "serious" literature of our time is largely created in and for a special educational bureaucracy.

All these discussions vary a single theme: the "Q" question I considered in the previous essay. In a chapter about the *Lady Chatterley* trial, Kernan poses it directly, and as relentlessly as George Steiner. Those who profess literature cannot begin to describe what it does to or for us, as the floundering attempts by scholarly expert witnesses illustrate. "What the *Lady Chatterley* case showed so dramatically was literature's lack of any theoretical basis, any systematic organization of its parts in a way that makes it real and meaningful to the eyes of the beholder and in the social world at large."[14] Chafed, like Steiner, at the death of "literature," he feels yet more vexed that he cannot explain why he should feel so.

The Curmudgeon is a classic *laudator temporis acti*. Here's a sample rant:

> The most inventive and powerful words heard in modern America are used in an openly immoral fashion, without, that is, any real concern for truth or logic or decency.
>
> Not only do our fools coin words and turn phrases in a kind of national logorrhea, but our most skilled users of words, the "hidden persuaders," are unashamed and unrepentant verbal fudgers, exaggerators, if not outright liars, distorters, and cynical manipulators. ... [T]he language that matters nowadays is made by ... the public relations flacks, entertainers, media specialists, television personalities, advertising hypesters, bureaucrats, celebrity manufacturers and marketers, politicians and their image makers, technocrats, and singers of popular songs. (169–70)

Behind this explosion lurks the Clarity-Brevity-Sincerity or "C-B-S" conception of language I discussed earlier. This pure and true use of language belongs, presumably, to the professors, rather than the filthy scum who actually run the world through the media. Back to Allan Bloom's conception of the virgin university and the debauched society. But, given the picture of the professors which the Satirist draws, where does that leave us? Do the professors have a lock on "truth or logic or decency"? If not, who does—or doesn't? This outburst is, like so much literary philosophizing these days, the purest pastoralism. There once was a time when people were straight and true to each other; that was when the world was run by people like Us. Now it is run by people like Them, and it is full of dirty rotten lies.

But the techniques that people like Them use—let us have done with euphemism and call these techniques by their right name, *rhetoric*—are these not the techniques that Western literary education has depended on since the Greeks? Kernan argues from the Weak Defense I discussed in the last chapter: when *we* use it, we talk sense; when *they* use it, they offer "only rhetoric." When Kernan uses it, we might ask, as he does in his three overlapping voices, what is it then? Back to the "Q" question. The Analyst (at least I think it is the Analyst) has staked a position on the other side of this question too: "Words are not pale isolated things but magical in their ability to evoke, shape, control things. To the eye of the philosopher it is all a vast swindle, but what privileges the casuistries of the philosopher over the evidence of all our lives to decide what is real and true?" (188).

In Kernan's book, the Satirist and the Curmudgeon always color the Analyst's efforts to understand. As a result, an unease pervades the book; it has an air of not coming clean about its own hatreds. Often, what the Curmudgeon gives, the Analyst takes away. For example, the Curmudgeon bemoans on several occasions the takeover of literature departments by composition—basic instruction in reading and writing. This is bad. But the Analyst argues the other side: "Criticism has wanted and acknowledged no relationship between its own sophisticated intellectual activities and the grungy business of adults who can't read …" (145). But it is the composition people who have tried to establish exactly this relationship. In this respect, in not coming clean to others or to itself about its real hatreds, Kernan's book accurately reflects much humanist response to technological change. The change in technology liberates a set of preexistent resentments about the other streams in our convergence, democratization and the return of rhetorical theory and practice. Again, the technology debate triggers a deeper one.

Such self-contradictory waffling runs deep in the traditional humanist argument about the word, an argument based, as we saw in chapter 7, on the Weak Defense. You can state the inconsistency in different ways. Opaque figurative language is all right in poetry but not in prose, which has to be transparent. Or, "good" rhetoric (or good "ornament") is good when it is serving Truth (when the "ornament" is "integral to the argument") but otherwise not. This is the true Socratic arrogance, but Plato, at least, came clean.

And so Kernan flinches at the same point Hardison does—when he confronts the bi-stability of genuine two-sided argument. He will argue one side of the case at one point and then, having forgotten the theoretical under-pinnings of his argument, later on argue the other side. But, as with Hardi-son standing before the Red Lion development, the Strong Defense never occurs to him even as a possibility. He never tries to explain his own self-contradictions to himself. When he comes to discuss "the critical iconoclasm that ripped the guts out of the old literature" (85), it is either the villainous, valueless world of deconstructive *aporia* or it is "Humanism's long dream of learning, of arriving at some final truth by enough reading and writing, [which is] breaking up in our time" (135). That humanism's long dream of learning involved both of these polar positions, put into fertile oscillation, never emerges as an alternative. Starting out to ponder the influence of new electronic technology on literary education, Kernan ends up simply choos-ing sides in the old fight between the philosophers and the rhetoricians. *Ter-tium non datur.*

His diatribe against television falls victim to the same polarization, but cast in a different form. He concludes his discussion this way: "Television, however, is not just a new way of doing old things but a radically different way of seeing and interpreting the world. Visual images not words, simple open meanings not complex and hidden, transience not permanence, episodes not structures, theater not truth" (151). *Theater not truth.* We are back at the antitheatrical prejudice whose history Jonas Barish has chroni-cled. Television is theater. Reality is something other. But elsewhere in the book Kernan takes some pains to defend Shakespeare. Is Shakespeare not theater? And do Shakespeare's plays offer "simple open meanings not com-plex and hidden" ones? How can villainous TV deceptions become simple and obvious here?

I emphasize again that this argument *is not really about technology at all.* Kernan's remarks a page or two earlier about broadcast television—that it is "never put together with much care," that "the pictures on the tube are con-stantly improved, but the speakers remain rudimentary," that it produces "not classics but entertainment consumables that seldom have any existence beyond their brief moment on the screen," and other suchlike opinions—are ignorant and silly, but they are at least *about what they think they are about.* Kernan ranting about television is like a Puritan divine ranting about the Elizabethan stage, or like Jane Austen disapproving of amateur theatri-cals in *Mansfield Park.* Drama threatens the stable central self. "Technolo-gy" is only the current stand-in for that threat.

Kernan also speculates on how electronic technology will affect uni-versity structures and learned disciplines. He fears that literary study may lose its traditional place, but we can stand this fear on its head and wonder what disciplinary and departmental accommodation multimedia study will find in the modern university. In all of large-scale corporate American enterprise, no craft guild has proven more hidebound than the professoriate. The tidal wave of social pressure now inundating the public school system will soon flood colleges and universities. Its demands for increased productivity, greater quality-control, and new work rules seem repellant by themselves, but they will inevitably come with a technological component. Response to the electronic word, here too, will be confused with much older fears, fears about the proper nature of corporate learned enterprise.

As I pointed out in chapter 5, digital technology promises to exert on the bureaucratic structures that sustain the *study* of the arts and letters a solvent force as great as that it already exerts on the *practice* of the arts and letters. When words, images, and sounds blend together into a new presentational mode, the "corporate structure," as one might call it, that supported the old mode must reinvent itself. The present university and departmental structure seems as ill-suited for what we will need as the old compartmentalized, seven-tier General Motors management structure was for making cars in a global economy. Academic humanists disdain to view themselves as resembling other large corporate structures in American life, and this disdain has blinded us to how antiquated and inelastic our management system is. Since the professoriate spans both management and labor, its self-enclosure proves doubly hermetic, and we ignore changing labor practices as well.[15]

Again we return to the "Q" question. If we are talking about literacy as basic economic training—educating a competitive work force—we have at least some reference points. The marketplace will tell us how we are doing and force needed changes. But what standards measure the "liberal" part of the liberal arts? If liberal education will increasingly depart from an electronic base, it becomes doubly vital to answer the "Q" question and embody that answer in a new rhetoric. There is no alternative. We cannot sustain one expressive mode for "art" and another for "life." Kernan worries about preserving the old job and the old work rules; putting the issue in a positive form—what will the new jobs and work rules be like?—only poses the problem more insistently.

◻   ◻   ◻

George P. Landow's *Hypertext: The Convergence of Contemporary Critical Theory and Technology* begins to sketch an answer.[16] Landow's book has a particular authority because it emerges from his deep experience with the most mature hypertextual instructional system yet assembled, the Intermedia program at Brown University. In a chapter called "Reconfiguring Literary Education," he singles out the pressures on disciplinarity and departmentality we have just remarked. "Inevitably, hypertext gives us a far more efficient means than has previously existed of teaching interdisciplinary courses, of doing, that is, what almost by definition 'shouldn't be done'" (124). Students in an instructional system like this, facing not the finality of textbooks but the raw perplexities from which scholars assemble textbooks, become collaborative authors of a continuing textbook.

A "course" in such an environment (Landow does not develop the argument in these terms) acquires for the first time a history. It becomes a separate sub-culture, in which students can review comments and writings by previous students, and track how those students' interests have shaped the evolution of the course. The design of the course *evolves* rather than reflecting a single instructor's original conception. It takes on the properties of an emergent system, and in its evolution undermines a standard building block of all current American university curricula, the equivalence of one course with another. Such courses will outgrow disciplinary and departmental boundaries. And, as Landow points out, the time frames within which study is pursued become individualized in a system where each student works at an individual pace.

This customization threatens the idea of a "course" from yet another side. Gerald Graff has argued in *Professing Literature* that American universities handle disagreement by departmentalizing it. When differences within a department become intolerable, a new department siphons off the insurgents; since departments talk to one another only in stately bows and flourishes, no one learns anything from the disagreement. Hypertextual instruction threatens this method of departmental fission.

It is not university structures that provide the main argument of Landow's book, however, but the surprising ways in which electronic text embodies the teachings of current literary theory. Kernan touches on this convergence from a contentious point of view, but Landow discusses it at more disinterested length. The role of networked rather than linear thinking, the changed status of the author, the talismanic and imperiled status of the codex book, the now familiar *aporia* before a now-volatile text deprived of its canonical authority—the full critical agenda is reviewed.

◻   ◻   ◻

For those who have trouble focusing Landow's diffuse citational discussion, a more concentrated one ("Critical Theory and the New Writing Space") can be found in another recent book, Jay David Bolter's *Writing Space: The Computer, Hypertext, and the History of Writing*.[17] Bolter's book is, on balance, the best general discussion of electronic text that has yet appeared. A classicist with a degree in computer science, Bolter projects his discussion of electronic text on the entire history of Western literacy.

Electronic technology, he argues, "offers us a new kind of book and new ways to write and read" (2), a "fourth great technique of writing that will take its place beside the ancient papyrus roll, the medieval codex, and the printed book" (6). Bolter does not demonize any of these historic forms but puts their various powers into useful comparison. Thus he remarks on the extraordinary expressive richness of the medieval manuscript and, by contrast, the self-imposed visual poverty of the printed book. And thus he can, like George Gilder,[18] put Kernan's television anxiety to rest: "In fact, hypermedia is the revenge of text upon television. ... In television, text is absorbed into the video image, but in hypermedia the televised image becomes part of the text" (26). If the "printed book is an extreme form of writing, not the norm," then the norm—if such there be—can be constituted only by surveying all the expressive forms now before us. This he does.

Bolter places computer writing in the historical context of alphabetic and iconic notation. His discussion of writing in Western culture makes clear what is new and old about electronic text and also reappraises Western writing *in terms of* electronic text. He uses electronic text, that is, as a perspective from which to look backward as well as forward. In considering the literate/oral debate which encapsulates the history of electronic text, he returns to the original stimulus: "Electronic text is, like an oral text, dynamic. Homeric listeners had the opportunity to affect the telling of the tale by their applause or disapproval. Such applause and disapproval shared the aural space in which the poet performed and became part of that particular performance ..." (59), and later, "It is no coincidence that many ancient poetic and historical texts do not have climactic endings" (86). In the light of hypertextual conventions, he recaptures traditional printed texts that have seemed in one way or another to strive against print: Wittgenstein's *Philosophical Investigations* and Derrida's *Glas*, Joyce's *Ulysses* and *Finnegans Wake*, and Sterne's *Tristram Shandy*.[19] We spend a great deal of time today talking about the canon but, as I've argued in chapter 1, we have yet to consider the enormous canonical reform implied in an electronic reassessment of the past.

What strikes me most about Bolter's book, however, is the way it reconceives the philosophers/rhetoricians debate in terms of electronic text. I've suggested in chapter 2 that the visual arts created an aesthetic for the electronic screen before that screen was invented. Bolter argues that the philosophy of mind embodied in a computer was similarly created before the computer was invented.

> As a new writing technology, the computer is yet another instance of the metaphor of writing in the mind. With the aid of the computer, the writer constructs the text as a dynamic network of verbal and visual symbols. These electronic symbols in the machine seem to be an extension of a network of ideas in the mind itself. More effectively than the codex or the printed book, the computer reflects the mind as a web of verbal and visual elements in a conceptual space. When technology provided us with printed books and photographs, our minds were repositories of fixed texts and still images. When the contemporary technology is electronic, our minds become pulsing networks of ideas. ... [E]lectronic technology fits perfectly with the semiotic view of language and thought in the tradition from C. S. Peirce to Umberto Eco. ... [I]t is not simply the mind as computer, as the artificial intelligence specialists propose, but rather the mind as a network of signs, of which the computer is the embodiment. (207–8)

On the one side we have the semiotic view of language as self-referential, of human thinking as "kiting checks" rather than making deposits. Electronic text encourages this, takes the dramatistic view of human self and society which the rhetorical paideia has always taken. On the other side, we have the philosophers' argument for a Platonic central self and intentionality, and a "reality" which is somehow or another really out there. Print technology encourages this view. "Perhaps even the Cartesian notion of the ego depends on the metaphor of the author and the text. ... When Descartes claims 'I think therefore I am,' he is claiming that the text validates him as author" (221).

And so emerges from yet another point of view the polarization of Western thought between rhetoric and philosophy, and yet another suggestion that electronic text enfranchises the oral/rhetorical/dramatistic/semiological world in the same way that print did its literate/philosophical/positivist opposite. The oral world returns in a hyperliterate form.[20]

◻   ◻   ◻

Gregory Ulmer's *Teletheory: Grammatology in the Age of Video*[21] carries the convergence of literary theory and electronic expression several steps further than Bolter, and constructs a new university pedagogy from it. Ulmer's argument is subtle and complex, and (though often expressed with the trademark obscurity of Derridean prose) it represents the first substantial attempt to rethink university discourse in terms of electronic expression rather than print.

Ulmer begins by accepting as fact, as do Kernan, Hardison, and Bolter, that a "communications revolution" has occurred, and one that has deep cultural roots. It mixes images and words in new ways, and, as in an oral society, substitutes narrative for conceptual argumentation. Unlike Kernan, however, Ulmer applauds its results rather than damning them.

> During the Renaissance, humanists led the educational reforms associated with the rise of literacy and the new technology of the press. Humanists today are no less responsible for developing the educational potential of the new technologies of memory and communication. (viii)

> Television is indeed a rival didactic institution, promoting an alternative mode of thought, just as the critics warn. But what should the response of the schools be? I would like us to participate in the invention of a style of thought as powerful and productive as was the invention of conceptual thinking that grew out of the alphabetic apparatus. I want to learn how to write and think electronically—in a way that supplements without replacing analytical reason. (ix–x)

As an intermediate goal, Ulmer aims at academic discourse. It has, he argues (as do Kernan and many other critics), abandoned the way people "think" outside the academic world. This is specially true of the humanities, the only group still irrevocably committed to the printed word.

Ulmer proposes a new genre of academic discourse, "mystory." A "mystory" combines elements of personal autobiography, oral history, and expert conceptual analysis. A collage, it claims originality only from the particular pattern of juxtaposition it offers. Good Derridean that he is, Ulmer argues that pun and wordplay should figure more strongly in university writing: "The ground of teletheory is the research pun, bringing together two unrelated semantic fields on the basis of one or more shared words" (63). "Mystory" puns on "mystery": a good mystory should surprise us by its juxtapositions and changes in declaratory and stylistic register.

One does not have to be a card-carrying television-hater like Kernan to detect problems in Ulmer's argument. In the first place, the meaning of "video" remains unclear. He seems, most of the time, to be talking about broadcast television, and so to be basing his new discourse on an obsolescent technology. But broadcast TV is not the same expressive form as "video," with which he makes it synonymous. His thinking seems, in fact, to have been formed as much by film as by broadcast television. The emergent digital "multimedia" mixture of word, image, and sound he does not consider at all. Yet this rich new signal should supply the real substance of his "teletheory."

For someone who is trying to write a new chapter in the history of education, Ulmer seems curiously ignorant of his curricular forebears. Much of the book's argument for narrative and visual signals as against discursive argument amounts to a restatement of progressive education. Much, too, comes directly from the arguments for "right-brain" activity that have figured strongly in discussions of education in the arts for some time now. But the argument for progressive education has been developed far more clearly by conventional historians.[22] The argument for right-brain intellection is made—and illustrated—much more clearly, with less terminological fuss, in Betty Edwards' *Drawing on the Right Side of the Brain*. Rudolf Arnheim has spent a career developing this argument for a unified human "reason" without the benefit of complicated Derridean machinery.

Again and again the critical machinery cranked up so ponderously to develop the argument obscures far more than it illuminates. Underneath the machinery, we find the same polarity the rhetoric/philosophy debate has always posed, between a social self and a central self, a dramatistic society and an unselfconscious one. Starting with electronic technology, like Hardison, Kernan, Bolter, and McLuhan before him, Ulmer ends up talking about rhetoric. On the one hand Ulmer equates the television world with the social self and dramatistic society of oral rhetoric, simply applauding it where Kernan despises it. On the other hand, he wants to preserve both sides and toggle between them. Like Hardison and Kernan, he cannot make up his mind whether he wants a single pure state or toggling between two opposed ones. And so he waffles about whether mystories are going to supplement ordinary academic discourse or replace it entirely. And so he vacillates about whether he is suggesting an alternative to print-based linear, logical "reason" or merely a supplement to it.

Ah, but Ulmer is entitled to reply that this discussion of his—as things are now called—"project," is unfair. A mystory is not a logical discussion and must not be read as such. So, too, a discourse built on pun and wordplay must be willing to follow those literary coordinates. But what happens when you do so in his book? You must then apply the alternate standards of literature as against discursive prose. You are entitled to comment on the prose style. If the "creative" elements of a mystory are boring, tedious, and ill-written, this flaw must necessarily compromise the core of things. Such boredom does not constitute an ornamental periphery. If the jokes and puns are dreary and pedestrian, they hamstring the entire "project." If you build your book on puns, you had better not be humorless. If you aim to invent a new style of academic discourse, you had better not model it in peanut-butter prose. If you are trying to revolutionize a bureaucracy, even an educational one, you cannot afford to write like a bureaucrat. In a deep, but absolutely obvious, sense, Ulmer's book undermines its own argument not only logically, by the waffling I have noted, but stylistically as well.

In spite of all this, the pressing need to which the book responds can hardly be denied. The academy cannot do business in a different expressive language, using a different definition of reason, than the world it serves. That expressive language is changing, and academic discourse must change with it. The best framework in which to understand these changes is the rhetorical one, even if, as here, rhetorical theory is seen through a Derridean diffusion-filter.

◻   ◻   ◻

A sixth book on this common theme has recently appeared which takes issue with many of the arguments advanced by Lanham, Bolter, Landow, and company. Myron Tuman, in *Word Perfect: Literacy in the Computer Age,*[23] brings to the transformation wrought by electronic texts some penetrating questions. He argues, for example, that the optimism some of us express for electronic text reflects an experience of print literacy that an electronic generation will lack. "What happens," he asks, "to future generations of students who differ from Lanham, Landow, and Bolter in not having spent the first forty years of their lives mining the vast cognitive and psychological resources of print literacy?" (80). Those future generations may lack the training in "literate" reason, "linear" argument, left-brain conceptualization, whatever we want to call it, which allows us to consider electronic text a fulfillment, a completion of expressive register, a balancing of the brain, if you like. In the argument I have been making for literacy as an oscillation between these two kinds of thinking, of reading, of perception, I have opposed shutting down one side, stopping the oscillation. This, Tuman charges, is precisely what hypertext—as described by Bolter and Landow, as enshrined in Ulmerian mystory, as sketched in my chapter 1—threatens to do.

"Hypertexts," he contends, "are not really texts at all, not documents prepared by authors to convey a distinct world view to readers; they are systems for storing and retrieving information, in much the same way that an online version of the Library of Congress catalogue is a system for shelving

217

and subsequently locating library materials" (75). They sacrifice the integrative function of discursive prose, of utterance itself. It is, he argues, as if Ken Burns had presented his Civil War photographs just as he collected them, and left the arrangement up to us. Some highly praised multimedia programs do exactly this. I recently had occasion to comment upon the new "Columbus" and "Illuminated Books and Manuscripts" programs IBM has underwritten to demonstrate its educational multimedia equipment. They resemble, in every respect, the disassembled "Civil War" Tuman hypothesizes.

I shocked a multimedia conference where these programs had just been demonstrated with full showbiz fanfare—darkened room, big color screen, sound so loud it made your chest cavity vibrate—by suggesting that these were intrinsically *mindless* products. Using arguments not unlike those developed by hypertext enthusiasts, they were billed as the brilliant new teacher of the future: self-paced, permissive learning, deep database of reference material for students, the invitation to infinite networking. Their primary developer described these programs as a cultural Noah's ark floating in a sea of illiteracy and bad teaching. My response to the program I played around with for a couple of hours was like Tuman's. The programs offered not a teacher or a curriculum or a book or a lesson plan, or even the table of contents for any of these. They supplied only the raw material, the parts list, for them. These programs employed every animated effect that multimedia can have except the animation of a human mind. They were the perfect incarnation of Whitehead's curricular chaos, "a rapid table of contents which a deity might run over in his mind while he was thinking of creating a world, and had not yet determined how to put it together."[24]

The question implied by Tuman's critique is surely the "Q" question. Whatever it is that constitutes the value of literary experience, does not electronic text sacrifice it? "Is it possible for the ascendancy of hypertext to do anything but push literacy in the direction of information management? Will literary hypertext ever be more than a diversion in the computer age, a relic or craft from an earlier time, occupying something of the status of calligraphy in the age of print?"[25] To answer this question we must answer the "Q" question.

At the beginning of his book, Tuman takes strong issue with several of my essays in this one—I'm altogether too cheerful about the postmodern threats to textual authority and stability, for a start—but he could have pressed me even more strongly, had he been aware of how I develop the argument, on the "Q" question. It is on his mind too: "What do we really mean by related phrases that we so often use unreflectively: to have *insight*, to think *deeply*, not superficially, and, possibly most important of all, to think *critically*? Why is remaining on the surface, where we spend almost all our lives interacting with friends and family, bad, and burrowing ourselves deep beneath the surface in a dark and lonely spot far from all other human beings, good?" (27).

He wants to protect the rich interiority of the Western self, the "rounded character" as he says at one point, that E. M. Forster talks of. I can't do justice to his argument here; it seeks to project the complex self against a screen not only of print but of industrial capitalism as well. But we can glimpse what he is after from his discussion of an electronic classroom. "The technology driving the networked classroom, just like that driving hypertext, seems to lead inevitably to a redefinition of literacy. In the long run, just as hypertext is ill-suited to support a traditional author, so networking undermines the central status of the teacher" (89). And, by moving up one level, of the curriculum as well. No teacher and, finally, no curriculum either. The student must do it all.

This troubles Tuman because the student is given no role models to imitate; again, the nature of the self and how it is formed stands at risk. Tuman wants to argue, along with Castiglione and, much later, George Herbert Mead, that the self is formed from the outside in, by imitating a series of models and gradually interiorizing them into a central self. He takes as his opposition a 1987 monograph by Anne Gere, *Writing Groups*, which argues for a collaborative rather than a hierarchical mode of learning. "What is at stake in Gere's contrast between hierarchical and collaborative modes is, in the final analysis, a conflict between alternate ways of being in the world. What Gere and, by extension, more direct advocates of computer-mediated writing are promoting is a new form of social relations—the world of print is rejected mainly for its moral deficiencies" (97). Back again to the philosophers and rhetoricians quarreling about the nature of the self.

Something in this repeated discussion about self and society in the electronic classroom and, by extension, in electronic society needs to be set straight.[26] The central self is threatened not by a lively social self but by the lack of one. Electronic networks permit a genuinely stylized public life, one with formal roles that we can play and that are *not* isomorphic with our "real selves."[27] They allow us to create that genuine social self which America has discouraged from the beginning. Our Clarity-Brevity-Sincerity theory of style has been a theory of identity too. We have in America always resisted a formal public self and society: that represented the kind of European insincerity America meant to escape. For this reason, American academic utopias have always tried to do away with the false authoritarian relationships between student and teacher and to speak without the "rhetoric" of polite public conversation.

But this rhetoric allows us to have a genuine private self. The one extreme *creates* the other; the oscillation between the two creates the complex Western self. If computer networks allow us to play roles with no fear of exposure, so much the better. We should push them in that direction. We needn't worry that the private, central self will be impoverished. Private selves are created by public ones. In America, every time we create a means of communication that allows us to create a separate public self, we spoil it by making it more intimate. So, for example, we are periodically threatened with a TV screen for the telephone. If you try to be your unadorned "real self" on a network, you start "flaming," as it is called. Perhaps we will throw away this fresh opportunity to formulate a proper public life and self, much as we now throw it away in political life, but it will be a great shame if we do. Those who feel that the computer classroom, or network, will abolish the central self and create a genuine collective enterprise, fall victim to the characteristic American delusion that the oscillation of the self can be shut down, that the private self can exist without a public doppelgänger. We should make computer conversation more formal and ritualized, not less so.

If we seek to protect the central self, its rich interiority, as Tuman does—as I think we all do—we shouldn't do it by singling it out, but by focusing on the rich, tense interaction between central and social self which creates that interiority in the first place. If print created that rich sense of self, it must have done so by intensifying the oscillation, not by shutting it down. Writing gets its power from the *role* it allows the writer to play. The writer seems to speak as we do, but actually speaks from a different time scale, one that condenses years of work and thought into minutes of reading time. The rush we get from reading great writing comes from that sudden, almost instantaneous transfer of power. No writer's role, no transfer of power. Most defenses of the "individual" against the predations of electronic expression seek, as here, to defend the wrong kind of "individual" in the wrong kind of way.

◻   ◻   ◻

These six books create an interesting hypertext. Ulmer advocates everything that Kernan loathes. Tuman shares Kernan's fears but from an opposite political and cultural position. Bolter forms a neutral analytical median toward which one part of Hardison yearns. Another part of Hardison, however, passes a tendril back to the vexations that Kernan expresses with satirical waspishness. Landow's narrow literary focus profits from a connection with Hardison's broad cultural one. And, since Landow develops his argument entirely in terms of literary theory, he naturally leans toward Ulmer's world at about the same angle Hardison leans away from it. Elegies for the book as they all are, they develop very different arguments from very different patterns of interest. Yet, taken together as a single hypertext, they all suggest that the convergence of technology, democratization, and the return of rhetoric provides the dominant reality for the arts and letters in our time.

But how can one argue that rhetoric, an education built on the word, has regained its centrality when the word itself shows every symptom of radical decline? When the test scores that measure popular literacy worsen each year? When the *logos*, the long-lasting Western centrality of the word, seems to evaporate before our eyes, and the characteristic Western conception of self and society with it? I consider these arguments in the next chapter.

NOTES

1. Richard A. Lanham, *Style: An Anti-Textbook* (New Haven: Yale University Press, 1974).

2. Jonas Barish, *The Antitheatrical Prejudice* (Berkeley and Los Angeles: University of California Press, 1981).

3. George Gilder, *Life After Television* (1990; New York: Norton, 1992).

4. Jane M. Healy, *Endangered Minds: Why Our Children Don't Think* (New York: Simon and Schuster, Touchstone, 1990).

5. George Steiner, "On Reading Marshall McLuhan" (1963), in *Language and Silence: Essays on Language, Literature, and the Inhuman* (New York: Atheneum, 1970), 251.

6. Philip Marchand, *Marshall McLuhan: The Medium and the Messenger* (New York: Ticknor and Fields, 1989); see, for example, 58–59.

7. See Adam Parry's introduction to his father's *The Making of Homeric Verse: The Collected Papers of Milman Parry*, ed. Adam Parry (Oxford: Clarendon Press, 1971).

8. See, for example, Sylvia Scribner and Michael Cole, *The Psychology of Literacy* (Cambridge: Harvard University Press, 1981), and Robert Pattison, *On Literacy: The Politics of the Word from Homer to the Age of Rock* (New York: Oxford University Press, 1982).

9. Marchand (n. 6 above), 54–55.

10. Unlike the philosophical argument, which Plato created and preserved for us, the rhetorical argument has come down to us only in fragments. Eric Havelock recreated this rhetorical argument, as both educational and political pro-

gram, in his most important book, *The Liberal Temper in Greek Politics* (New Haven: Yale University Press, 1957).

11. O. B. Hardison, Jr., *Disappearing Through the Skylight: Culture and Technology in the Twentieth Century* (New York: Penguin, 1989), 264.

12. Alvin Kernan, *The Death of Literature* (New Haven: Yale University Press, 1990), 9.

13. Jay David Bolter, *Writing Space: The Computer, Hypertext, and the History of Writing* (Hillsdale, N.J.: Erlbaum, 1991), 2.

14. Kernan (n. 12 above), 57.

15. It makes for an interesting exercise to ask oneself how the techniques of "lean manufacturing" that have proved so effective in the automobile business might apply to the university world. "Lean" as against "mass" production stresses more horizontal communication between various parts of the corporate enterprise—as if the economists regularly talked to the chemists and both to the philosophers. It insists that with lifetime employment must come an emphasis on more job rotation—as if I should be able to teach Tudor history, or medieval economics, if need be. It creates an intimate connection with suppliers—as if university professors were to develop our random and bureaucratized connections with the schools into a permanent conversation. It conceives its relationship with its customers to be a lifetime affair—as if colleges and universities conceived their students to be clients for lifetime learning, rather than one-time customers. It insists on tracing each manufacturing defect to its cause and remedying it, rather than making the product badly and then fixing it at the end of the line—rather like educating students right the first time, so as not to plague the system with "remediation." It stresses dynamic teamwork rather than the lone worker trading on special skills—a system the complete opposite of our present professoriate. Even to make these analogies with corporate enterprise will rile the academic soul. But we may be sure that, sooner or later, they will be made. In suggesting them, I have drawn upon the MIT five-year study of the future of the automobile, *The Machine that Changed the World*, by James P. Womack, Daniel T. Jones, and Daniel Roos (New York: Rawson, 1990).

16. George P. Landow, *Hypertext: The Convergence of Contemporary Critical Theory and Technology* (Baltimore: Johns Hopkins University Press, 1992). Landow has also, with Paul Delany, edited a volume of essays about particular hypermedia applications, *Hypermedia and Literary Studies* (Cambridge: MIT Press, 1991); it includes excellent amplifying essays by Landow, Bolter, and others.

17. Bolter, *Writing Space* (n. 13 above). Perceptive comments on the relationship between literary theory and digital text are to be found, in fact, throughout the book.

18. See above at n. 3.

19. See, for example, the discussion of *Tristram Shandy*, 132–35.

20. The oral world returns in another way through a current technological rage, "virtual reality." This digital technology allows someone wearing a special helmet and glove or bodysuit to enter a three-dimensional digital space and act in it. We can finally creep inside the television set. The inventors of this incredible technology have conceived it as the ultimate communicative medium, one that will contribute zero distortion to human interaction. Jaron Lanier, a main player in the virtual-reality world, remarked at the TED2 Conference that virtual reality allows us at last the luxury of uninterrmediated communication (*Technology Entertainment Design: The Second Conference, 22–28 February 1990, Monterey, California* [Voyager videodisc, side 2, chap. 15]). But, as Bolter points out, such a conceptualization omits the semiological element of all human communication: "The problem is that virtual reality, at least as it is now envisioned, is a medium of percepts rather than signs. It is virtual television" (230). This is bad news for those who wish to make virtual reality into an an art form. Semiological play is what people seek in vicarious experience. Eliminate that entirely and you have not simplified human communication, you have eliminated it. Virtual reality strikes a deep chord in American thinking about communication. It embodies perfectly what I have called above the C-B-S theory of language: finally we get rid of deceptive symbols and get down to reality itself. Once again, we come across an attempt to shut down that vital oscillation between AT and THROUGH vision which constitutes the full human reality.

21. Gregory Ulmer, *Teletheory: Grammatology in the Age of Video* (New York and London: Routledge, 1989).

22. See, for example, Lawrence A. Cremin, *The Transformation of the School: Progressivism in American Education, 1876–1957* (New York: Vintage, 1961).

23. Myron Tuman, *Word Perfect: Literacy in the Computer Age* (London: Falmer, 1992).

24. See chapter 7 at n. 10.

25. Tuman (n. 23 above), 78. This point is developed in Neil Postman's new attack on electronic technology, *Technopoly: The Surrender of Culture to Technology* (New York: Knopf, 1992), and also in a slightly earlier book by Theodore Roszak, *The Cult of Information: The Folklore of Computers and the True Art of Thinking* (New York: Pantheon, 1986).

26. I depend, in this argument, on Richard Sennett's profound and brilliant *The Fall of Public Man* (New York: Random House, Vintage, 1974).

27. When I worked online circuits around the globe in the Signal Corps thirty-five years ago, we were able to formulate such a public persona, even within the stylized confines of military communication. Top Secret formats covered a multitude of sins.

9

When I went in to get my final grade in freshman calculus, the conversation went something like this:

Professor: *Mr. Lanham, I'm giving you a D, and frankly, it is a gift.*

Lanham: *I know it is, sir, and I thank you from the bottom of my heart. I don't think I could take another year of this.*

Professor: *No, Mr. Lanham—nor could I, nor could I.*

That, I thought, was the end of that, a peril past. It took a long time for my mathematical blindness to catch up with me. First, it was population genetics that I couldn't follow. Then information theory. Then the arcanities of computer science. And now, unable to wield even the basic Newtonian instrument, I cannot follow in a proper formal way the post-Newtonian thinking in chaos theory and complex systems that seems most closely to parallel my own thinking about rhetoric and stylistics.

When I read in Waldrop's **Complexity: The Emerging Science at the Edge of Order and Chaos** that George Cowan had started the Santa Fe Institute to bring the sciences back together into a common centripetal theory,[1] the picture that I had been trying to draw over the last twenty years finally snapped into focus. There it was. What had been happening for the last twenty years in the humanities—the gradual return to a central body of common theory—was happening in the sciences as well. In both cases, the basis of the theory was evolutionary, bottom-up, not Platonic or Newtonian and top-down. In both cases, the new was a return to the old: for the humanities, to the oldest body of thinking about language, formal rhetoric; for the sciences, to a kind of thinking that had much in common with pre-

Socratic Greek science, and with Eastern religion as well. And—again it seemed immediately clear to me—the basic theory informing complex systems held for language, too. Whether the template you fitted over it was called "Saussure" or "postmodern" or "rhetoric," the correlations were astounding. Language, indeed, was a complex system—perhaps (for homo sapiens sapiens at least) the complex system. And to really understand this isomorphism, no mathematically handicapped people need apply.

I try, nevertheless, at the end of this chapter, to suggest how important the new convergence of C. P. Snow's "two cultures" promises to be. The argument for complexity is still being developed, yet for me it provides the spring from which genuine optimism can flow. Here, at last, the larger post-Newtonian landscape begins to come clear for both the mathematically based and the word-based sciences. Better yet, the two worlds seem to be part of one world, to make sense in terms of each other. Here, at last, is a large design within which our current technophobic jeremiads and political stinkfights can be seen in true proportion. Here, at last, is a new curricular design, and a new evolutionary path to it. Here, even— though I have not unraveled this strand of thinking—we glimpse a new way to relate the characteristic modalities of Western thinking with those of the East. In such a world, even the mathematically blind must try to see.

Operating Systems, Attention

Structures, and the Edge of Chaos

Operating Systems

*I*n the previous essays, I've been trying to track a fundamental change in what we might call the "operating system of the humanities," a movement from the fixed and silent signal of the printed book to a richer but more volatile signal, writing + voice + image, of digital display. This changed operating system is now called upon to function in a society that has itself suffered a similar digital transformation. In a society based on information, the chief scarce commodity would presumably be information not goods. But we are drowning in information, not suffering a dearth of it. Dealing with this superabundant flow is sometimes compared to drinking from a firehose. In such a society, the scarcest commodity turns out to be not information but the human attention needed to cope with it. *Intelligenda longa, vita brevis* should be the motto of the information age— life is short, but long indeed the list of things to be known in it.

We have in the West a venerable tradition of studying how human attention is created and allocated: the "art of persuasion" which the Greeks called rhetoric. A better definition of rhetoric, in fact, might be "the economics of human attention-structures," for whenever we "persuade" someone, we do so by getting that person to "look at things from our point of view," share our attention-structure. It is in the nature of human life that attention should be in short supply, but in an information economy it becomes the crucial scarce commodity. Just as economics has been the study of how we allocate scarce resources in a goods economy, we now will use a variety of rhetoric as the "economics" of human attention-structures. Whatever we choose to call it—and almost certainly our name will not be the now-discredited "rhetoric"—the construction and allocation of attention-structures will be a vital activity in our information society.

It is not as if we haven't had warning that this new economics has supervened. Was not Pop Art all about the replacement of goods by information as the main scarce commodity in an information society? That was Andy Warhol's message, however various his medium. So his infatuation with movie stars, and especially with "personalities," people famous for being famous. So, too, the infatuation with signage that James Rosenquist carried to epic dimensions: his immense canvases take the scaling of attention-structures as their great subject. "Target" paintings, preoccupied with central focus, and alphabet paintings, depicting letters as opaque objects rather than transparent symbols, both "imitate" the "information" in an information society. Robert Irwin's minimalist paintings and environments are all calculated to bring human visual attention to acute self-consciousness.[2] "Happenings" were contrived yet spontaneous and participatory attention-structures. The shift of emphasis from object to beholder in contemporary art and letters bespeaks the same sensitivity to a new scarcity. Indeed, much of the strangeness and "experimentality" of twentieth-century experimental art comes from the relative difficulty of "imitating" human attention as against the objects we attend to.

In this experimental world, a training in rhetoric turns out to be of real use, and an intellectual framework frankly rhetorical condign to describe the society as a whole. In an information society, then, the arts and letters, the "humanities," move from background to foreground, become essential rather than ornamental, and the "Q" question poses itself with a new urgency.

To argue thus is *not* simply to repeat the usual combination of self-pity and self-satisfaction that humanists use when asking the government for more money. It is not clear that the humanist world really wants to become central, for a start; it often relishes the marginality it pretends to deplore. Nor is it clear that the humanities will embrace the new order of business which their changed status in an information society thrusts upon them. The "humanist" task may pass to other groups while the humanities dwindle into grumpy antiquarianism. But it is now possible to develop a new kind of argument for the relationship between society and rhetoric, and hence between society and the arts and letters, the "humanities."

An information society brings with it a different *theory of communication* from that prevalent in an industrial society. Newtonian science reinforced a venerable Stoic theory of language to which I have given the dyslogistic epithet "C-B-S." Newtonian science was built, that is, on Clarity, Brevity, and Sincerity. In a goods society, words are derivative; the goods are the thing, the "things" you can point to and touch. In the sixteenth century, as we saw in chapter 7, Peter Ramus split off rhetoric from philosophy, rhetoric being relegated, that is words themselves being relegated, to a derivative and ornamental role. This paved the way for Bishop Sprat's famous injunction a century later that we should have one word for one thing, that we should abolish verbal ornamentation. Since Newton had shown "nature" to be a closed and complete system, words should be too. Ideally, in a Newtonian society, you wouldn't need words at all, sincere feelings and clear ideas of physical entities would do it all. You look through the words to the goods that are really out there in the real world. It should hardly surprise us that such a theory of verbal style, such a systematic devaluation of the verbal surface, should create a "literacy crisis" of the sort we face now.

All this changes in an information society. There, the words *are* the "goods." They operate in an ambiguous fashion, overlapping, bumping into one another, creating unintended meanings, making more meaning come out of an utterance than the author put into it.[3] Walter Wriston has remarked recently that we need both a new economic terminology and a new accounting system for our new information society. We need to get rid of the C-B-S way of thinking about language for the same reasons, as linguists from Saussure onward have been telling us—albeit, in the public mind at least, to no avail. The immateriality of information brings with it a new set of boundary conditions: "When the world's most precious resource is immaterial, the economic doctrines, social structures, and political systems that evolved in a world devoted to the service of matter become rapidly ill suited to cope with the new situation. The rules and customs, skills and talents, necessary to uncover, capture, produce, preserve, and exploit information are now mankind's most important rules, customs, skills, and talents."[4] Aren't these rules and customs what humanism has been about since Erasmus formulated it at the beginning of the sixteenth century?

In our present educational crisis, the popular clamor has been for more technological education. Doesn't this miss the mark? Shouldn't we be after a generalized ability to manipulate symbolic reality? In our society, this symbolic reality depends on precisely the rich signal of mixed word, sound, and image we have been considering in these essays. Teaching us how to live within this reality will be the job of a new kind of humanistic education. Perhaps we shouldn't use the charged word "humanistic," since such an education will involve a new mixture of the arts and sciences altogether. But "technological" or "technical" or "scientific" are not the right words either. They are all part of an old educational and disciplinary nomenclature that is as obsolete and confusing in an information age as industrial bookkeeping conventions prove to be. About this new mixture, the humanities have a great deal to say, but they cannot say it until they understand that both their operating system and the society within which it operates have undergone a state-change.

Attention-Structures

Not surprisingly, many thoughtful people have written cautionary tales about both parts of this technological revolution, the change in operating system and the new importance of human attention-structures. Perhaps the first to discern how deep the change in humanistic operating system would run was George Steiner. Marshall McLuhan is usually regarded as an exuberant advocate of electronic expression, but in fact, he was an extremely conservative man who loathed the world he saw acomin'.[5] This mixed insight, foresight, and regret, if nothing else, McLuhan shared with Steiner. In a remarkable series of essays, mostly from the sixties and seventies, Steiner zoomed in on a pop "literacy" which he saw replacing the genuine culture of the book.[6]

In tracing this change in operating system, Steiner goes back beyond McLuhan to Marinetti, and projects his story on the broad screen of Western culture. His view of the book as operating system, for all that, is surprisingly narrow: "Our style of reading, the unforced currency of our business with books, is not easy to document before, say, Montesquieu. It climaxes in Mallarmé's well-known pronouncement that the true aim of the universe, of all vital impulse, is the creation of a supreme book—*le Livre*."[7] I asked in chapter 1 whether it was the book itself, the physical construct, that was essential or only what it does. Steiner makes the classic case for the book itself as a full operating system. It requires a private library, full sets of the great classics, and a servant to dust them.[8] Steiner argues that when the book dies as an operating system, it takes a lot of suppliers with it.

In an essay called "Future Literacies" he laments the lack of what, after Hirsch, we now call "cultural literacy," the ability to participate in the deep intertextuality of literary texts. We possess now only "an archival pseudovitality surrounding what was once felt life; a semi-literacy or sub-literacy outside, making it impossible for the poem to survive naked, to achieve unattended personal impact. Academy and populism. The two conditions are reciprocal, and each polarizes the other in a necessary dialectic. Between them they determine our current state."[9] This semiliteracy, we are told later in this essay—and often elsewhere in Steiner's work—characterizes mass democracies like the United States. Thus he tries to read the increasing layers of cloud that the great information storm-front sends out before it. People are trying their hand at symbolic processing who never used to do this sort of work before. They pay attention to it in different kinds of ways.

But then he confronts his own golden-age yearnings: "The challenge is: was it ever different?" (427). Choosing as his cultural litmus test the knowledge needed to read Milton's *Lycidas*, he concludes that circumstances vary but that "none of Milton's imitations and pointers would have been outside the scope of my father's schooling in a Vienna *Gymnasium* before the First World War, or indeed outside my own in the *section lettres* of the French *lycée* system of the 1930s and 1940s" (428). The Golden Age is to be found, as always, in the particular background of the Golden Ager. Just as Allan Bloom found his ideal university in the American university of the fifties where he was educated, so Steiner returns to his roots for an ideal pattern. He looks back to a goods-and-services economy of attention and finds all the subsequent changes distasteful. Is it merely accidental that his golden age of reading corresponds so closely to the great age of manufacturing?

Steiner the golden-ager is Steiner at his narrowest and most narcissistic. At least as often, he exhibits a remarkable breadth of view. In an essay from 1965, for example, "Literature and Post-History," he turns his back on the quiet library full of full sets, their bindings dutifully smeared with British Museum preservative goo by silent servants, and looks out at the new operating system and its richly mixed signals:

> Unquestionably, nothing is more important to an understanding of the future forms of artistic communication than the simple, immense fact that hundreds of millions of human beings are now, for the first time, entering the world of reading and writing. By comparison with this fact, examinations of literary schools or fashions, of the *nouveau roman* or the theater of the absurd, look trivial. There is a profound logic in the historical coincidence between the emergence of the hitherto illiterate peoples and the simultaneous development of graphic mass-media. To the new literates, with their native traditions of oral and pictorial communication, the patterns of meaning and emotion conveyed by radio, television, comic strip, or film will carry far more immediacy and significance than the silent book.[10]

He verges here on acknowledging that we may be in the midst of a major expansion of the imaginative franchise, the expansion which an information society requires. In the same essay, as well as in several others, he explores the issues that have occupied us in previous chapters—volatility of text, failure of authority, the interactive audience, and so on. But he will never allow the electronic world of "readers and writers" in new media to have any connection with his golden-age paradisiacal library.[11] For Steiner, as for Hardison and Kernan, whose diagnoses we've examined in chapter 8, the new electronic world is separated by a cataclysm from the old. Once again, our characteristic pattern: the view forward skewed by a skewed view of the past.

This strict division pleads directly to another main Steiner theme, one which we explored in chapter 7. The passing of the old information system, which Steiner sketches with broad learning and penetrating foresight, is not only sad but tragic. The cultural system of the book, that whole "*Lycidas* world," was a moral failure. In "Humane Literacy," he confronts the fact that the Vienna whose *Gymnasium* so well equipped him and his father to read *Lycidas* was the same Vienna that welcomed Adolph Hitler with marked cordiality. To reflect thus "compels us to ask whether knowledge of the best that has been thought and said does, as Matthew Arnold asserted, broaden and refine the resources of the human spirit."[12]

Like many European scholars who have found temporary or permanent refuge in the United States, Steiner has had to reconcile a popular American culture which he despises, but which has offered academic succor in time of trouble to him and the European culture he embodies, with a beloved Europe that drove him out and has not always preserved its own values with the zeal he would wish. "Nowhere has the debilitation of genuine literacy gone further," he writes, than in America, but no country has so preserved classic European culture either.[13] America becomes, then, a "museum-culture" of the old literacy and a depraved embodiment of the new. The two can have no evolutionary connection. A cultural cataclysm separates them. Like Hardison, he wants to polarize, to shut the vital oscillation down. He cannot admit that the forces that would preserve European culture were the same ones that wanted to pour it into a new information mold.

Both of these dichotomies emerge from the same conception of high literacy. What that conception is, we can imagine when Steiner comments on the decline of eloquence: "There *is* a comprehensive decline in traditional ideals of literate speech. Rhetoric and the arts of conviction which it disciplines are in almost total disrepute. Pleasure in style, in the 'wroughtness' of expressive forms, is a mandarin, nearly suspect posture."[14] But at the same time, along with everyone else, he condemns the popular rhetoric of advertising, the media, every evidence that human attention is the new scarce ingredient in an information society. He cannot recognize that "pleasure in style" which Tom Wolfe has spent a lifetime chronicling in modern American life.[15] He laments the departure of the very rhetoric that surrounds him on all sides in American culture. He too, that is, believes in the "Weak Defense" for rhetoric. He believes in eloquence if it serves the causes with which he agrees, the tastes that please him, but not otherwise. The new economics of attention-structures demands the "Strong Defense," a genuine belief in two-sided argument. Steiner's lack of it desolates the cultural pageant he sees before him. He cannot glimpse an answer to the "Q" question he has posed with such impassioned learning and so, like Sidney Hook, like Grafton and Jardine, he turns away from it.

Steiner subscribes, that is, to the self-contradictory conception of rhetoric that undermines modern liberalism, the political faith emerging from that Vienna *Gymnasium*. And it is the "Weak Defense" for rhetoric that prevents him even from conceiving that the two sides of American culture, the "good" museum side and the "bad" mass-culture side, either have a relationship now or ever could have one in the future. If the only seriousness he can envisage is Arnoldian "high seriousness," the seriousness of the high print culture that runs from Montesquieu to Mallarmé, then he can find no hope in the expanded literacy he glimpses in genteel horror. His mistake comes from his misconstruction of that Western culture of which he is so superb an example: he reads it through "print" spectacles, through the Arnoldian seriousness which, he himself admits, characterizes only a small part of it. His golden-age vision blurs the entire picture. Because he misreads the past he can have no hope for the future. He will naturally view the return of the rhetorical ideal of life as an ending, not a new beginning or even the possibility of a new beginning. The new operating system of the humanities, and the self-conscious attention-structures it creates can, in his view, only look like the end of the world.

◻   ◻   ◻

A recent study suggests that perhaps it is. Jane Healy's *Endangered Minds: Why Our Children Don't Think*[16] bases its argument on the structure, and more explicitly on the plasticity, of the human brain.

> The primary thesis of this book is that we are rearing a generation of "different brains" and that many students' faltering academic skills—at every socioeconomic level—reflect subtle but significant changes in their physical foundations for learning. These fundamental shifts put children in direct conflict with traditional academic standards and the methods by which they are usually conveyed. *Particularly at risk are abilities for language-related learning (e.g., reading, writing, analytic reasoning, oral expression), sustained attention, and problem solving.* (45–46; emphasis mine)

The "different brains" she describes belong to children who form a clear group: they have shorter attention spans; they dislike reading, avoid it wherever possible, and can't read very well when forced to; they can't write well either, dislike it, and avoid it too whenever possible; they have special trouble with complex, "periodic" (my word) syntax of any sort; nor can they speak well, commonly starting an utterance vaguely, interrupting it with "like" now and again, and finishing it with gestures and a terminal "You know?"; their social skills remain as undeveloped as the conversational ones they mirror; they cannot think successfully about complex problems in science and mathematics, or indeed about any problem that involves higher-order reasoning, especially if it requires verbal skills; they don't listen attentively and so cannot remember what they have just heard; they have great difficulty switching from a written to a colloquial stylistic register, since they have mastered neither one; they learn much more easily and comfortably from pictures than from words; they are accustomed to a bombardment of loud sounds and scintillating visual images; they seem—most alarming of all—not to have had much real-life social experience of any sort. They embody the multimedia nightmare come true.

Dr. Healy waffles about the conclusions her survey of research suggests: "Kids today are no less intelligent than those of former years, but they don't fit the same academic molds" (278). She urges us not to blame these students for being what they are, since society has made them so, but her discussion leaves no doubt that these children and now, indeed, young adults and (as I can testify myself) university students pay attention to the world in new and unsettling ways. The tale she tells—of declining test scores, of simplified tests and dumbed-down textbooks, of a rapidly aging ten percent of Americans who read eighty percent of the books, of a new generation of "language arts" teachers who "dislike reading and avoid it whenever possible," of television narcosis, of poisons in the environment and the medicine chest, and inevitably of "recreational drugs"—is a familiar but none the less frightening one.

She makes it scarier still by putting a new argument at its heart—the plasticity of the brain. She cites a broad range of research which argues that the brain forms itself, actually takes physical shape, around experiences, and that it needs certain kinds of experiences at certain ages to develop fully. If, during certain critical periods, the brain does not get the experiences it needs, vital neural pathways will not be formed. The window closes, forever. Especially is this so of the pathways needed to use language in complex ways—the complex ways required in formal schooling of any sort. "The brains of today's children are being structured in language patterns antagonistic to the values and goals of formal education. The culprit, which is now invading all levels of the socioeconomic spectrum, is diminished and degraded exposure to the forms of good, meaningful language that enable us to converse with others, with the written word, and with our own minds" (86).

Dr. Healy waffles, too, about the *irreversibility* implied by the research she cites: "Since one of my favorite jobs is teaching writing to young adolescents, I personally refuse to believe that all hope is lost when we enter the gates of puberty. ... I take considerably less pleasure in trying to teach remedial grammar to mainstream university juniors who will be language-arts teachers within two years" (132). Since both these tasks form part of my job, too, I don't want to believe in irreversibility either. But it provides the rock-bottom fear that animates Healy's argument: "The brain is ravenous for language stimulation in early childhood but becomes increasingly resistant to change when the zero hour of puberty arrives" (86). An atmosphere of rich linguistic stimulation is not inevitable. The culture must provide it; that is how plastic brains work.

We can view her argument as taking the Ong/Havelock thesis one step further. Ong and Havelock argued that literacy changed the "noosphere," the interiority of the self. Healy argues this case in terms of the developmental structure of the brain. The children she describes represent, presumably, the oral world whose transformation into alphabetic literacy Ong and Havelock have traced. "Orality" is for neither a dyslogistic term, and Healy takes pains to disclaim any such intention either. Surely, though, they are talking about the same thing. Because of her neurological focus, Healy casts her argument in the framework of the brain's asymmetrical hemi-sphericality.[17] It is the right brain that popular culture, and especially television, stimulates. Dynamic electronic text pleads to the right sphere, too. Healy's scathing "Sesame Street" chapter, for example, argues that far from teaching children how to read, animated print does the opposite: "Words in books do not jump about, transform before one's eyes, or call attention to themselves" (226). She argues that the acculturation which children receive now, reinforced as it is by massive doses of electronic technology, badly imbalances the brain's asymmetrical powers.

This new acculturation of attention goes much deeper than electronic text. She sees the breakdown of the American family as the taproot problem, though here too she flinches before the logic of her own argument. What the family no longer does, the school must do. But the linguistic acculturation she finds lacking is so labor-intensive that no school could do it. Nevertheless, she argues that the schools, in shouldering this impossible burden, appear to have three choices:

1. Keep the traditional "standards" and continue to cram children into them. Let prisons and the welfare system handle the overflow.
2. Throw out the standards.

3. Maintain the goals represented by the standards, but prepare students more effectively. Expand the schedule of expectation and the teaching methods to honor children's latent abilities.

The first two alternatives should be unthinkable. We are left with the third. (304)

Healy seems to provide, then, a perfect complementary proof of Steiner's case for cultural decline. His perspective is a magisterially cross-cultural survey from a university vantage; hers is a neurologically based argument seen from the elementary and secondary school. Steiner argues from the library, Healy from the trenches. Steiner would think all three alternatives "unthinkable." He would preserve traditional literacy for a very small élite of readers who do not need to be "crammed" into the traditional standards and give it up for the rest. His analysis of the problem, though, agrees exactly with hers.

Healy has indeed found the only three alternatives, even if "the standards" are those of print literacy, the ones which not only electronic expression but all of postmodern culture call into doubt. The Left will argue that the third alternative seeks to preserve the values of late capitalism which it seeks to abolish; it chooses the second—throw out the standards. The Right will argue that the third seeks to abolish the Great Books of Western culture; it chooses, instead, to keep the traditional standards. So both the first and the second choices are thinkable enough. And much easier to think about than the third. The "traditional standards" are not, in fact, preservable under present cultural pressures; they *are* being thrown out. Nor will all those "language arts" instructors who hate to read lament their passing.

If we wish to preserve Western culture in the bi-stable definition I have been advancing, then we must embody it in the more complex signals of a digital information system. No one, I think, yet knows how to do this. And, however well it is done, it will not solve the deep problems in American family life that provoke Healy's critique. Nor, in spite of her touching faith in it, would print if we were to return to its reassuring bosom.

◻   ◻   ◻

Perhaps the most clamorous of the humanist voices questioning the new operating system for the arts and letters has been Neil Postman's. His *Amusing Ourselves to Death* hopes to persuade us "that the decline of a print-based epistemology and the accompanying rise of a television-based epistemology has had grave consequences for public life, *that we are getting sillier by the minute"* (emphasis mine).[18] America has become, according to Postman, a culture of glitz and false values symbolized by Las Vegas, much as we used to be a culture of sober good sense, symbolized by Boston (3). Our great "Age of Exposition" (the eighteenth and nineteenth centuries) has been usurped by an "Age of Show Business" (63). The usurper, of course, is television. Postman believes a fundamental break has occurred in our cultural life.

We have met this cataclysm before. It is the sure sign of someone sensing the presence of a new operating system and a new economics of attention. Kernan finds it all across the cultural landscape, Hardison in a more unified pattern of cultural change; Bolter fixes its cause in electronic text, George Steiner (like Hardison) woven into the fabric of twentieth-century thought. Postman, like Ulmer, finds it in broadcast television: "We have reached, I believe, a critical mass in that electronic media have *decisively and irreversibly changed the character of our symbolic environment.* We are now a culture whose information, ideas and epistemology are given form by television, not by the printed word" (28; emphasis mine). Postman's technological focus is as narrow as Steiner's print focus. He simply ignores, indeed appears ignorant of, all the digital technologies that have emerged to change expression; multimedia, in all its forms, plays no part whatsoever in his attack. Here he resembles Ulmer, whose book seems Postman's written in a mirror, with all its moral polarities reversed 180 degrees. Analogue broadcast television is the target. Postman ignores not only digital expression in his "magic of electronics" but cable television as well, with all its "narrowcast" attributes, distance-learning educational nets, proprietary television circuits for business and professional training—everything but TV.

Yet, for all his narrow focus, Postman's central argument resembles the standard humanist ones we have been considering. Print is the hero: "I must, first, demonstrate how, under the governance of the printing press, discourse in America was different from what it is now—generally coherent, serious and rational; and then how, under the governance of television, it has become shriveled and absurd" (16). The "image," in both its visual and its social meanings, provides the villain for his neo-iconoclasm: "The God of the Jews was to exist in the Word and through the Word, an unprecedented conception requiring the highest order of abstract thinking. ... People like ourselves who are in the process of converting their culture from word-centered to image-centered might profit by reflecting on this Mosaic injunction" (9). Unlike Healy, he does not argue for neurological change: "[A]t no point do I care to claim that changes in media bring about changes in the structure of people's minds or changes in their cognitive capacities" (27). Broadcast television has made people irretrievably silly but not actually brain-damaged.

Like Steiner, Postman looks back to a golden age of informational purity. His lasted a little longer, a pretechnology America communicating entirely by the printing press: "There were no movies to see, radio to hear, photographic displays to look at, records to play. There was no television. Public business was channeled into and expressed through print, which became the model, the metaphor and the measure of all discourse" (41). The Golden Age is everything an information society is not. It lasted until 1858, when the photograph and telegraph appeared, the "advance guard of a new epistemology that would put an end to the Empire of Reason" (48). In this golden age even advertisers were honest, and "assumed that potential buyers were literate, rational, analytical" (58). People were more reasonable then because print was the only means of communication. "This point cannot be stressed enough," he tells us. In this golden age of typography there was, presumably, no public oratory, no oral folktale and folksong tradition, no preaching tradition, no Chautauqua tradition, no training in formal rhetorical theory and practice. And, since advertisers were honest and consumers rational, there were no snake-oil salesmen. Even the lawyers, in this golden time, "tended to be well educated, devoted to reason, and capable of impressive expositional argument" (56).

Like Steiner, and like Bloom too, having described his golden age Postman sees it for what it is—at least for a moment. So he goes on, in a chapter called "The Typographic Mind," to talk about the oratorical tradition in America, but *as a creature of print.* He praises one of Lincoln's periodic sentences as representing the pure spirit of print (46), as if periodicity had been invented by Gutenberg, instead of by Isocrates as a neat oratorical trick in classical Greece. The silliness of what he is saying about nineteenth-century political debates does sometimes strike him, but fleetingly: "there were elements of pure orality in their presentations. ... Nonetheless, the resonance of typography was ever-present" (49).

It's odd, isn't it, how often periodic syntax has cropped up in these critical presentations? For Postman, it provides a basal model, the leitmotif almost, of real—that is to say print—literacy. For Healy, it provides the external proof that the neural circuits for higher-level thinking have been wired. For Steiner, it provides an example of the genuine literacy mass culture can never attain. One might almost believe that at the core of "higher," or "real," or "print" literacy stands—good heavens!—the rhetorical figures! The High Style! Eloquence!

Let's harken back for a moment to chapter 7, to the distinction Richard

McKeon makes between the two basic definitions of rhetoric: "When the philosophic arts are conceived of as arts of being or of thought, rhetoric is not treated as a philosophic art, although it is used extensively in the controversy and refutation which constitutes communication among philosophies. When the philosophic arts are arts of communication and construction, rhetoric is made into a universal and architectonic art."[19] Rhetoric can either be a cosmetic art which ornaments a truth preexistent to it, or it can be the means of arriving at truth. It can either be Plato's villain, or the architectonic system of genuine two-sided argument that animates Anglo-Saxon jurisprudence. In chapter 7, I call the cosmetic argument the Weak Defense, and two-sided argument the Strong Defense, of rhetoric. Steiner, who praises eloquence too, adopts the Weak Defense. So does Postman. He realizes, or at least begins to, that his argument about technology replays the longstanding argument between the philosophers and the rhetoricians: "like the printing press, television is nothing less than a philosophy of rhetoric" (17). In this conversation, he stands with Plato—or does he? "But to the people who invented it, the Sophists of fifth-century B.C. Greece and their heirs, rhetoric was not merely an opportunity for dramatic performance but a near indispensable means of organizing evidence and proofs, and therefore of communicating truth" (22). At this point he verges on understanding the Strong Defense. Then he chooses the other side: "To disdain rhetorical rules, to speak one's thoughts in a random manner, without proper emphasis or appropriate passion, was considered demeaning to the audience's intelligence and suggestive of falsehood. Thus, we can assume that many of the 280 jurors who cast a guilty ballot against Socrates did so because his manner was not consistent with truthful matter, as they understood the connection" (22). Rhetoric was merely a set of sterile rules and Socrates, the Platonic saint, went to his doom because he did not follow them.

But how can the complex, figurative use of language symbolized by the periodic sentence be at one and the same time a product of print's sweet reason and a creature of the tradition that martyred Socrates? Postman returns to the self-contradiction at the heart of rhetorical theory. There have to be two completely separate versions of a rhetorical pattern, one good and one bad, yet both composed of the same words. And he returns to the "Q" question, as well. Except that where Quintilian says "rhetoric," Postman substitutes "print." The "print"-trained man is the natural man of reason and virtue. And, like Quintilian, Postman offers no proof for his case; he simply reiterates it.

This inconsistency runs through Postman's entire argument and vitiates it at every point. We can observe how this happens by examining his use of the classic American antitechnology remark, Thoreau's dismissal of the telegraph in *Walden*. "We are in great haste to construct a magnetic telegraph from Maine to Texas; but Maine and Texas, it may be, have nothing important to communicate." Postman's comment:

> The telegraph made a three-pronged attack on typography's definition of discourse, introducing on a large scale irrelevance, impotence, and incoherence. These demons of discourse were aroused by the fact that telegraphy gave a form of legitimacy to the idea of context-free information; that is, to the idea that the value of information need not be tied to any function it might serve in social and political decision-making and action, but may attach merely to its novelty, interest, and curiosity. (65)

There are, that is, good and bad kinds of *information* as well as good and bad kinds of verbal ornamentation! The bad kind, which appeals to "novelty, interest, and curiosity," is the kind, Postman tells us later, that TV retails. The good kind is the kind that print offers. Good information is "tied to the problems and decisions readers had to address in order to manage their personal and community affairs" (66). Good information, then, is *purposive* information. And bad information? Bad information is the "context-free" information that we use for game and play. Postman does not seem aware that he has, like his godfather Plato, banished poetry from his commonwealth.

Thoreau's now-shopworn remark denigrated what Malinowski called "phatic communion," the conversation we pursue simply to maintain social contact. In an oral culture, phatic communication is vital—Gregory Bateson calls it "ticking over" behavior. It reassures both parties that the social engine is still "ticking over," still running. From it various other purposes can be created, but its main purpose is creating social cohesion. When the Pacific islanders sailed vast distances to trade their shells for somebody else's shells, they were after social interchange not new shells. The shells were the decoration, the interchange was the essence. Rabelais makes this point through Panurge's great *declamatio* on debt in book 3 of *Gargantua and Pantagruel*. Debt *held people together* and therefore was good. Rabelais makes it a metaphor for all social obligation. He perpetrates the same play/purpose reversal we saw on the façade of the Beaubourg. Economics is not purposive but playful. The shells are not the driving force; it is the social situations that the shell game creates. In an information economy, economics is an affair of attention-structures. This aspect of communication Postman would prohibit.

The chance-driven visual and musical patterns we examined in chapter 2 all capitalize on playful motive, on "novelty, interest, curiosity." Bateson has argued (see chapter 3) that we need playful motives to control our overweening purpose. I argued, therefore, in favor of the *irenic*, the peacemaking, force of much postmodern formal experimentation. All this Thoreau outlaws: we must have "real things" to say or the telegraph isn't worth inventing. And real things can as easily be sent in a letter. The deep creativity built into technology, working though chance juxtaposition, is simply denied. In writing, too. We are never to make a discovery in the act of writing. A piece of writing never takes off and takes us in a direction we had not anticipated. Writing is, ideally, a simple and sincere transference of descriptive fact from one person to another. So Thoreau's theory of style:

> As for style of writing, if one has anything to say, it drops from him simply and directly, as a stone falls to the ground. There are no two ways about it, but down it comes, and he may stick in the points and stops wherever he can get a chance. ...
>
> A sentence should read as if its author, had he held a plough instead of a pen, could have drawn a furrow deep and straight to the end.
>
> The word which is best said came nearest to not being spoken at all, for it is cousin to a deed which the speaker could have better done. Nay, almost it must have taken the place of a deed by some urgent necessity, even by some misfortune, so that the truest writer will be some captive knight, after all.[20]

This is the world out of which Thoreau's condemnation of the telegraph comes. Ideally, in such a world, there would be no language at all; we could communicate directly, concept-to-concept, through mathematics perhaps, or feeling-to-feeling through pure sympathy.

This conception of a self-effacing, ideally transparent, in truth ideally nonexistent, language we have met before—the "C-B-S" or Clarity-Brevity-Sincerity model for language which fits so well an industrial society that makes *things*. Such a theory of style has no place for periodic structures, for all the careful and "sophistic" rhetorical figures which symbolize ... which symbolize the higher patterns of thinking that literacy creates! Which we must defend in the face of electronic technology!

Postman builds his case for the decline of public civility on the C-B-S theory of style. When he argues that "as typography moves to the periphery of our culture and television takes its place at the center, the seriousness, clarity and, above all, value of public discourse dangerously declines" (29), he is arguing that print communication is clear, brief, and sincere and TV the opposite. People pay attention to the dramatic interest of things, to—as he fulminates later—their *entertainment* value, rather than to their purpose. People, that is, start looking at life *poetically*. From a *literary* point of view. In my terms, they start looking AT it rather than THROUGH it. As for using the C-B-S theory as a model for human society, just think about it. It wouldn't last a day. Imagine waking up in the morning and being entirely clear, brief, and sincere to everyone you met. You'd lose your spouse the first day, your job the second, and your "reason" the third.

We present ourselves in different ways to different people. We temper the wind to the shorn lamb. We use a soft answer to turn away wrath. We do not, as Sarah Churchill once said, owe the whole truth to everybody. As I've been arguing in these essays, human society depends for its survival on a self-conscious/unselfconscious oscillation between AT and THROUGH vision. It is a bi-stable illusion, a shared drama. Postman, like the biblical prophets, wants to shut that oscillation down. Artifice is the very Devil!

Postman's great concern is the inundation of meaningless information created by electronic media. (He returns to it in his new book, *Technopoly: The Surrender of Culture to Technology*.) Information must be immediately useful, purposive, or it is no good. But what is useful to one person is dross to another. Under Postman's scorn for mere information lurks good, old-fashioned social snobbery. We need not worry about people's being swamped by useless information. They will pick out what is germane to their needs. Their psychological marketplace will work as it always has. But it is a wider marketplace now. We are free to make up our private reality from a much, much wider public one. We are paying a new kind of attention to attention-structures. We have come to recognize that different people make up different realities. Postman's citation of Thoreau leads to a praise of provincial thinking. In the golden age of print, people stayed home and paid attention to local concerns. That way, the global society would just go away.

In pleading for the provincialism of his golden-age America, Postman is sometimes simply silly: "Prior to the age of telegraphy, the information-action ratio was sufficiently close so that most people had a sense of being able to control some of the contingencies in their lives" (69). Life was less chancy before the telegraph? The Eastern bankers were kinder to the Western farmers? Better the pneumonia you knew than the penicillin you didn't? Better the local flood than the distant government dam that controlled it or the telegraph that warned you of it?

Postman's antipoetic Platonism leaves one breathless. Look at this example of how he "reasons":

> For the first time in human history, people were faced with the problem of information glut, which means that simultaneously they were faced with the problem of a diminished social and political potency.
>
> You may get a sense of what this means by asking yourself another series of questions: What steps do you plan to take to reduce the conflict in the Middle East? Or the rates of inflation, crime and unemployment? What are your plans for preserving the environment or reducing the risk of nuclear war? I shall take the liberty of answering for you: You plan to do nothing about them. (68–69)

Speak for yourself, Neil. I do a number of things, from recycling my trash to designing new writing curricula, from talking to my congressman to giving money and (though he seems to denigrate this) casting a ballot. Small things these, but actions. Most people act on the "information glut." They pick out what looks vital to them and try, in whatever ways they can, to do something about it. That is what the humanities are all about in an information society—attention-structures.

But social action is not the vital point. The "information glut" vastly expands the dramatic stage upon which all of us live. Electronic media, yes, including TV, have expanded this stage enormously. I may not be able personally to stop the breakup of Yugoslavia, but this new chapter in the history of central Europe still interests me very much. I put it in a context of European political history I began to learn as a schoolboy. Such information makes life more interesting. All this no one would make a point of affirming unless Postman had made the opposite case. Is it automatically more virtuous to inhabit a small, closed world of purely private purpose?

Postman bills his book as a defense of propositional thought against the mindlessness of TV. It is fair, then, to examine his basic propositions as such. As we asked of Allan Bloom's Platonism,[21] we may ask of Postman's Old Testament prophecy: What has a lifetime of print-based reasoning made of Neil Postman's mind? We've seen a characteristic pattern emerge already; he imagines a golden age of print and then, whenever defending it gets too silly—as it always does—he starts to weasel and waffle. He comes across like a biblical prophet condemning artifice of every sort, and then demonizes TV into a devil of artifice. He poses, however, not as a biblical prophet preaching a divine truth imparted to him, but as a Man of Reason. It is both instructive and fair, then, to present his arguments in raw propositional form.

Proposition: Typographical culture = human reason. If this is so, why wasn't the world more "reasonable" when typography reigned supreme? We return speedily to Steiner's paradox: does the "literacy" you seek to defend bring the benefit you claim? Was the reign of print remarkable for the sweet reasonability of its life? Plato's idea of "reason," which Postman follows in many respects, led to the tyrannical model of the *Republic.* The eighteenth-century triumph of reason led to the Civil War. The nineteenth-century triumph of reason led to World War I.

Proposition: Typographical culture was more moral than electronic culture. Back to the "Q" question, the redemptive power of literature. Back to Steiner's tragic view of European culture. Where's the proof that print makes people better? The argument that the Clarity-Brevity-Sincerity theory of prose style underlying print—if it does—can serve as a model for human social decorum is preposterous, as two minutes' reflection shows. Do the illiterates in our own culture seem morally inferior to the semiliterates, who are in turn inferior to heavy readers like us?

Postman loathes TV preaching, but is there any evidence that it works less well than viva voce preaching, itself an oral not a print technique? Or the preaching that Postman himself does in his books? Why, if they are not comforted, do people send so much money to these programs? Why is it bad to mix preaching and pleasure? Pulpit oratory did so all through the age of print; why is it automatically bad on TV? Did not the biblical prophets, of whom Postman is a latter-day alembicated mutant, depend on dramatic pleasure? Doesn't Postman depend on it in his own condemnation of human amusements?

Proposition: Commercial broadcast TV = electronic media. The telephone and telegraph make the list of demons in Postman's antitechnology world, but he ignores the entire digital universe and all the powers that it offers to us. What happens to his argument if broadcast TV disappears, as it well may? You cannot build a strong argument on so artificially restricted a sample of the evidence. Has he staged his biblical rant on an epiphenomenon?

Proposition: Print was the only *communicative medium during the golden eighteenth and nineteenth centuries in America.* This is simply silly, as well as hopelessly ignorant.[22] One might make a case for the opposite: that the "local knowledge" for which Postman argues was in fact communicated, as for so long before, orally, through folk sayings, songs, tales. The hunger for the oration as a social pleasure waxed as strong in "golden-age" America as it did in classical Greece. He knows all this and yet states the opposite case categorically.

Proposition: TV has become the dominant means of communication in America. This is now popular wisdom, but is it true? Any balanced attempt to answer this question would have to consider not only books but conversation at all levels, and daily life from office to pulpit. It would have to consider digital communication of all sorts. What Postman really objects to is pop-culture TV, and, like an exasperated monarch, he wants to kill the messenger.

Proposition: TV news is glib and superficial; print news is deep and concerned with the issues. (Not "sometimes" for both, mind you, but intrinsically.) Stories may be deep in the *New York Times*, the *Washington Post*, or the *Los Angeles Times*, but in most of the local newspapers I've seen across America, they are no more detailed than any TV snippet. TV news is built on collage techniques, but so is the columnar structure of a newspaper. And what of the great American tradition of yellow journalism?

Proposition: Visual thinking is inferior to verbal thinking. Ulmer is quite right that Postman ignores everything we have learned about the nature of visual thinking, but Postman goes further than that. He is a religious iconoclast. We must cleave to the Word and only the Word. What about all those medieval manuscripts with the demons dancing a marginal commentary on the text?[23] What about the biblical stories in stained-glass windows? What about the cathedrals these windows illuminate?

Proposition: Behavioral thinking is inferior to verbal thinking. If Postman is ignorant of the inquiry into "visual thinking" he is even more ignorant of the inquiry into behavioral biology. We evolved as a species which learned to "think" in terms of specific behavioral situations. This behavioral thinking stands much closer to the surface of life in an oral culture than in a literate one, but it is essential to human thought of any kind. The long tradition of literary allegory—as common in the age of print as before or since—attests to this. "Thinking" in behavioral terms—with all the reliance on appearances, local knowledge, private interest, that it brings with it—is our native mode of thought. Conceptual thinking rides on top of it. Surely any full definition of "reason" wants to integrate the two, not separate them and prohibit the older and more vital of the two. Even Swift's savage anger did not drive him to define reason as the Houhynyms do. Postman rightly sees that behavioral allegory, rather than disinterested price-comparisons, stands behind modern advertising, but so what? What would you expect? Aren't people free to make their own stylistic decisions? Must we buy everything from a *Consumer Reports* review?

Proposition: Political debate has been degraded by commercial TV. Print political debate was intrinsically more rational, more issue-oriented, more sincere. Again, this has become proverbial wisdom. But is it true? A fat man could not be elected to public office today, Postman says. What about an eighteenth-century politician with a pip-squeak voice? He wouldn't have made it either. Conversely, can we learn nothing from appearance? Do we not, have we not always, judged by appearance in daily life? Is this to be outlawed? Is it always deceiving, even on TV? I cannot for the life of me comprehend how this argument survives an hour of TV-watching. Never has there been a more mercilessly revealing medium. Presentation of self has special rules on TV, but so it does everywhere else, too. Was the Lincoln of the Lincoln-Douglas debates, periodic syntax and all, really more "sincere" when he was bellowing out his arguments across a tent-strewn meadow? Are misleading TV political commercials any worse than misleading print ads or slogans? Do ordinary people have so weak a crap-detector as Postman thinks? Like his mentor Plato, what Postman actually objects to is politics itself. Political argument always proceeds from, and pleads to, mixed motives—game and play, appearance and interest—as well as the issues. TV hasn't changed the mix. An antipolitical prejudice is not a proof.

Proposition: Theatricality is bad in human life and sincerity is good. Behind Postman's attack on TV stands not only a religious iconoclasm— destroy the image that desecrates the Word—but an equally religious hatred of the theater. "Show business is not entirely without an idea of excellence, but its main business is to please the crowd, and its principal instrument is artifice" (126). Every moralist in the Judeo-Christian world returns to the antitheatrical prejudice, as Barish so exhaustively chronicles. To prove this proposition, one would have to prove several things: that human life itself is not deeply theatrical; that sincere religious convictions always lead to the good life and never to religious war; that sincerity never falls victim to pharisaical dramatization of its own virtue; that self-conscious theater always leads to moral evil; and many more. The antitheatrical prejudice is a prejudice not a proof. Perhaps Shakespeare was right in dramatizing, as he so often did, that moral reform must come through theatrical role-playing.

◻   ◻   ◻

Postman proves none of these propositions. It is very odd that someone who makes such extravagant claims, historical and theoretical, for propositional thinking should be so bad at it. When you disentangle his arguments from the waffling self-contradictions, the golden-age wishful thinking, the religious iconoclasm, and the biblical prophet's rants against artifice, and express them plainly, they seem self-confuting. Furthermore, Postman does not really consider electronic technology at all. As we have seen, he doesn't know very much about it. He simply detests television, and the pop culture which it expresses. To give this snobbish detestation argumentative depth, he reconvenes the philosophers vs. rhetoricians debate and, like so many others, demonizes the rhetoricians, this time as broadcast TV. "Culture-death," he tells us, "is a clear possibility" (156), but, like the other critics we have examined, he caricatures and distorts, cuts in half, that bi-stable Western culture which he seeks to defend.

The antitechnologists we have considered all rehearse, in their different forms, the same debate between the philosophers and the rhetoricians. They all know that rhetoric stands at the center of the current technology debate, and that the "Q" question stands at the center of rhetoric. They all reincarnate, in their different forms, our persistent hunger for a golden age when rhetoric had not yet been invented. They all flirt with religious iconoclasm and religious antidramatism. They all stumble over the basic bi-stability of Western culture and, while trying to accommodate it, want to shut it down. They would all defend traditional Western culture but don't understand what that "tradition" is about. And so they cannot imagine how it might survive translation into a new operating system and a new economics of attention.

The Edge of Chaos

The phrase "information society" has been given a new meaning in the last several years and, appropriately enough, the new meaning has been created by a new computer-driven science, the science of complex systems. This emerging way of thinking about how life organizes itself argues that life itself is information. Not the particular embodiment but the information embodied provides the essence of life. The carbon-based "life" which we as human beings happen to know, and embody, is but one possible printout of general rules about how life evolves and organizes itself. Thus the movement from object to beholder, from static perfection to dynamic interchange, which has occurred so often in twentieth-century art, finds a scientific counterpart. Thus, too, the long process of removing *homo sapiens* from the center of the universe finds its most recent, if not its last, manifestation.

This new science is far from easy to describe, and I place myself at the limits of adhesion in trying to do so. But I must try, for this new way of thinking stands to the sciences as the return of the rhetorical paideia stands to the arts and letters. Putting the matter at the highest level of generality—which is where we must begin—the sciences now seem to be undergoing a convergence very like the convergence I have sought in this book to describe for the arts and letters. C. P. Snow's "two cultures" seem to be undergoing similar reversals from centrifugal specialization to centripetal reintegration, and in the process they seem themselves to be coming together into a common center. Since this common digital center affects each argument I have tried to develop—democracy, technology, rhetorical theory, and a university curriculum that might embody their new relationships—I must at least sketch its broad outlines. It provides a framework within which the antitechnologists' discomforts can be located and understood. And, more important than that, it makes clear the real and present grounds for optimism that their views ignore—the truly extraordinary similarity between the world view of classical rhetoric and that which we now find emerging everywhere in the sciences, hard and soft, physical and social.[24]

In chapter 6, I talk about the hunger for some common theoretical center, some possible "core curriculum" for the humanities, which many of us have shared as we saw specialization dominate formal inquiry. George A. Cowan had often had similar thoughts about the physical sciences: "The traditional disciplines had become so entrenched and so isolated from one another that they seemed to be strangling themselves."[25] So, when in 1982 he stepped down as head of research at the Los Alamos National Laboratory, he decided to do something about it. He sensed an underlying similarity in different fields of inquiry, and wanted to start an institute to precipitate that similarity out into public view. I have described a similar effort for the human sciences in chapter 3, where I picked out, from a variety of fields, a common rhetorical center which could constitute the "useful miracle," to borrow again Clifford Geertz's phrase, that might locate the increasingly centripetal disciplines of the word in a common frame of reference.

In the archetypal quarrel between the philosophers and the rhetoricians to which I have so often returned, the rhetoricians took human society as it was, messy with conflicting interests and attention-structures, and tried through the stylized techniques of two-sided argument to bring some order—always temporary and shifting—to the human barnyard. The Sophists accepted human nature as it was and tried, through a rhetorical judo, to use its forces to bring some order into human life. They trusted to the free marketplace, both of goods and of ideas, to make the infinitely many decisions required in a system as complex as human society. Plato taught the philosophers to take the opposite approach, to despise the messy human reality and imagine a much tidier one, a republic where people had single roles and obeyed clear rules about who could interact with whom.

Social policy in the West has ever since vacillated between these two ways to think about social order. The statists have wanted to create a large, central plan that ordered human life from the top down, according to a pre-arranged design. People needed to be straightened out and up. This kind of top-down thinking, utopian thinking, has always been a favorite humanist entertainment. Imagine the ideal prince; imagine the ideal state. If human nature was recalcitrant to the design, it was to be coerced. If an ugly slum had grown up, it was to be bulldozed and a more orderly set of high-rises in the International Style put in its place. The planner decides where the paths should be and people are made to walk on them.

The opposite idea, bottom-up thinking, has always accepted the messiness of human nature and started from there. The planner waits to see where people wear a path, then paves it. Robert Venturi and his team looked at Las Vegas, and instead of deciding to tear it down and start over, they pondered it as a new city of signage that revealed new patterns of public attention. A contemporary urban-redevelopment plan begins with what is on the ground, buildings and the people who live in them, and tries to reweave that basic fabric. When you stand at a high point in the Jerde Associates' Horton Plaza shopping center in downtown San Diego and look out over the city, the new plaza design, though it does not exactly imitate earlier buildings, makes you look at them in a newly self-conscious way. The older architecture has been re-possessed rather than destroyed. Old and new talk to each other. The cityscape spread out before you from a high-rise looks like a skillful reweaving of the historical urban fabric, not a brand new design thought out to the last detail.

What seemed to be happening in the sciences was a movement from the "philosophic" thinking of Newtonian physics to the "rhetorical" thinking of molecular biology or nonlinear physics. Physical science had spent three hundred years looking for its lost keys under a Newtonian lamppost, not because it had lost them there but because, as the old joke has it, the light was better. In the Newtonian world, the whole was the sum of its parts. "If a system is precisely equal to the sum of its parts, then each component is free to do its own thing regardless of what's happening elsewhere. And that tends to make the mathematics relatively easy to analyze. (The name 'linear' refers to the fact that if you plot such an equation on graph paper, the plot is a straight line.)"[26] In such a system, as in Plato's *Republic*, things don't get out of hand and go off in unexpected directions. You can foresee everything; the system is designed to guarantee it. The physicists "had spent the past three hundred years having a love affair with linear systems," just as the humanities had spent three hundred years in the same Newtonian interlude cherishing a similar theory of language, one where one word = one thing, and where human communication was clear, brief, and sincere. Or ought to be. And if it wasn't, well, then, people should change until it was. And if, in fact, the system didn't adequately describe how a great deal of human communication went on, well, tough. So, too, if the Newtonian equations could not cope with the "three-body problem,"[27] and hence with a great deal of nature—the weather, for example—well, tough. Hard science would concentrate on what they could cope with. This is not an alien distinction to anyone engaged in formal inquiry. Every field has its "hard" and "soft" branches. The "hard" branch is theoretically rigorous, mathematically based if possible. But it can prove strong theorems only for trivial problems. The softies take on real problems but come up with nonrigorous solutions.

Cowan thought he saw the same thing happening in many different fields—a new willingness to deal with messy, real-world, "rhetorical" (my term) problems. Chaos theory was confronting nonlinear problems like weather systems and the flow of turbulent fluids. Computer simulation, almost by now a third branch of science standing between theory and experimentation, could model nonlinear equations as well as linear ones. And people here and there were trying to recreate, through the time-scaling powers of digital computers, the very processes of evolution which had created the self-replicating system molecular biology was trying to study.

> And yet, as intriguing as molecular biology and computer simulation and nonlinear science were separately, Cowan had a suspicion that they were only the beginning. It was more a gut feeling than anything else. But he sensed that there was an underlying unity here, one that would ultimately encompass not just physics and chemistry, but biology, information processing, economics, political science, and every other aspect of human affairs. What he had in mind was a concept of scholarship that was almost medieval. If this unity were real, he thought, it would be a way of knowing the world that made little distinction between biological sciences and physical sciences—or between either of those sciences and history or philosophy.[28]

To institutionalize this vision, or the search for it, Cowan organized the Santa Fe Institute. It would explore this notion that the natural laws of complex systems—a.k.a. messy reality, human and otherwise—were the same across many disciplines and many patterns of order. Its scientists, by creating "genetic algorithms" that modeled biological processes in a digital computer, would grow "artificial life" and see how it worked. These evolutionary systems would start out with a very few simple rules and, using the immense iterative powers of digital computation, compress time-scale and see what evolved. The Institute would do the same "bottom-up" thinking in other fields, economics for example, or robotics. Its manner of proceeding was bottom-up, too; it would bring together scientists who never went to the same meetings, and see what they had to say to each other. The first such confab took place in September of 1987, and it brought together physicists and economists. What "emerged" was a new conception of economics, messy, inelegant, but more useful than the old one.[29]

To grasp this way of computer-driven "thinking," it may help to contrast it with AI, artificial intelligence. The AI movement was Platonic, top-down. It sought to foresee every consequence and to protect any individual outcome from self-interference and hence to prevent unwonted behavior. The ace programmer who did this got to play Platonic god. Complexity modeling worked the other way, from the bottom up. It did not try to foresee consequences but instead noted what unforeseen results came from simple generative rules. It looked for novelty; as John Cage had for so long recommended, it coaxed chance.

More information emerged from a complex model than was put into it. It was not like the closed Newtonian universe in which the whole equaled the sum of its parts. It was like a poem, where the words on the page generated different kinds of "information" in different readers. It didn't try to design a universe, like Plato. It tried to evolve one in the Darwinian way. Computer programs themselves, in such a world, are not designed; a digital universe is created in which they can evolve into maximal utility. The programming techniques thus created are often nonintuitive, not the kind a human programmer would have created at all.

From the complexity movement emerges a scientific way of thinking about the world that has a lot in common with the rhetorical way of thinking we've been considering in these essays. Let me chart some of this common ground.[30]

Both ways of thinking seek to make sense of the world as it is, rather than rearranging it into a pattern that is easier to make sense of. Or (as with Ramus's separation of logic from rhetoric, words from things) easier to teach. Rhetoric had always billed itself as a way to make decisions based on incomplete information, on probabilities, on the kind of knowledge we have in the everyday world. Complex thinking, too, starts from a universe of incomplete knowledge. A group at the University of Michigan is trying to develop "flight simulators for policy" which would give politicians some realistic sense of the choices they face "without taking 250 million people along for the ride."[31] A training like this was precisely what the Greek Sophists tried to provide their students—a general skill in political decision-making.

Both approaches proceed by a bottom-up, evolutionary method of problem-solving. The art of persuasion in a free society tries to create "public opinion" by a series of local conversations that build from level to level, formulating a consensus that emerges rather than being imposed. The flexible "politicians" whom we are so fond of despising act as catalysts for this process. Christopher Langton, a pioneer of what is called "artificial life" (silicon-based, computer-hosted "life" rather than carbon-based, earth-hosted "life") comments about the same bottom-up process in nature: "It's the way nature works. It's what makes atoms and what makes molecules. Co-operative structures, the formation of co-operative structures, localized in time and space. You have these little packets of co-operation, and then packets of packets, and packets of packets of packets." As Steven Levy goes on to say, "Bottom-up was everywhere in biology. It was the way life began, from the formation of organic molecules, to the formation of bacteria, to the emergence of multicell organisms. ... Emergent behavior was the payoff of the bottom-up approach. ... Something had to happen that was not specifically programmed in."[32] This is how persuasion drives thought in a free society, allows democratic social thought to grow and mature.

In thinking about how living systems emerge, John Holland, the dominant figure in the field, stresses the complementary role played by competition and cooperation. "Competition and cooperation may seem antithetical, but at some very deep level, they are two sides of the same coin."[33] In the information system created by classical rhetoric, the systematic use of competition, of two-sided argument, aimed to create from the bottom up a social cooperation which could not, except with violence, be imposed from the top down. The same push-pull process inheres in how life bootstraps itself up into organization and self-reproduction. Variety and richness emerge from competition; the Platonic urge to shut it down impoverishes life at every level.

I have argued in chapter 3 that the rhetorical view of life has always been an evolutionary view, not an Edenic one. It does not look back to a vanished utopia or forward to one built by whittling human beings down to size. The rhetorical version of a utopia, in fact, looks very like a richly emergent evolutionary system.[34] Such a system is poised, to borrow a phrase from Langton, on "the edge of chaos."[35] It does not aim at *stasis*, as does the utopian tradition that descends from Plato, at finding an ideal pattern of life and then *shutting the developmental process down*. The developmental process *is* life. To shut it down is to kill it. Stasis is the death by ice. The death by fire is real chaos, driving the system into total incoherence. The evolutionary niche that favors life poises itself in the interface between the two. That is where deep, rich, vigorous life is to be found. So I have argued that the Western self oscillates between two basic modes of being, central and social. The oscillation is inherently unstable but controlled; neither static nor chaotic. Poised, as perhaps we can now conceive all living systems to be, on the edge of chaos.

It is suggestive to project this evolutionary thinking back onto the world of twentieth-century art I discussed in chapter 2. The dissatisfaction with the masterpiece psychology of Arnoldian "great art" is a dissatisfaction with a top-down method of creating beauty. Tinguely's interactive machines create a simulacrum of the evolutionary bottom-up system of creation. His machine that creates you an abstract drawing for sixpence has found a digital equivalent in the work of Karl Sims. Sims began with the "biomorph" system of Richard Dawkins; this was a computer-based system for evolving natural organic shapes. Sims, whose job it was to create striking computer graphics for the Thinking Machines Company, decided to grow them, evolve them, rather than create them. For Sims was after "a computer artist's tool, one that allowed a person with no programming ability and no drawing acumen to create complex and compelling images."[36] The result was this: "In only a few generations, anyone capable of manipulating a computer mouse could create hauntingly beautiful visual artifacts. The power to search ... all possible *images*—a dizzying concept in and of itself—coughed up pictures that displayed the hard-earned distinctiveness of great modern artists. Sims had a portfolio of evolved images that evoked Dalí, Klee, Picasso, Mondrian, and Rothko."[37]

John Cage's effort to put chance and randomness into the heart of music reflects, surely, the same return to a pattern of evolutionary thinking. Cage saw music not as a great effect but as a current, evolving, real-time human system in which chance played a role as well as design. The dethronement of the Great Composer operated here much as the dethronement of the Great Programmer in the world of artificial intelligence. The movement from static to dynamic, from changeless perfection to continual change, that appears again and again in twentieth-century art shows up as the crux of scientific thinking about complex systems poised on the edge of chaos. Scaling, too, stands at the center of both contemporary art and the new science of complexity. Thinking about complex systems is made possible by the computer's ability to compress time-scale; what is the music of Philip Glass or the operatic drama of Robert Wilson but a similar manipulation of time-scale, only this time in the opposite direction? The more one looks, the more one sees twentieth-century art as an exploration of the edge of chaos.

The place to situate Jane Healy's critique of a changing human attention-structure is right here, on the edge of chaos. This new way of attending to the world may indeed *be* chaos; it is too early to tell. But it may be a new form of dynamic stability whose real boundary-conditions we cannot as yet detect. Perhaps it has evolved to cope with the new demands exerted by a digital information society. The Edenic yearnings of George Steiner and Neil Postman are easier to locate. They clearly belong to the death by ice, to the urge to live in stasis. Steiner's talismanic attachment to the book, and to the social operating system that allows the book to communicate, cherishes a closed system, fixed and comprehensible. It is no accident, I think, that both locate their Edens in the heyday of an industrial economy.

It is the intrinsic volatility, the intrinsically democratic volatility, of the particular edge of chaos on which an information society lives that so disconcerts them.

The rhetoricians, the "Greek Liberals" as Havelock calls them, built their world on the *logos*, on the word, or more largely on what we would call "information." It was there that they found their natural home, not in a "real" world beyond language, either in Platonic Forms or Newtonian bodies. It was words that constituted life, not embodiment. This assumption now has returned to the sciences as well. Life is information; life is the *logos*. It is an evolutionary system, dynamic, perpetually emergent. It *creates* new meanings, as does poetry, rather than simply communicating preexisting knowledge in a transparent capsule.

I have tried to describe, in chapter 2, a didactic pattern in the arts that tries to teach this lesson. I sketched an undergraduate curriculum in chapter 4 built on the return of rhetoric, of the centripetal vision, to the humanities. It appears now that we can expand this vision to the sciences as well. They are undergoing a similar reversal from a centrifugal to a centripetal mode of thought. And surely, when we have all had time to ponder these issues more fully, we will see that the two centripetal modes of thought are built on the same intellectual structure, a science of complex adaptive systems. This new convergence between the arts and sciences is deeply democratic—"bottom-up" from the bottom up. It is digitally driven. It is capable of generalization. Like the rhetorical paideia that forms part of its emergence, it *aims for* generalization. It *aims to be* a theory that can be put into practice, can explain practice, can cure the split between the two.

Surely here we must find what Ortega y Gasset called the "height of the time,"[38] which ought to animate a liberal education. When we have this *altitud vital* clearly in mind, we'll know what kinds of attention-structures we would like to coax, to persuade, into being in the minds of our students. We will then learn how to thrive on this new edge of chaos. This emergent understanding of *where we stand,* dangerous as it is, I find extraordinarily exciting and heartening. I can't, therefore, share the deep nightmares, Edenic or otherwise, that now cloud the electronic word. We have begun to understand what the phrase "information society" really means and can prepare ourselves to live in it. And, as Pasteur said, "Chance favors the prepared mind."

NOTES

1. M. Mitchell Waldrop, *Complexity: The Emerging Science at the Edge of Order and Chaos* (New York: Simon and Schuster, 1992), 67.

2. This becomes very clear in Lawrence Weschler's perceptive study, *Seeing is Forgetting the Name of the Thing One Sees: A Life of Contemporary Artist Robert Irwin* (Berkeley and Los Angeles: University of California Press, 1982).

3. This reversal of the customary words/deeds relationship is behind much of the current dispute about literary "theory." The "theorists" have advanced the theory of style implied by an information economy—even if many of them do so from a Marxist orientation based on a goods economy.

4. Walter B. Wriston, *The Twilight of Sovereignty: How the Information Revolution Is Transforming Our World* (New York: Charles Scribner's Sons, 1992), 19–20.

5. "'I find most pop culture monstrous and sickening,' McLuhan declared in the sixties. 'I study it for my own survival.'" Philip Marchand, *Marshall McLuhan: The Medium and the Messenger* (New York: Ticknor and Fields, 1989), 43.

6. See, for example, "The Language Animal" (1969) and "In a Post-Culture" (1970), reprinted in *Extra-Territorial: Papers on Literature and the Language Revolution* (New York: Atheneum, 1971); the "Humane Literacy" section of six essays from the sixties, reprinted in *Language and Silence: Essays on Language, Literature, and the Inhuman* (New York: Atheneum, 1970); "On Reading Marshall McLuhan" (1963), in the same volume; "After the Book?" (1972), reprinted in *On Difficulty, and Other Essays* (Oxford: Oxford University Press, 1978); *In Bluebeard's Castle: Some Notes towards the Redefinition of Culture* (New Haven: Yale University Press, 1971), esp. chapter 4, "Tomorrow"; and "The End of Bookishness?" *Times Literary Supplement*, 8–14 July 1988.

7. "After the Book," *On Difficulty*, 188.

8. Ibid., 189–90.

9. "Future Literacies," *George Steiner: A Reader* (New York: Oxford University Press, 1984), 427.

10. "Literature and Post-History," *Language and Silence*, 384–85.

11. Steiner later elaborates this golden vision into a full monastic fantasy, a "house of reading" where "full" reading goes on, in many languages and with full intertextuality always as dependably on call as the silent servants who fetch and dust the books—the old operating system, preserved in amber. See chapter 1 n. 9 above.

12. "Humane Literacy," *Language and Silence*, 5.

13. "Future Literacies," *A Reader*, 429.

14. *In Bluebeard's Castle*, 112.

15. The locus classicus of Tom Wolfe's study of style is his essay on the Southern California custom-car scene, "The Kandy-Kolored Tangerine-Flake Streamline Baby," first published in *Esquire* and reprinted in his essay collection of the same title (New York: Farrar, Straus and Giroux, Noonday, 1965).

16. Jane Healy, *Endangered Minds: Why Our Children Don't Think* (New York: Simon and Schuster, Touchstone, 1990).

17. Here is Healy's breakdown (125–26):

Right Hemisphere
- responds to *novelty*
- works with wholes, not parts
- is visual, not auditory
- is associated with intuition and the ability to "size up" social situations
- in music, picks up the melody and disregards the lyrics or the sequential details of notation patterns
- is specialized for understanding the relative position of objects in space and mentally turning around three-dimensional figures (remember those items on IQ tests that showed you a funny-looking shape and then asked, "Which one of these, if upside down, would be the same as the first?"). Many video games probably call heavily on these abilities.
- in language processing, is well adapted for:
    —understanding general meaning and some aspects of word meaning (e.g., content words)
    —getting the "gist" of the speaker's intent
    —picking up the contours and melodic pattern of spoken language (prosody)
    —gesturing and "body language"
    —thinking metaphorically

Left Hemisphere
- deals with "*automatic codes*" (quick recall of specific words and letters, accurate spelling, math tables)
- analyzes and arranges details in order, e.g., time concepts, cause-and-effect relationships (first X, then Y), and the sequential patterns of small motor movements (e.g., tying shoes, forming letters with a pencil)
- is auditory rather than visual
- in music, it mediates the notation and lyrics rather than the melodic patterns
- in language processing, it mediates:
    —fine distinctions between sounds (phonology)
    —the order of sounds in words
    —the order of words and their relationships (syntax)
    —some types of word meaning (e.g., function words)
    —other aspects of language comprehension

18. Neil Postman, *Amusing Ourselves to Death: Public Discourse in the Age of Show Business* (New York: Penguin Books, 1985), 24.

19. Richard McKeon, *Rhetoric: Essays in Invention and Discovery*, ed. with intro. by Mark Backman (Woodbridge, Conn.: Ox Bow, 1987), 108.

20. The first sentence occurs in the *Letters*, ed. Emerson, 158; the second and third come from "Sunday" in *A Week on the Concord and Merrimack Rivers*.

21. See the discussion of Bloom's book in chapter 7.

22. As a reading of David S. Reynolds' *Beneath the American Renaissance: The Subversive Imagination in the Age of Emerson and Melville* (New York: Knopf, 1988) makes strikingly clear.

23. They are discussed in a new book by Michael Camille, *Image on the Edge: The Margins of Medieval Art* (Cambridge: Harvard University Press, 1992).

24. In attempting to chronicle this new "rhetorical" science, I depend heavily on two books published in 1992, Waldrop's *Complexity* (n. 1 above) and Steven Levy's *Artificial Life: The Quest for a New Creation* (New York: Pantheon). I have also used James Gleick's *Chaos: Making a New Science* (New York: Viking, 1987), and two books by my UCLA colleague N. Katherine Hayles, *The Cosmic Web: Scientific Field Models and Literary Strategies in the Twentieth Century* (Ithaca: Cornell University Press, 1984) and *Chaos Bound: Orderly Disorder in Contemporary Literature and Science* (Ithaca: Cornell University Press, 1990).

25. Waldrop, *Complexity*, 61.

26. Ibid., 64–65.

27. Hayles, *Chaos Bound* (n. 24 above), 1.

28. Waldrop, *Complexity*, 67.

29. Ibid., 136ff.

30. To flesh out the "rhetoric" side of these etiolated comparisons, the reader may want to follow the reconstitution of "rhetorical" thinking that Eric Havelock provides in *The Liberal Temper in Greek Politics* (New Haven: Yale University Press, 1957).

31. Waldrop, *Complexity*, 267.

32. Levy, *Artificial Life* (n. 24 above), 106.

33. Waldrop, *Complexity*, 185.

34. I have discussed these two opposed kinds of utopias in an earlier book. See "The Choice of Utopias: More or Castiglione?" in *Literacy and the Survival of Humanism* (New Haven: Yale University Press, 1983), 24–40.

35. Waldrop, *Complexity*, 230. One might think of the entire "complexity" argument as finding focus in this concept.

36. Levy, *Artificial Life* (n. 24 above), 212.

37. Ibid., 214.

38. See José Ortega y Gasset, "La altura de los tiempos," in *La Rebelión de las masas* (1929; Madrid: Revista de Occidente, 1968).

10

The movement from book to screen, from fixed print to digital volatility, presents so many surprises, anomalies, opportunities, and dangers that none of us can see how it will play out. The only framework within which to pursue such an elusive quarry is open-ended argument. The pros and cons have been vigorously aired in the thinking I've reviewed in the last two chapters. I wanted to conclude by interiorizing these grave reservations about, and bright hopes for, the electronic word, putting them into an internal dialogue with myself. For if I feel optimistic about how we might use digital technology to sustain our public and private discourse, I also share the fears and longings for the book. A dialogue seemed the appropriate form for such a divided self.

Conversation with a Curmudgeon

urmudgeon. Well, Lanham, even if you think Neil Postman is a papier-mâché Jeremiah, can you doubt the accuracy of Healy's composite portrait?

Lanham. No, I can't. Too much evidence, coming from too many places, supports it. All those teachers in her survey. All that behavioral neuroscience. She could have summoned a lot of behavioral biology to support her argument, too, if she had thought to look there.

C. She is departing from a print-based conception of human reason, all right, but don't you find a generation of students that lacks this old-fashioned commodity a little scary?

L. Yep. I didn't run a composition program for seven years without learning something.

C. And do you doubt that her thesis really supports all the things in Kernan's argument that irritate you the most?

L. Which ones? There are lots!

C. The title argument, for a start: "the death of literature." The literary world depends on the university; the university depends on literate students—otherwise nobody to teach; and clearly the Healy generation will grow up and be our students. You teach Chaucer and Shakespeare—how will you teach the new differently abled student?

L. Not "will grow up." *Have* grown up. The portrait Healy draws fits my Chaucer and Shakespeare students right now. Syntax is their main problem; function words trip them up; they haven't the foggiest idea how to build an argument. They'll watch the video of a Shakespeare play but hate to read the text.

C. Is this not the death of literature? Wasn't Kernan right? And even Postman?

L. Well, literature is not isomorphic with print, is it?

C. No, but can you really teach it, whatever it is, to people who hate to read and do so only when compelled by the instructor?

L. No. I'm as committed to the third alternative as Healy is, and as you are. What else is there to do? But mixing the philosophers with the rhetoricians is very hard. In fact, as I argue in these essays, you really can't *mix* them. You have to oscillate between them. Build a literary structure that holds these two opposite worlds in dynamic interchange. That's why the curriculum has to have an *artistic* structure, not a bureaucratic one. Balancing the hemispheres of the brain is like balancing central self and social self, like holding together the "rhetorical" and the "philosophical" views of the world. As I keep arguing, they form a bi-stable illusion. They alternate but don't mix. That immiscibility surely must stem from asymmetrical hemisphericality as an evolutionary strategy. Separating these two modes of apprehension and then letting them exchange information must have had survival value. That, at least, is how I read Corballis's new book on the subject.[1]

C. Do you think the hypertextual universe Jay Bolter describes will aid in this oscillation? Seems to me that it will more likely destroy it.

L. If taken by itself, it will. Just as Ulmer's new definition of "reason" will. But Ulmer, at least some of the time, argues for his "videocy" as alternating with old-fashioned "literacy." And, as hypertextual "writing" works itself out, I think the two modes will mix, that they will alternate.

C. How can you be sure this alternation will take place? And won't there always be many tasks that conventional linear reason must perform all by itself?

L. Sure. I have never meant to argue otherwise.

C. And isn't that ability—to reason in conventional linear fashion—what "Healy's children," if I may so style them, so clearly lack?

L. Yes. In fact, when you think about it, Healy's argument interrogates Ulmer's in some tough ways. She is arguing, for a start, that the baby he sees as being born, with Derrida as midwife, has already been born and grown up. No need for academic revolution at all. In the same way that electronic text makes a lot of "theory" unnecessary, Healy's children will make Ulmer's revolution in academic text unnecessary. It has already happened. You don't have to worry, as Edwards does in *Drawing on the Right Side of the Brain*, about liberating the right brain from the domination of the left. If Healy's worst fears about irreversibility are true, her children won't *have* a left brain, or any to speak of. Simply adopt her second choice, open the gates (some of the time, at least, Ulmer argues for this) and everything will happen naturally.

C. And if students hate to read and write, will they be able to read and write a "mystory," or will they have to make only videos? Ulmer is like all you electronic prophets: you neglect the basic print-platform you speak—ah, read and write—from.

L. Doesn't your criticism run even deeper? Consider Hardison's picture of the postmodern electronic culture. It seems, at least to me, full of excitement and verve and interest. I'm not afraid of it. But what if it ends up producing Healy's children? Are they the first crop from this wonderful new cultural tree?

C. Isn't that inevitably so? And what do you think of them?

L. They scare me just as much as they scare you. But let me try to weasel out of this corner. Aren't Healy's children the product of an educational system, and a family, which has disintegrated and doesn't teach much of *anything*, left-brained or right?

C. And then pop culture takes over and does the right-brained job she talks about. We're back to our need for a balance that is very hard to achieve, much harder than your glib generalities about the "electronic word" would lead an innocent reader to believe. You're back in your corner.

L. Okay. Another try. Healy's arguments from behavioral neuroscience begin to suggest an answer, or part of one, to what I call the "Q" question. What literary experience, if we take that in the widest sense (starting from childhood with nursery rhymes and fairy stories), supplies for us may be the complicated set of neural pathways that sustain higher-level thought. It may not be moral choice, as such, but the neural framework this choice requires, that humanistic education constructs. I've been arguing for this oscillation as fundamental for a long time—way before personal computers were invented, in fact. I think of electronic text as able, at least in some instances, to *enhance* this oscillation, to support it better than print does.

C. Well, maybe you are out of the corner, but you still haven't faced up to the real and critical neural imbalance that Healy makes so convincing a case for—and the *irreversibility* that lurks at the heart of it. And so you haven't faced up to the real implications of "postmodernity," either.

L. You're right. Whether we're looking at Andy Warhol or Paul de Man, I've always taken the postmodern arguments as a didactic corrective, not as an outrageous revolution, and perhaps that is not altogether correct. Certainly it's not how most people read it.

C. And to make them read it your way, you really must be more specific about your version of Healy's third alternative. How can the rhetorical paideia be returning, as you keep insisting, if the *logos* on which it is based, the Word, is dying, as Steiner predicted and Healy's children seem to embody? What agenda can you construct that will make their world into anything but a catastrophe? Spell it out, my friend.

L. Yes, all right. I'll try. Okay to start by seeing if we can "stipulate," as the lawyers say, the basis of the agenda, find what we can agree on?

C. Sure.

L. Would you agree that there has been a convergence of the sort I sketched out in chapter 4: that electronic technology, our theory of discourse, and the democratization of higher education have converged into one single cultural manifestation?

C. Yes, for better or worse. Worse.

L. And would you agree that the move of electronic technology from print to screen has democratized, or as you would put it, degraded, public discourse?

C. Yes, the movement has occurred. Kernan, Hardison, Bolter & Co. are right about that.

L. Would you agree that, in some areas at least, the move from print to an interactive digital screen seems a positive gain? I'm thinking now of do-it-yourself books, cookbooks, books of manners, "how-to" manuals of all sorts. Here, the combination of visual instruction, alphabetic text and, where needed, sound (You want to hear what a mistimed engine *sounds* like? Listen up!) does the job much better than an ordinary codex book.

C. I'll agree to that. And I'd add travel books too, sometimes; I've watched some very interesting programs on that travel channel they have on cable TV.

L. These same genres have formed a large part of the printed-book market almost from the beginning. Now they are available to people who would not use them, or not use them so readily, in print form.

C. The sitcom audience, you mean?

L. Not necessarily. We all know people who are "good with their hands" but not so good at dealing with complex prose exposition. Interactive video provides a perfect instructional format for people like that. Is there anything intellectually degrading about such instruction?

C. No. I honestly agree with you there. But what about other types of books that have formed a huge part of the market—such as romances, to take what may be the biggest category?

L. Don't TV soap operas feed the same hunger?

C. Yes, but they involve no imaginative recreation from the word.

L. So it is *literary* texts that cannot be translated? The movie is never as good as the novel?

C. Yes, but also any extended conceptual argument, an economics text for example, or a medical treatise.

L. Have you seen the way medical texts now use bar codes? You read the bar code with a light pen and that fetches a video picture, animated or live when appropriate, to illustrate the argument. Will that necessarily degrade the "rationality" that Postman thinks comes automatically with printed text?

C. No. I've never seen that technology, but why can't it apply to any illustrated text? Art history, for example.

L. It can. And then you can manipulate those illustrations, zoom in on details, etc.[2] Will such powers compromise the automatic "rationality" of print? If you are writing a history of World War I, and can refer your reader to a film segment on trench warfare when you are discussing it, will that injure our Postmanesque print rationality?

C. Well, if Postman is right that print is always rational and pictures always a second-rate form of information, then it would have to. But that's a pretty stupid conclusion, isn't it?

L. Indeed it is. In fact, the more you think about conceptual argument, the more methods of visual and auditory enhancement occur to you. I think the law will get there first on this one. They are already beginning to use digital media for courtroom demonstrations, compiling complex evidence in new ways so that jurors can understand it. And why shouldn't complicated financial arguments, impossible for a jury to absorb under current courtroom practices, be presented with visual accompaniments? I've even heard that one author of a copyright text is creating a multimedia version that shows film sequences rather than stills. And think what you could do when trying *music* copyright cases! All kinds of direct comparisons possible in no other way.

C. Okay. I'll stipulate that mixed forms of presentation, even of conceptual argumentation, are now widening and democratizing our general literacy.

L. And so when I said in one of the essays that digital display could help bridge the gap between the "museum culture" and the pop culture, I was not dreaming. It is happening now. That impassable gulf between the two which Steiner posits has been bridged.

C. Yes. Maybe I should learn more about it.

L. At least don't automatically assume that broadcast TV is the whole story, or anything like it. Anyway, let me summarize our agenda thus far. We've agreed that a convergence is taking place between electronic media, current theoretical thinking in the arts and letters, and the democratization of American society. We've agreed that, through the electronic word, public discourse at least *can* be opened out to new constituencies without necessarily degrading it, or them.

C. Not likely, but possible, yes.

L. Okay, now that we've basked in this "sunny interval" (as the BBC weatherpersons call it) let's get back to Healy's children. We agree that they have now come up through the schools to the colleges and universities? Or are you now *emeritus?*

C. Not yet, but by God it can't come soon enough. Yes, it's as you say. My students fit Healy's profile, too. On my last quiz in the Milton class, I put the usual "Milton b._____; d._____" question and one student came up and asked what "this *b* and *d* nonsense" was. Must have been one of your "visual learners"!

L. And can we agree that some productive, or at least neutral, or at least suggestive, ways have emerged to describe this change? Can we agree, for example, that the various cultural pairings that have been used to describe this movement do lead in some interesting directions?

C. You mean the oral/literate distinction, for example, and how it correlates with the left-brain/right-brain model?

L. Yes, and also the way we can map these onto the "linear" and "hypertextual" contrast and the "serious/rhetorical" opposition that I used years ago in *The Motives of Eloquence*.[3]

C. Yes, yes. That's the only one of your arguments that makes sense to me. It all emerges out of the Greek debate between Plato and the Sophists— what you call the philosophy/rhetoric debate. You did some sensible thinking before you disgraced your classical education with this electronic text nonsense.

L. You're dead right about that, Mudge. If I hadn't bought the Osborne in 1981, I'd have finished that book on Plato's prose style by now. But onward. Are we agreed that Healy was right on the money when she said alternative #3 was the only possible choice? That is, we can neither preserve the educational system unchanged nor throw out the "literate" ways of thinking. We have, in some way, to move the humanities from the old to the new operating system.

C. Yes. That follows from admitting that the move from book to screen is happening.

L. Okay. Now, one more stipulation, but a big one—you probably will dig your heels in at it. I've been arguing that it is the pivotal oscillation between the two basic opposites we've now agreed on—whether you conceive of them as sides of the brain, sides of the self, or opposite kinds of society—that establishes Western reality. That is, I've been trying to put the philosophy/rhetoric quarrel *back into time*. Don't let Derrida jiggle your bag of spleen here. It's Chaucer's argument, Castiglione's argument, Ovid's argument, that I'm developing.[4] And certainly Shakespeare's—you did say that one time that you agreed with me about *Hamlet*, didn't you?

C. Yes, I'll agree to that if you'll explain one thing you've always waffled about in that matrix of yours.

L. Okay, shoot.

C. It's about the "motive" spectrum. You usually argue that rhetoric depends on game and play while philosophy depends on ordinary purpose—food, shelter, etc. That's a polarity I can understand as part of the bi-polar pattern we've been talking about. But then you change the rules and argue that "the rhetorical paideia," to use your somewhat hyperventilated phrase, advocates an *oscillation* between the two. Which is it? What does "rhetoric," in this scheme of things, actually stand for?

L. Good question. Nuclear question! This difference is one of the things that screws up Postman's argument. Let me go back to Marrou's crucial remark in *Education in Antiquity* that although philosophy has always won the arguments, rhetoric has always controlled the curriculum. Not precisely true. Rhetoric did control the curriculum, but that was because it coopted the philosophical point of view. That explains why rhetorical theory, as well as education, has always been deeply self-contradictory—as I've argued in chapters 3 and 4, and especially in 6.

C. Sorry, I don't follow.

L. Think about how we teach language and argumentation even now, in the rare times when we still do. We teach a fundamental contradiction. On the one hand, we hold up Clarity, Brevity, and Sincerity as the god-terms of prose style; on the other, the history of rhetoric can be seen as the ever-increasing proliferation of terms for stylistic ornamentation. On the one hand, we have stressed that every public speaker and writer should strive to appear sincere, open, and unrehearsed. On the other, we have devoted most of our verbal training to creating that *appearance* of sincerity. We've seen Postman repeat the contradiction: he argues for a periodic style as high literacy and then adopts a C-B-S theory of style that would prohibit the very patterns he valorizes.

C. You work both sides of the street, too. You compile a list of rhetorical terms with, what is it, a thousand of them,[5] and at the same time you do textbooks on revising prose.

L. It's not inconsistency; it's oscillation!

C. Ah! Yes, of course! But I'll accept the oscillation argument if it comes from Castiglione rather than you—he is, after all, the most underrated thinker in the Italian Renaissance.

L. You'll get no argument from me about that. More Platonic prejudice getting in the way. Now, I need some industrial-strength Socratic stooging if I'm to get on with things.

C. I'm up to it.

L. Does it not seem to you, then, Curmudgeon my friend, that Healy's alternative #3 puts us right back in the hands of rhetorical education?

C.   Sorry. You do not carry me with you.

L.   Let me put it another way. She is trying to preserve the values of print in an electronic age; of literacy in an oral one; of the left brain when the right is in the ascendant. Is this not the case?

C.   Yes, I've admitted that.

L.   Well, then, since this base-pair does not mix but only oscillates, isn't the oscillation what *must* underlie any education based on our now-familiar #3?

C.   I guess you are right. Really right.

L.   Wow. Let me laminate that for my wallet!

C.   Point to you.

L.   Since you are in so compliant a mood, let me run some other comparisons by you.

C.   Run on—not that you need any encouragement to do that!

L.   Think about Ulmer's reconceptualizing of university discourse: he argues for a mixture of creative and analytical modes, personal and impersonal argument, alphabetic and imagistic discourse. Right?

C.   Yes. At least when he is not defining "reason" entirely in video terms.

L.   But rhetorical education has always striven for precisely this, for an alternation of theory and practice. That's what the endless practice in *declamatio*, in the practice oration, was all about. To me, a mystory looks suspiciously like a new version of *declamatio*.

C.   Well, maybe. It seems, at least, a slightly more accurate analogy than your absurd comparison of Christo's fence project to a classical oration. And the "theory" world is forever taking bits of classical rhetoric and tarting them up in new French frocks.

L.   A mystory is much closer, I'll give you that. A rehearsal oration involved a particular presentation of self mixed with a presentation of issues, all put in a specific local context: what a great man would have said at a particular place and time.

C.   The great man here being Derrida, I suppose, and the particular place the Little Bighorn?

L.   Now, don't make a travesty of it.

C.   Or, like Socrates when someone gives him a real argument, you'll send me back to stooge mode?

L.   Exactly.

C.   Well, to escape that, I'll agree with you. Certainly a literary historian of my traditional principles couldn't doubt that the much-heralded remix of criticism and creation comes right off the rhetorical agenda. The great book hasn't been written yet on how rhetorical theory *drives the cre-*

ation of literature, but literary history is full of examples, from the Homeric poems onward. The inner logic of both arguing from rules and insisting that rules are there to be broken—as rhetoric has always done—makes the use of examples part of the core argument. And from there, voilà, it's only a step to the plays of Shakespeare. Arthur Kinney makes an excellent case for this movement in *Renaissance Poetics*—a book you treated a bit roughly, I thought.

    L. No, no. I give him his due there. But you do understand that Ulmer is asking for what Kinney argues the Renaissance delivered? Neat, isn't it, this postmodernity—what goes around, comes around.

    C. And, since I am in so agreeable a mood, couldn't you argue that Jane Healy's suggestions for new ways to implement—God, now *I* am doing it: implement, facilitate!—new ways to carry out her alternative #3 all come from traditional rhetoric? Look at what she argues for: children today need formal training in speaking aloud, not only public speaking but private conversation as well. The rhetorical curriculum emphasized both, including the very practice in focused oral argumentation which she feels children today need. She points out that children cannot form syntactically complex sentences, either in speech or in writing.

    L. And there's the periodic sentence ready to hand! That same periodic sentence, the model of complex syntax, which figured so strongly in oratorical training since the days of Isocrates.

    C. And her argument about new ways to relate verbal and visual thinking. ...

    L. The very relationship debated, and exercised, in rhetorical training from its earliest attempts to create all the figures of speech that aimed at "speaking pictures."

    C. And the basic system of memorization, the memory theater, was built upon the visual cortex. As well as all the "figures of arrangement."

    L. And what about the theory of gestures? She points out that our students leave sentences incomplete and content themselves with vague, muddled gestures. Rhetorical training supplemented syntactically complete utterance with an equally detailed training in gestural communication. The gestural register was catalogued, organized, and taught as a separate type of communication. It provided precisely the training our, as you call them, "grunt and wave" students need.

    C. Yes, though it pains me to agree with you. But since we are talking about something very old rather than very new, maybe it's all right. Think of it. Healy complains that students have trouble discriminating between stylistic registers, and especially between written and spoken utterance: she's really lamenting the loss of the classical three-level conception of style! It's as if it hadn't been debated since the Greeks! And memory, too. Healy's children have none. Maybe, in this absurd project you're about—to revive rhetorical education, no less!—we could resurrect memory to its old stature. If we are truly in an oral culture again, as you all say, won't we need to do this?

    L. No, no, the hip argument now is that the silicon will do it for us.

    C. But it *can't* do what the memory training did. That was a matter of making—to borrow Healy's argument—new pathways in the brain. There is no silicon substitute for that training. Can't they see that?

    L. No, alas, so far they can't. But maybe they will. For Healy's argument about how language literally forms the brain fits perfectly rhetoric's concentration on language. Healy's argument does it by presenting all that research about how language forms the "plastic" brain. Rhetorical education was built upon language, and every subdivision of the modern curriculum has exfoliated out from that traditional core. Now the core has dwindled away into one term of "freshman English," and we wonder why we have a literacy crisis.

    C. And that "whole language" movement she talks about. Why must they go on reinventing the wheel? Honestly! Look. The "whole language" movement is an answer to the linguistic breakdown she describes. It has three parts, and they're all parts of the rhetorical paideia. *First,* the learner is viewed as an active constructor of knowledge not a passive receiver of information; rhetorical education was an education in finding arguments, organizing them, and performing them. *Second,* reading, writing, speaking, and listening are to be taught as integrated rather than separate disciplines— as the rhetorical curriculum insisted upon from the beginning. *Third,* examples of excellent writing and speaking must be made available to the student, as objects of imitation. As you said, rhetoric has always reached out to literature for exemplification. From Homer onward, it was rhetorical education that formed the reading environment in which literature could be created, heard, read. Did we really need the French to tell us about "intertextuality"? Merciful heaven! Rhetorical education has always emphasized stylistic imitation. While we ask our poor freshpersons to look in their heart and write, rhetorical education asked them to look at texts, find out what was good in them, and learn to imitate it. Much easier and more sensible procedure. You said that yourself in the Renaissance rhetoric course you took from me all those years ago.

    L. Yes, and I still think so. So we're together on this. It is astonishing, when you look at the remedies Healy suggests for the present inarticulate generation, to see how easily and naturally they map onto the main ingredients of traditional rhetorical education. Kernan and Steiner regret the passing of classical eloquence, and Ulmer and Healy want us to resurrect it!

C. You could make the same argument for that "hypertextuality" you people go on about, too.

L. How so?

C. Come on, Lanham, you're not thinking. Classical rhetorical training is full of associational or, as you call them, "hypertextual" patterns! By the way, let me get something else off my chest. How can you fall for all this new terminology when you've spent a goodly chunk of your life making lists of all the old terms? And now "theory" adds more, and the computer world more still.

L. But, Mudge! I'm an educational bureaucrat! More terms, more explanation, more work! But back to hypertext.

C. Okay, I'll spell out the obvious. The history of rhetorical figuration is a history of verbal patterns to think by, right? And these patterns, for a trained writer or speaker, often *determine* the direction of thought as well as follow it. A memory theater, too, is an *associational* method, isn't it? Looking at a list of the topics of argument and picking to suit distracts us from linear thought in a "hypertextual" way. The method of assembling an argument from the various resources offered by formal rhetorical theory is itself— if we were to diagram it—"hypertextual." You want in the end to present an argument that is linear, moving inevitably from one stage to the next but, as Kenneth Burke often pointed out, the way we arrive at arguments is hardly the way we present them. We arrive at them intuitively, hugger-mugger, taking one thing from one place, another from another. Then we line the pieces up to simulate a logical inevitability. The same argument you make for human civility: an agreed-upon illusion. It's your favorite "oscillation" again. Doesn't the central doctrine of rhetorical performance—inspired but carefully prepared improvisation—continually coax chance much as a hypertextual sequence does?

L. *Peccavi!* I didn't see it. But it makes sense.

C. You can carry it a step further. I'll use your own arguments. The hypertextual narrative strand Bolter sees in novels like *Tristram Shandy* only begins to tell the story. You're right in saying that Western narrative uses as its basic pattern the narrative-speech-narrative oscillation you talk about in the *Motives* book.[6] The narrative segments are literate, the speeches oral; the speeches work against the narrative to invite the analogical, associational reasoning characteristic of hypertext. So "hypertext" is built into Western literature from the beginning. Even the curmudgeons can understand that!

L. Yes, and that's why I argue that the "screen" of print has distorted this hypertextual alternation, and that electronic display may in fact present it better.

C. Well, I'm with your friend Myron Tuman there: Says who? It's not going to be presented better. Worse!

L. Okay, okay. Can I get this argument back on the rails? We have agreed that there *is* a convergence. We have agreed that it has *not* led to any great resurgence of eloquence, at least of verbal eloquence, but rather the reverse. This failure does not seem to inhere in the nature of things, since oral cultures have in the past seemed to *breed* eloquence, verbal and gestural. But it has happened. Healy's children are upon us. We have also agreed, and agreed with her, that her alternative #3 is the only possible one. We must isolate what is valuable and at risk in print literacy and transfer it to the new media.

C. So your "Q" question turns out to be what Healy is talking about too, doesn't it?

L. Absolutely. Venerated teacher, our hearts again beat as one. So we agree upon that, too. And to answer the "Q" question, we have to build structures that put the two great contending parties of our time, and past times, the philosophers and the rhetoricians, in a fruitful oscillation. These structures will have to be artistic, because logical argumentative structures exist out of time, and will simply reproduce the polarization. The curriculum will have to be a work of art.

C. Yes. You wrote an article about that once.[7] As I remember, it didn't get much response, did it?

L. Sank like a stone.

C. Was it that dumb?

L. Well, I hope that wasn't the complete explanation. Partly, at least, it's the old problem: it's hard to *contend* for a bi-stable ideal since the *principles of contention* require that we choose sides. Partly, too, we want to *mix* the two sides rather than alternate them. We want to shut the oscillation down because it causes too much pain. We want one Edenic simplification or the other, truth or skepticism, Plato or Oscar Wilde, or as I sometimes put it to myself, Eleanor or Franklin. We *don't want to know* that both sides exist, or that one is viewable only from the other, that they constitute one another.

C. That's what your "matrix" wants to plot?

L. Yes. And the matrix is where I, at least, have to start in trying to make up an action program, a real *agenda,* to fulfill, implement, and deploy alternative #3.

C. But how are you going to do it? Isn't it about time you got down to real proposals?

L. Well, haven't I advanced some "real proposals" in these essays? We're going to need a new administrative structure, a new "informational structure" instead of a "library,"[8] and a new lower division with a new curriculum. I'm willing to bet, though it's early days yet on this issue, that the arts and sciences are converging on a common "science of complex systems." That common science will be the new "core" curriculum, the basis of a real lower-division *general* education.

C. Why is talk about curriculum always so tedious? Even if I agreed with you—and I see nothing wrong with what we've always done or how we've always done it—I'd begin to nod off.

L. I know, I know. We ought to have a motto: "When Sominex fails—try Curriculum!" Maybe some of us carry a gene for curriculum-talk, the way some people seem programmed to open a boutique. You have to do it. But it should be resisted. Utopian curricula fare about as well as boutiques—no, worse.

C. It is because the plans are all very detailed, and no one agrees with anybody else on the details.

L. Yes, so you have to work the opposite way—create a generative set of rules and then turn people loose. That's why I consider Venturi's architectural thinking the best curricular thinking around. The people experimenting with artificial life by modeling evolution on a computer are proving the same thing. John Holland's genetic algorithms are the model here; you don't plan a curriculum, you evolve one.

C. But then what are the generative rules?

L. As near as I can make out, we're going to need a new rhetoric of the arts and letters to answer that question, a rhetoric which applies some bottom-up evolutionary thinking to the the radical mix of word, image, and sound that is implicit in digital technology. Classical rhetoric works fine as a beginning point, and often as more than that, since it was originally devised for an oral society and works pretty well in a secondarily oral one like ours, too. But we clearly need much more than this.

C. Like what?

L. First, I don't think we have to be so afraid to open the issues up. Hypertextual and linear processes of thinking are surely the two basic processes of the human mind. We are not going to abjure either one. Fixed text accumulates its power through a compressed time-scale; we read in an hour what it took a year to think through and create, and the rush of that compression we will want to preserve. Volatile text pleads to a different constituency, to that chance which always favors the prepared mind; we don't want to forgo this source of power, either.

C. But you immediately hit a gigantic iceberg. Any rhetoric built on the AT/THROUGH oscillation must take self-consciousness as its primary variable. People don't like self-consciousness. They want to escape it.

L. Well, I think it has to be reinstated. There is no reason why a rhetoric—an organized system of expressive effect—cannot be built around the matrix I've outlined above. It works as well for images and sounds, art and music, as it does for literature. It would become, in fact, as rhetoric always does, a poetic. Put that at the heart of the lower division.

C. Hey, Lanham, give me a break! You're proposing that the Renaissance *aristocratic* idea of education be reinstated in the great age of egalitarianism?

L. Why not? Thanks to the digital technology which you so despise, we now have the means genuinely to democratize music and visual art. And to teach reading and writing and speaking in new ways, too, if we want to. There's an infinite number of new mixes out there awaiting exploration. We have the theory, we have the technology, we know what this "convergence" is all about. There is nothing inevitable about Healy's children. We lack only the will to solve the problem.

C. Honestly! It's not that simple! What do you mean by teaching reading and writing in new ways, for example?

L. Can't we rethink what "reading" might be in a new environment, both technological and theoretical? Is it truly beyond our powers to factor out the yield of alphabetic information from its present printed codex format? After all, we still don't know what it means to be "lost in a book."[9] Perhaps we shall find out when we "lose ourselves" in a new environment. If we can understand the structure of self that underlies all such discussions, we will certainly have a better chance of understanding what "reading" has been about since print and before. We need not oppose the current campaign to "Read more books, damn you!" but surely we need a more thoughtful and less retrogressive approach to preserving the value of "reading." Healy objects, in her attack on "Sesame Street," that words don't jump around on the page in books. Well, is it the death of reading if they do? I've written two videos for teaching prose style in which words do just that, and change color besides. Those videos teach some basic lessons of prose style far better than my printed textbooks can. No reason inheres in the nature of things that prevents us from using the techniques of digital multimedia to teach higher-order thinking of all sorts. Of course, we can continue to use it for the idiot diversions that vex you so, but that is an affair of our will and imagination, not of the technology itself.

C. That's where your behavioral neuroscience comes in; that at least I can agree with. Surely we'll begin to learn what happens to the brain, how its pathways are formed and reformed, when it learns to process language, spoken and written, and how it mixes its inputs of sound and visual image. All of this ought to give a better answer to the "Q" question than your theorizing.

L. I hope so. I think it will. I'd also want to mix in (though I know how much you loathe and despise sociobiology) what we are learning from behavioral biology as well. Havelock's profound insight about Greek sophistic thought—that it was based on an evolutionary conception of humankind—must enter our conversation about the humanities. The arts and letters clearly work in the domain of game and play, and game and play are "vacuum behaviors," as Lorenz called them, which reveal the basic hungers of the human biogrammar. Any reconceptualization of rhetoric in the age of multimedia must return to these reformulations of the human nature that are coming to us from other fields. Behavioral neuroscience and behavioral biology seem the most needful places to begin. It's madness to keep ignoring them, if we want to preserve literate culture in these new ways.

C. Well, I'm not going to let you get me started on sociobiology. But what about music? You've been arguing that digital technology democratizes it. Honestly, now, aren't you kidding yourself? Can you democratize genius?

L. No, but I think you can democratize music-making. Let me take refuge, since eight years of piano lessons beat in vain on my lack of musical talent, behind the arguments of a genuine musical genius, Glenn Gould.

C. Oh, have you read Otto Friedrich's biography?[10] I know you are a Gould collector.

L. Yes, I've read it; it's a delight. Friedrich's explanation of the enfranchising act of Gould's career, his withdrawal from the concert stage, is much to my purpose. Gould made a crucial distinction, and one that Friedrich doesn't quite understand. He wanted to split off "perfection" from "perfect performance." He hated, despised, the tightrope-act part of public performance.

C. You mean when he said that the audience always came smelling blood, wanting the performer to fail, to fall off the tightrope?

L. Yes. You could still aim for the perfect performance, but you would do it by editing the tape. A performer would edit her performance in the same way a writer would edit her prose.

C. The same condensation of effort, the same transfer of power, that happens in writing.

L. For sure! In that famous article in *High Fidelity*,[11] Gould argued for an interactive listener who would splice the tapes in his collection into new composite performances. "I'd love," he said, "to issue a kit of variant performances and let the listener assemble his own performance." All this in 1966.

C. But that's cheating!

L. Why? What is sacred about a concert performance? As a tradition, it's only, what, two hundred years old? Gould wanted to junk it and return, via modern technology, to an older tradition of collective music-making. Digital technology allows people to do this. We can assemble a piece of music as a rhetorician assembled an argument, from topoi, from a stock of ready-made phrases. We can vary them in limitless ways. To compose and play, we don't need to be a genius or devote our lives to cultivating manual dexterity. This puts music back into ordinary people's lives in a fundamentally new way. And into our educational practices in a new way, as well. A curriculum that teaches the arts and letters as a single entity is now possible for a democratic educational system.

C. And the same thing is going to happen for the visual arts—Good God!

L. Just so. She has finally given us a break.

C. And you would put these new "democratic" techniques to work as part of a new rhetoric of the arts and letters, based on the matrix of self-consciousness you've been plumping for?

L. Yes. I know you don't agree, but at least follow the pattern: Convergence suggests a new curriculum for the arts and letters; a new rhetoric is thus required, and it must be built on digital technology. There is no point—provided that you really are committed, as you say you are, to alternative #3—in building a new education on the printed word, and its corollaries in music and the visual arts. That leads only to the obsolete curriculum debate you guys are having with the Left.

C. A debate which you say is pointless.

L. Pointless, yes, but not harmless, since it distracts us from the real business at hand—that pesky alternative #3, the transfer of power from page to screen.

C. So the curmudgeons and the revolutionaries are the main obstacles to human progress.

L. No, not even that, though maybe the most tiresome. The main obstacle to the agenda I would advance is the chaos of copyright law.

C. You've mentioned that several times in these essays.

L. Yes, but I didn't carry the argument far enough.

C. Is it the literate/oral distinction that causes all the confusion?

L. Not all, but some. In its largest magnification, the two conflicting parties are a literate culture where works of the imagination can be private property, and an oral culture which by its very nature insists that all intellectual property be public property. That is what orality is all about, how it works. So we have two kinds of culture, and the two conceptions of intellectual property that depend from them, in direct opposition to one another. They are so different in this respect that statements meaningful in one domain will by definition be nonsense or worse in the other.

C. And everybody can copy everything in your wonderful new digital world, anyway.

L. Again, right on! Another fundamental opposition appears. On the one hand we have a body of copyright law that is making ownable, "privatizing," more and more of the imaginative world. Not only the *ipsissima verba* of a text are now protectible but the "total concept and feel" as well. Famous figures can own their own public images and voices. The networks own most of the images from which our future history will be constructed. In a very real way, they own the history. Copyright law has traditionally said that *ideas* are not protectible, only the *expression* of those ideas. Increasingly, though, because of the way "originality" is marketed in the Hollywood world, through "treatments" of one sort or another which are in fact only ideas, protection is reaching out toward "ideas" as well. Computer software is now being protected by patent law as well as copyright law, a very significant extension. Opposing this, we have the full force of digital technology, which makes expression infinitely replicatable at extremely low cost. What we *can* do grows larger and larger; what the law allows, smaller and smaller. Another impossible opposition.

C. But what about Ulmer's idea that we are coming to a new definition of human reason itself? How will that affect, for example, the cases you've worked on?

L. It makes things worse yet. The pivotal term for copyright law has always been "substantial similarity." In the twenty years I've been working as an expert witness, I have never found a central meaning for this central term. But now it is subject to new and intolerable stresses. First, the "substance" has evaporated. No more print and ink and binding and unalterable image and sound. All can be and regularly are metamorphosed in the act of "reading." In the cases I've worked on, the "substance" in "substantial similarity" has often been patterns of plot and characterization. Now these are presented not as fixed, i.e. "substantial," but as suggestions for imaginative re-creation. Comparisons based on beginnings, middles, and ends—a routine way to start putting two properties into comparison, the very *flos ac robor* of many parallel-column charts of similarities—are not possible in a hypertextual environment. In fact, all the constants that lend substance to "substantial similarity" dissolve in the digital environment. If we have to do with a redefinition of human *reason,* as it seems clear that we do, then what has changed with the electronic word is not only the property that copyright law seeks to protect but the means of thought itself, the "reason" that formulates and resolves such disputes. The difficulty becomes one order of magnitude harder than we thought.

C. It occurred to me, when you were describing Healy's arguments, that there were copyright implications there too.

L. That I hadn't thought of.

C. Well, look at it this way. Copyright law depends on print, yes, but more generally on left-brain intellection. Now, this new "concept and feel" criterion I've read about in the Apple/Microsoft dispute, the one about the desktop arrangement and icons, seems inane to left-brained types like me. But what if it takes a step toward "right-brained" property—where the global "feeling" seems to be the same?[12] The implications of this for what can and cannot be protected are extraordinary. The courts, to their credit, have always taken a jaundiced view of literary experts like you, building instead upon the judgment of the common reader or viewer.[13] But how will Healy's children play the role of a common reader if they can't, or won't, read? How do you compare if you cannot remember, if you cannot organize and prioritize knowledge, if you cannot isolate elements from the general background noise, if you don't pay attention to the lyrics except as they reinforce the thump-thump of the beat? Won't everything look, and sound, alike to Healy's children? If we insist that such people are not real common readers, we are making up a false "expert" version of the common reader, and all the strictures against the literary expert will once again supervene. In a culture of secondary orality, the felt sense of imaginative property will be oral. What will that do to jury verdicts?

L. I don't know—but it certainly should mean that literary experts will be more important than ever. Vital, in fact! And it means one other thing, too. We need a proper rhetoric of the digital arts and letters not least in order to have a framework within which meaningful statements can be made in copyright disputes. Without one, copyright law will not know what kind of intellection to use in its debates. The referential thinking in copyright law turns out to be, oftentimes, thinking based not only on print, but on literature itself.[14] Applications to films, television shows, visual artifacts, have seemed strained even while still operating in the domain and with the expectations of print. Now they're going to be intolerably stressed. We will doubly need an organized matrix within which to make comparisons between the arts of words, images, and sounds.

C. But if these issues need to be thought out, wouldn't it make sense to do it somewhere besides the courts? Since the university world itself is so tied up in knots about reprint permissions, duplication permissions, customized textbooks, and the like, couldn't we do something ourselves? Work out an educational system that might then be generalized outward to the more contentious entertainment world?

L. Good thinking, Mudge. Why don't you make it your retirement project? There might be some consulting in it, to cushion that reduced income.

C. There you go, talking about money again. But it needs to be done, and I'd be doing it for its own sake, really.

L. Of course you would. That's why we'll work through this daunting revolution. That, and to lead Healy's children out of the darkness.

NOTES

1. Michael C. Corballis, *The Lopsided Ape: Evolution of the Generative Mind* (New York: Oxford University Press, 1991).

2. For an interesting example of such techniques, see the *Piero Project* created by Marilyn Aronberg Lavin, of the Department of Art and Archaeology at Princeton University, and her associates.

3. Richard A. Lanham, *The Motives of Eloquence: Literary Rhetoric in the Renaissance* (New Haven: Yale University Press, 1976); see chapter 1, "The Rhetorical Ideal of Life."

4. I develop this argument for all three authors, as well as for Shakespeare, in *The Motives of Eloquence.*

5. Richard A. Lanham, *A Handlist of Rhetorical Terms,* 2d ed. (Berkeley and Los Angeles: University of California Press, 1992).

6. I have discussed and illustrated this pattern extensively in *The Motives of Eloquence* (n. 3 above).

7. Richard A. Lanham, "The Rhetorical Paideia: The Curriculum as a Work of Art," *College English* 48, no. 2 (Feb. 1986): 132–41.

8. For the most recent discussion of this problem, see *Synopsis of an Invitational Symposium on Knowledge Management* (27–29 Oct. 1991), sponsored by the Council on Library Resources, Johns Hopkins University, and the University of California, San Francisco.

9. In this connection, see Victor Nell, *Lost in a Book: The Psychology of Reading for Pleasure* (New Haven: Yale University Press, 1988).

10. Otto Friedrich, *Glenn Gould: A Life and Variations* (New York: Random House, 1989). My discussion departs from chapter 6, "The New Life."

11. Glenn Gould, "The Prospects of Recording," *High Fidelity*, April 1966.

12. See, in this regard, two cases that figured strongly in this reassessment of nonprint materials: *Sid & Marty Krofft Television Productions, Inc. v. McDonald's Corporation,* 562 F.2d 1157 (9th Circuit 1977), and *Walt Disney Productions v. Air Pirates et al.,* 581 F.2d 751 (9th Circuit 1978).

13. The role permitted an expert witness in copyright cases has been discussed in a number of cases, including the *Krofft* case cited in n. 12. A case often cited in this regard is *Arnstein v. Porter* 154 F.2d 464 (2d Circuit 1946), but I challenge the reader to extract from it any sensible guidance on how literary analysis, expert or lay, might best illuminate a copyright case. The use of expert testimony is yet another area that is further obscured by the digital desubstantiation of intellectual property.

14. For an interesting early discussion of this problem see Bayard F. Berman and Joel E. Boxer, "Copyright Infringement of Audiovisual Works and Characters," *Southern California Law Review* 52, no. 2 (Jan. 1979).

Index